COLLEGE VOCABULARY SKILLS

COLLEGE VOCABULARY SKILLS

FIFTH EDITION

James F. Shepherd
Queensborough Community College,
Professor Emeritus
The City University of New York

HOUGHTON MIFFLIN COMPANY   Boston   Toronto
Geneva, Illinois   Palo Alto   Princeton, New Jersey

Senior Sponsoring Editor: Mary Jo Southern
Senior Associate Editor: Melody Davies
Project Editor: Danielle Carbonneau
Associate Production/Design Coordinator: Jennifer Waddell
Senior Manufacturing Coordinator: Priscilla Bailey

Cover Image: Ulf Deutsch, Hamburg-Hopen (Germany)
Cover Design: Linda Manly Wade
Book Design: George McLean
Part-opening photographs: Part I John Henley/The Stock Market; Part II Antonia
Deutsch/Tony Stone Images; Part III Hashimoto/Photonica; Part IV Ulrike Welsch; Part
V Eric Roth Studio/The Picture Cube; Part VI Lightscapes/The Stock Market.

*We would like to acknowledge and thank the following sources for permission to
reprint material from their work:*

Extracts featuring the words *omnipotence, nomadic, dispersed, depopulation,
subsisted, omnipotent, ethnocentric, polygyny, supplanted, irrevocably, inescapable,
phenomena, irreversible, nonconsumption, intimidate, dilemma, stamina, prevailing,
benevolence, modifications, ceremoniously, semifreedom, exploratory, anti-European,
restraint, interstate, paternalistic, motifs, precocious,* and *self-sufficiency* in Chapters
9 and 14 are from Norton, Mary Beth, David M. Katzman, Paul D. Escott, Howard
Chudacoff, Thomas G. Paterson, and William M. Tuttle, Jr., A PEOPLE AND A
NATION: A HISTORY OF THE UNITED STATES, Third Edition. Copyright © 1990
by Houghton Mifflin Company. Used with permission.

The thesaurus entry for *enormous* in Chapter 17 is from THE RANDOM HOUSE
THESAURUS by Jess Stein and Stuart Berg Flexner, editors. Copyright © 1984 by
Random House, Inc. Reprinted by permission of Random House, Inc.

The thesaurus entries for *old, new, like,* and *hate* in Chapter 17 are reprinted by
permission from THE RANDOM HOUSE THESAURUS, COLLEGE EDITION,
copyright © 1984 by Random House, Inc.

The dictionary entries for *symposium* and *tuxedo* in Chapter 4 are reprinted by
permission from MERRIAM-WEBSTER'S COLLEGIATE DICTIONARY © 1992 by
Merriam-Webster Inc., publisher of the Merriam-Webster dictionaries.

(Credits continued on page 227.)

Printed in the U.S.A.

ISBN (student text): 0-395-708494

ISBN (instructor's edition): 0-395-717345

3456789-B-98

Contents

UNIT FIVE   **Use Words Precisely**   *159*

UNIT SIX   **Improve Your Spelling**   *189*

Preface

College Vocabulary Skills teaches the vocabulary knowledge and skills that are essential for success in college and the work place. Written in a clear, straightforward style that students can easily understand, it contains more than one hundred practical exercises that help students to acquire skills through practice. In its various editions, *College Vocabulary Skills* has been used with great success by thousands of writing, reading, and study skills students, both in the classroom and in independent study environments such as learning centers and skills laboratories.

Organization of the Text

This new fifth edition has twenty-two chapters arranged in six units.

- Unit One, "Improve Your Vocabulary," teaches basic strategies for increasing vocabulary and introduces the variety of information contained in desk dictionaries.

- Unit Two, "Study the Context," explains how to locate the meanings of words that are stated in context and how to infer the meanings of words that are implied by context.

- Unit Three, "Analyze Word Structure," provides instruction on how to determine word meanings by analyzing them to identify the prefixes, suffixes, combining forms, Latin roots, and other elements contained in them.

- Unit Four, "Locate Word Meanings," explains how to locate definitions in dictionaries and textbooks. It also introduces students to the terminology of five subject areas: psychology and sociology, business and economics, language and literature, law and government, and natural sciences.

- Unit Five, "Use Words Precisely," provides students with an opportunity to learn how to use a dictionary and a thesaurus to locate the words they need to express their thoughts accurately and precisely in writing.

- Unit Six, "Improve Your Spelling," teaches a variety of strategies for learning and remembering the correct spellings of words.

Each chapter ends with exercises that were carefully field tested to ensure that they promote the understanding of information and the acquisition of skills that are explained in the text. Varied exercise formats sustain students' interest, and their ample number allows for paced repetition according to students' learning needs.

Each unit ends with a review that provides students with opportunities to learn the meanings of new words, to use new words in writing, and to assess their understanding of information about vocabulary presented in the unit.

Changes in the Fifth Edition

A distinctive feature of this fifth edition of *College Vocabulary Skills* is the inclusion of more than 300 entries from the acclaimed new third edition of *The American Heritage Dictionary*, which was published in 1992. In addition, exposition is updated, exercises are improved, and three new chapters are introduced:

- Chapter 9, "Using the Context," provides practice for transferring skill in locating and inferring word meanings to selections from college textbooks.
- Chapter 13, "Latin Roots," introduces elements such as *spect*, which means "to look," and explains how these roots differ from combining forms.
- Chapter 14, "Analyzing Word Structure," provides practice for transferring skill in analyzing prefixes, suffixes, combining forms, and other elements in words to the vocabulary in college textbooks.

In addition, the exercises feature 128 more words than previous editions and about twenty-five percent of the words in the exercises and in the word-learning programs are new to this edition.

Word-learning Program

College Vocabulary Skills provides the opportunity for students to learn the meanings of from 50 to 460 words, which are listed at the beginning of the first five unit reviews.

The Basic Word-learning Program of 230 words is appropriate for students who study *College Vocabulary Skills* as a supplementary text in a writing, reading, or study skills course. The Advanced Word-learning Program of an additional 230 words is intended for students who study *College Vocabulary Skills* as the basic text for a vocabulary course or who need more challenge.

Instructor's Edition

The Instructor's Edition of *College Vocabulary Skills* includes an Instructor's Resource Manual that contains teaching suggestions, quizzes, tests, and a complete answer key to exercises. The manual is printed on 8½-by-11-inch paper to facilitate duplicating the material for classroom use.

Acknowledgments

I am indebted to the talented staff of Houghton Mifflin Company for the expert guidance and assistance they provided me in preparing this revision: Mary Jo Southern, Melody Davies, Danielle Carbonmeau, Jennifer Waddell, Priscilla Bailey, George McLean, and Jennifer Huber. I am also grateful to the following reviewers who offered comments and suggestions that were very helpful to me in revising this book:

Janet R. Gilbert, *Delta College, MI*

Amy Henry, *Canada College, CA*

William J. McGreevy, *Ocean County College, NJ*

Joan Rodriguez, *El Centro College, TX*

Pamela R. Rupert, *University of Akron, OH*

Nancy M. Steward, *Del Mar College, TX*

Janet M. Wallet-Ortiz, *Western New Mexico University*

In addition, I thank my friend Earl Kemppainen and my students at Queensborough Community College for providing me with unfamiliar words they encountered while reading and who supported me with their enthusiasm for vocabulary improvement.

If you have any comments about this book or suggestions about how I might improve the text in its next edition, please write to me: James F. Shepherd, c/o Marketing Services, Houghton Mifflin Company, 222 Berkeley Street, Boston, Massachusetts 02116. If you write to me, I will reply.

J.F.S.

To the Student

As you read assignments for your college courses, you are likely to encounter many words that are unfamiliar to you. Also, as you write your papers, you may discover that you do not always have at your command the words you need to express your thoughts accurately and precisely.

College Vocabulary Skills offers help for these problems. As you study this book you will learn skills such as the following:

- How to learn more systematically the meanings of new words.
- How to increase the words you use for speaking and writing.
- How to figure out the meanings of unfamiliar words without consulting a dictionary.
- How to locate a wide variety of information about words in a dictionary.
- How to determine the correct pronunciation of any word.
- How to use a dictionary or thesaurus to locate words to express your thoughts accurately and precisely.
- How to learn the correct spellings of words.

You will learn about words and acquire vocabulary skills by doing many different types of exercises. Some chapters contain a series of similar exercises so that, in case you have difficulty with the first one or two, you will improve as you do the others in the series.

I wrote this book to teach you all the basic things you might like to know about English vocabulary and to make the study of vocabulary interesting and rewarding to you. I would like to know if I have succeeded. If you have comments about this book or suggestions about how I might improve the text in its next edition, please write to me: James F. Shepherd, c/o Marketing Services, Houghton Mifflin Company, 222 Berkeley Street, Boston, Massachusetts 02116. If you write to me, I will answer you.

J.F.S.

One

Improve Your Vocabulary

Learning Goals for Unit One

In studying Chapters 1 through 6 you will learn:

- How to increase the words you know when you read or listen (Chapter 2).
- How to increase the words you use when you write and speak (Chapters 2 and 3).
- How to use a dictionary to locate spellings, pronunciations, definitions, synonyms, and other information about words (Chapter 4).
- How to interpret the information dictionaries give about the pronunciations of words (Chapter 5).
- How to interpret the information dictionaries provide about the origins, or etymologies, of words (Chapter 6).

Assess Your Vocabulary

We ordinarily think of ourselves as having one vocabulary, but in fact we all have several vocabularies. You probably have a slang vocabulary that you use with your friends, an informal vocabulary that you use with your family, and a more formal vocabulary that you use when you transact important business, visit a doctor, or write papers for college courses.

In addition, you have two types of vocabulary that are of special interest in this book: the words you *know* when you read or listen and the words you *use* when you write or speak. These are sometimes called the **receptive vocabulary** (words you "receive" when you read or listen) and **expressive vocabulary** (words you use to "express" yourself when you write and speak).

There are many words that you know when you read and listen that you don't use when you write and speak; your receptive vocabulary is several times larger than your expressive vocabulary. For instance, if you have a receptive vocabulary of 14,000 words, the chances are that in 80 percent of what you write you rely on a vocabulary of fewer than 3,000 words, and that in 95 percent of what you say you use a vocabulary of fewer than 1,000 words.

No matter the size of your vocabulary, it can become larger—much larger! There are more than 500,000 words in the English language, and it is estimated that average college students make practical use of only about 10,000 to 30,000 of these words.

Thus, when you study, you must expect that any one of more than 450,000 words that you have never seen or heard before may suddenly appear. You must have at your command a variety of techniques to identify quickly and accurately the meanings of most of these words so that you will understand what is written in your books or spoken in your lectures. Also, in college you will be called on to express your ideas in writing and in class discussions. Unless you have a large writing and speaking vocabulary, these demands are likely to be consistent sources of frustration for you.

These, then, are two questions that you must ask:

- How can I quickly determine or find the meanings of unfamiliar words that I encounter when I read or listen?

- How can I acquire or locate the words I need to express my thoughts accurately and completely when I write and speak?

College Vocabulary Skills was written to help you learn the answers to these questions.

In addition, since you are not likely to use words that you do not know how to pronounce or spell, *College Vocabulary Skills* teaches how you can determine the correct pronunciation of any word, and gives suggestions about how you can improve your spelling.

This chapter provides an opportunity for you to assess some aspects of your vocabulary before you begin your study of English vocabulary in this book. Since your instructor may provide you with a special answer sheet for the following quizzes, do not answer the following questions until your instructor asks you to do so.

Quiz One: Vocabulary in Isolation

Check the boxes in front of the answers to the questions that best state the meanings of the words printed in boldface.

1. **ostracize**
   - ☐ a. crush
   - ☐ b. exclude
   - ☐ c. blend
   - ☐ d. polish

2. **maverick**
   - ☐ a. lazy individual
   - ☐ b. western cowboy
   - ☐ c. adolescent boy
   - ☐ d. independent person

3. **condone**
   - ☐ a. overlook
   - ☐ b. approve
   - ☐ c. encourage
   - ☐ d. uphold

4. **dilate**
   - ☐ a. enter
   - ☐ b. exit
   - ☐ c. enlarge
   - ☐ d. shrink

5. **curtail**
   - ☐ a. terminate
   - ☐ b. reduce
   - ☐ c. approve
   - ☐ d. expel

6. **inadvertent**
   - ☐ a. untidy
   - ☐ b. disorderly
   - ☐ c. inexact
   - ☐ d. unintentional

7. **benign**
   - ☐ a. charitable
   - ☐ b. universal
   - ☐ c. harmless
   - ☐ d. cherished

8. **euphoria**
   - ☐ a. relaxed mood
   - ☐ b. high spirits
   - ☐ c. kindheartedness
   - ☐ d. generous manner

9. **pompous**
   - ☐ a. superior
   - ☐ b. ridiculous
   - ☐ c. ill-advised
   - ☐ d. self-important

10. **congenital**
   - ☐ a. friendly
   - ☐ b. inborn
   - ☐ c. related
   - ☐ d. fun-loving

Quiz Two: Vocabulary in Context

Study the following excerpts from popular college textbooks and write the meanings of the boldface words on the lines provided.

Part 1

Experiments like Epstein's have demonstrated that **syntax,** the pattern of word order, plays an important role in the comprehension of sentences.

11. **syntax** _____

Indian religious beliefs varied even more than did their political systems. One common thread was that they were all **polytheistic;** that is, they all involved a multitude of gods.

12. **polytheistic** _____

The thing a word refers to is its **denotation;** the word *table* denotes a piece of furniture, and the denotation of *banana* is a yellow fruit.

13. **denotation** _____

The basic use of an **ellipsis** (. . .) is to mark the omission of one or more words from a quotation.

14. **ellipsis** _____

Both chemical and physical components constitute the "ground" factors that enable the **biotic** components, or living organisms, to grow.

15. **biotic** _____

Mead emphasized that the mind is a social product; and, indeed, one of the most important achievements of socialization is the development of **cognitive** abilities—intellectual capacities such as perceiving, remembering, reasoning, calculating, believing.

16. **cognitive** _____

Some of the adverse side effects of this type of therapy are **phlebitis**— vein inflammation—and certain types of anemia, or reduction in number of blood cells.

17. **phlebitis** _____

When she **critiques,** or evaluates, our written work, she emphasizes what is good about it and makes helpful suggestions for improvement.

18. **critique** _____

Speakers often use **hyperbole,** or exaggeration, to make listeners confront moral problems such as abortion and capital punishment.

19. **hyperbole** _____

The desire to be concise sometimes leads to the use of **maxims**—wise, compact sayings such as "A penny saved is a penny earned."

20. **maxim** _____

Part 2

Marshall was an **astute** lawyer with keen political sense. Throughout his **tenure** (from 1801 until 1835), the Court upheld federal supremacy over the states and protected the interests of commerce and capital.

21. **astute** _____

22. **tenure** _____

Most immigrants **gravitated** toward the cities, since only a minority had farming experience or the **means** to purchase land and equipment.

23. **gravitate** _____

24. **means** _____

We have seen that children get better at looking, listening, talking, reading, and remembering over the years from two to twelve. Within this general trend, however, there are large individual differences; some children are mentally **precocious**, while others lag behind their **peers.**

25. **precocious** _____

26. **peer** _____

In the United States, the infant **mortality** rate is among the lowest in the world, but one out of every hundred babies still does not make it through the critical first month.

27. **mortality** _____

The need to take a test **elicits** fear and a high level of anxiety in some students.

28. **elicit** _____

When students become bored in class, some daydream while **feigning** attention in order to appear polite.

29. **feign** _____

Since test questions are often based on class lectures, it is **imperative** for students to attend class and take good notes on what their instructors say.

30. **imperative** _____

Part 3

Religion was a constant presence in the lives of pious Puritans. As followers of John Calvin, they believed that an **omnipotent** God **predestined** souls to heaven or hell before birth, and that Christians could do nothing to change their ultimate fate.

31. **omnipotent** _____

32. **predestine** _____

The histories of popular governments in such places as Greece and Rome seemed to prove that republics could succeed only if they were small in size and **homogeneous** in population.

33. **homogeneous** _____

In July 1755 a combined force of French and Indians ambushed General Edward Braddock, two regiments of British regulars, and some colonial troops a few miles south of Fort Duquesne. Braddock was killed and his men **demoralized** by their complete defeat.

34. **demoralize** _____

People even learn to use facial expressions ironically or to hide or **miscommunicate** their feelings.

35. **miscommunicate** _____

The uncertainty of their social and **familial** position seems to have led some eastern girls to seek spiritual certainty in the church.

36. **familial** _____

Because their means were modest, they did not generate the **voluminous** legal papers, such as contracts, wills, and inventories of estates, that document the activities of the rich.

37. **voluminous** _____

In addition, it removed **intraparty** pressures for compromise and strengthened the hand of intransigent elements.

38. **intraparty** _____

The manager's sexist remarks revealed **insensitivity** toward the women in his department.

39. **insensitivity** ⎯⎯⎯⎯⎯⎯⎯⎯⎯⎯⎯⎯⎯⎯⎯⎯⎯⎯⎯⎯

As the customer was stating complaints, the salesperson developed her **counterarguments**.

40. **counterargument** ⎯⎯⎯⎯⎯⎯⎯⎯⎯⎯⎯⎯⎯⎯⎯⎯⎯

Assessing Your Vocabulary

Score questions 1–10, 11–20, 21–30, and 31–40, counting ten points for each correct answer. Write your scores on the lines provided at the beginnings of the following discussions.

⎯⎯⎯⎯ **Quiz One: Vocabulary in Isolation.**   The words in this quiz are examples of words that are introduced in exercises in *College Vocabulary Skills*; they are words that most high school graduates do not know but most college graduates do know. Your score for this quiz is a rough estimate of the percentage of words in the exercises in *College Vocabulary Skills* that you already know. For example, if your score is 40, you probably know the meanings of about 40 percent of the words. If your score is low, do not worry; one reason you are studying vocabulary is to learn new words. If your score is 50 or higher, consider learning the meanings of the words in the Advanced Word Lists on pages 57, 81, 154, and 185.

⎯⎯⎯⎯ **Quiz Two, Part 1: Meanings Stated in Context.**   The meanings of the boldface words in questions 11–20 are stated in the passages in which they appear. The average score for the quiz is 40; if your score is 60 or higher, you are better at finding the meanings of words stated in context than most students who study this book. Chapters 7 and 9 provide practice for improving your ability to find the meanings of words when they are stated in context.

⎯⎯⎯⎯ **Quiz Two, Part 2: Meanings Implied by Context.**   The meanings of the words in questions 21–30 are implied or suggested by the passages in which they appear. The average score for the quiz is 40; if your score is higher, you are better at figuring out the meanings of words suggested by context than most students who study this book. Chapters 8 and 9 provide practice in improving ability to infer the meanings of words that are implied by context.

⎯⎯⎯⎯ **Quiz Two, Part 3: Word Structure.**   The words in questions 31–40 contain prefixes, suffixes, and combining forms of the type you will learn about when you study Chapters 10 through 14. The average score for the quiz is 30; if your score is 60 or higher, you know more about prefixes, suffixes, and combining forms than most students who study this book.

Increase Words You Know

College Vocabulary Skills teaches a variety of ways for you to increase your **receptive vocabulary**—the words you know when you read or hear them.

- Chapters 7–9 teach how to locate or figure out the meanings of words that are stated in or suggested by contexts.
- Chapters 10–14 explain how to determine the meanings of words by analyzing prefixes, bases, suffixes, and other word parts.
- Chapters 15 and 16 describe how to locate the meanings of words in dictionaries and textbooks.

This chapter explains four steps you may use to learn the meanings of words you want or need to know: collect words to learn; make notes for words; recite from your notes; and review your notes often.

Collect Words to Learn

The first step in any learning program is to decide what to learn. Following are three methods for making these decisions:

1. Keep a list of words that you recognize when you read or listen but that you do not use when you write or speak. These are easy words for you to learn because you already know something about them. Search for these words whenever you read or listen to lectures, conversations, or television. For instance, you may read or hear the word *affable* and decide to learn that it means "easy to approach and speak to."

2. Learn the new words you need to know in order to understand the subject matter of your courses and to do well on tests. Your instructors will explain the meanings of words that are important to the subjects they teach. For instance, if you take an American politics course, your instructor is likely to explain the meanings of such words as *indictment, lobby,* and *libel.* Your textbooks also state the meanings of words. Chapter 16 explains how to identify the words in your textbooks that you should learn in preparation for tests, and it contains terminology for several college subjects.

3. Learn the words in the word lists that are provided in the Unit Reviews beginning on pages 57, 81, 154, 185, and 223.

You will learn many words quickly if you focus your attention on words you *want* to know so that you can use them to express your thoughts.

Make Notes for Words

After you have decided that you want to learn a word, make a note of the word and information that you want to learn about it. Use notebook paper or 3-by-5-inch cards.

Figure 2.1 illustrates how to make notes on notebook paper. Use the following procedure.

1. Draw or crease a vertical line 2½ inches from the left edge of the page.

2. Write words to the left of the vertical line.

3. Write definitions to the right of the vertical line.

4. Skip a line between each definition.

Figure 2.2 illustrates notes made on a 3-by-5-inch card. Use the following procedure to make notes on an index card.

1. Write a word, its part of speech, and its pronunciation on the unlined side of the card.

2. Write additional information on the lined side of the card, upside down in relation to the material written on the front.

If you use this procedure, information on the backs of cards will be in the proper position for reading when you turn the cards over.

When you write sentences to show how words are used, it is helpful to make the sentences about your experiences. For example:

■ Write sentences about yourself or someone you know. If you want to learn that *euphoric* means "high-spirited," you might write a sentence about an experience that caused you to experience extremely high spirits: "I was *euphoric* when I received an A on a chemistry test."

■ Write sentences about something you can visualize. If you want to learn that *retail* means "the selling of goods directly to consumers," write a sentence about something you can visualize: "Banana Republic is a *retail* clothing store."

Your notes should include only the information that you want to learn about a word. Figure 2.1 illustrates notes for learning only the definitions of words. In contrast, Figure 2.2 illustrates very complete notes that include a sentence showing how the word is used.

FIGURE 2.1

Notes on Notebook Paper

bicameral	Composed of two houses, such as the U.S. Congress which is composed of the Senate and the House of Representatives
deregulate	To remove or reduce government regulations from an industry or business
gerrymander	To draw congressional district lines to gain an unfair advantage in elections
libel	The use of print or pictures to harm someone's reputation
slander	The use of speech to harm a person's reputation or well-being

FIGURE 2.2

Notes on a 3-by-5-Inch Card

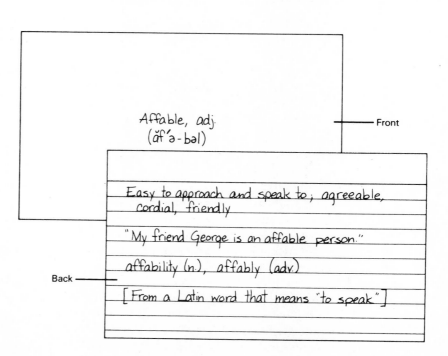

Affable, adj.
(ăf'ə-bəl)

Front

Easy to approach and speak to; agreeable, cordial, friendly

"My friend George is an affable person."

affability (n.), affably (adv.)

[From a Latin word that means "to speak"]

Back

Recite from Your Notes

Reciting is the act of repeating information silently or aloud so that you will remember it. By reciting from your notes, you will read and hear words as many times as you need to learn their meanings. Use the following procedure when you recite from notes.

1. Read the word or term that is written to the left of the vertical line on notebook paper or on the unlined side of a card.

2. Without looking at the information written to the right of the vertical line on notebook paper or on the lined side of a card, try to say the information silently or aloud.

3. Read the information about the word to make certain that you recited it correctly. If you did not, reread the information and then immediately try to recite it again.

4. Repeat this procedure at later times until you recall the information that you want to learn about the word.

The purpose of reciting is to learn information, not to memorize words. Since information may usually be stated in several different ways, you may often recite information correctly without repeating words exactly as they are written in your notes.

You may find that you learn words more quickly when you organize them into logical groups. *Fantastic, bizarre, grotesque,* and *exotic* are a logical group because they are synonyms that are used to describe something that is "very strange or strikingly unusual."

Experiment with grouping words. One student grouped *affable, compassionate,* and *gullible* because they all describe people's personalities, and she put *choreographer, actuary, meteorologist,* and *thespian* in a group because they all name occupations.

Review Your Notes Often

We tend to forget 30 to 40 percent of what we learn within about twenty-four hours of learning it. If you "learn" the meanings of twenty words, you can expect to have forgotten six to eight of them twenty-four hours later. That is why frequent review is necessary.

If your notes are on cards, maintain a set of "learned" words and a set of "unlearned" words. Each time you recite, begin with words in the "learned" set. If you have forgotten the meanings of any of those words, put the notes for them back into the "unlearned" set. Then recite the words in the "learned" set. Continue in this way until you can accurately recite the information that you want to learn about all the words.

If your notes are on notebook paper, place check marks in pencil next to words as you learn them. Each time you recite, begin with the "learned" words. If you have forgotten the meanings of any of those words, erase the penciled checks next to them. Then recite the "unlearned" words, attempting to put checks next to as many of them as you can. Continue in this way until you have learned the meanings of all the words.

NAME _____ DATE _____ **13**

EXERCISE 2.1   Notes on Notebook Paper

Make notes for learning the meanings of five words you need to learn for a psychology, chemistry, business, or other college course you are taking. See Figure 2.1 on page 11 for an example of the kind of notes you are to make.

EXERCISE 2.2   Notes on a 3-by-5-Inch Card

Select a word of general interest that you want to learn, and make notes for learning it on the form for a 3-by-5-inch card below. See Figure 2.2 on page 11 for an example of the kind of notes you are to make.

Increase Words You Use

In addition to helping you increase the words you know, *College Vocabulary Skills* will teach you how to expand your **expressive vocabulary**—the words you use when you write and speak.

- When you speak, you are not likely to use words that you are uncertain how to pronounce; therefore, Chapter 5 teaches how to pronounce words correctly.
- Chapter 17 explains how to use a thesaurus or dictionary to select words that express your thoughts precisely.
- Chapter 18 provides practice that will help you avoid misusing words that are frequently confused, such as *affect* and *effect, farther* and *further,* and *anecdote* and *antidote.*
- Chapter 19 teaches how to differentiate among standard, informal, slang, and nonstandard usages of words.
- When you write, you are not likely to use words that you are uncertain how to spell; therefore, Chapters 20, 21, and 22 explain how to spell words correctly.

This chapter explains how to improve your ability to jog your memory, so that you can recollect words you know and use them when you write or speak.

Recollecting Words You Know

You can improve your ability to recollect words you know by learning to ask yourself questions that help you to recall them. For instance, if you write about people swimming to shore because their boat has overturned, you might ask yourself the following question:

> Do I know a word that means "to turn a boat over"?

The chances are that you do know the word that has this meaning, but unless you go boating often, you probably seldom think of it. As a result, you may not recall *capsize;* it means "to turn over," especially a boat in water.

This chapter presents exercises that show you the kinds of questions you can ask yourself to recall words you know. In these exercises you are to supply words that have been deleted from each sentence. Write the word that correctly completes the following sentence.

To overturn a boat in water is to _____ it.

You should have written *capsize* on the line.

Expressive Vocabulary Exercises

The purpose of the exercises in this chapter is to help you increase your ability to recall and use more of the words that are in your receptive vocabulary. You do your best on an exercise when you recollect all the answers you know. For example, which of the words missing from the following sentences are words you know?

1. The hole in a needle is called an _____.

2. To cook a chicken in an oven is to _____ the chicken.

3. A period of ten years is a _____.

4. Those who are equal to you in most ways are your _____.

The words that are missing from these sentences are (1) eye, (2) roast or bake, (3) decade, and (4) peers. Your score is 100 if you gave all the correct answers you know. For instance, if you know two correct answers and you wrote both of those answers, your score is 100.

   If you do the following exercises carefully, trying to recollect as many correct answers as you can, you should notice improvement in your ability to recall words that are in your receptive vocabulary.

EXERCISE 3.1 **Recalling Words You Know**

Try to recall and write the words that are missing from the following sentences.

1. Washington, D.C. is the _____ of the United States.

2. The panel with gauges on it in a car is called a _____.

3. Oranges, grapefruit, and lemons are members of a class of fruit known

   as _____.

4. A lighting fixture that hangs from the ceiling and has branches for several

   lights is called a _____.

5. When someone's teeth have to be removed, dentists _____ them.

6. There are two pints of liquid in a _____.

7. The card game twenty-one is also called _____.

8. The meat from sheep is called _____.

9. The name and address of a person or firm printed as a heading on a sheet

   of letter paper is called a _____.

10. The transparent covering of the colored part of an eyeball is called a

    _____.

11. The shelter near the diamond where baseball players sit when not at play

    is called the _____.

12. A place that has docks for pleasure boats is called a _____.

13. The rules of behavior at social functions such as weddings are called

    _____.

14. The tax on imported products is called _____.

EXERCISE 3.2   Recalling Words You Know

Try to recall and write the words that are missing from the following sentences.

1. A period of one hundred years is a _____.

2. A person who is named to receive income from an insurance policy is called a _____.

3. To carve a name on a silver bracelet is to _____ the name.

4. The mark "-" which follows the fourth letter in *anti-intellectual* is called a _____.

5. A person in a court action who is accused of committing a crime is called a _____.

6. Macaroni and spaghetti are examples of a class of food known as _____.

7. A distance of 5,280 feet is called a _____.

8. The year 1747 was in the _____ century.

9. The part of the eyeball that is often colored brown or blue is called the _____.

10. In England, elevators are called _____.

11. The middle number in a series of numbers (such as 7 in the series 3, 5, 7, 8, 9) is called the _____.

12. There are four quarts of liquid in a _____.

13. A fancy bottle for holding wine or spirits is called a _____.

14. To accumulate and hide a much larger supply of food than one can possibly use is to _____ food.

EXERCISE 3.3   Recalling Words You Know

Try to recall and write the words that are missing from the following sentences.

1. Your skin will burn if you _____ it to the hot summer sun for a long time.

2. The window through which automobile drivers look while driving is called the _____.

3. The finger next to your thumb is your _____ finger.

4. Students in their fourth full-time year of college are _____.

5. A person or organization that brings a suit in a court of law is called a _____.

6. A bunch of cut flowers is a _____.

7. A knife attached to the end of a rifle is a _____.

8. There are four cups of liquid in a _____.

9. The outer layer of your skin is your _____.

10. People who derive pleasure from causing others to suffer physical or mental pain are called _____.

11. The tube in your body through which food passes into your stomach is your _____.

12. A list of words and their definitions at the end of a textbook is called a _____.

13. A factory that manufactures liquor is called a _____.

14. A woman opera star is called a _____.

EXERCISE 3.4   **Recalling Words You Know**

Try to recall and write the words that are missing from the following sentences.

1. The part of your leg between your knee and your hip is called your

   _____.

2. People who are forced to leave their countries are said to be sent into

   _____.

3. A round, flat object, such as a phonograph record, is in the shape of a

   _____.

4. The person who has the job of keeping records of students' grades at a

   college is called a _____.

5. Newspaper articles that state the opinion of the publisher appear on

   the _____ page.

6. A long speech by one character in a play is called a _____.

7. A drastic shortage of food is called a _____.

8. The uncured meat from pigs is called _____.

9. Initials on luggage, clothing, or jewelry are called _____.

10. A person with legs that curve out is said to be _____.

11. There are two cups of liquid in a _____.

12. Those who reject lovers after having accepted or encouraged them

    _____ their lovers.

13. A person who lives all by himself in a secluded place, especially for religious

    reasons, is called a _____.

14. When children look very much like their parents, we attribute the

    similarities to a process called _____.

Use a Dictionary

Dictionaries are alphabetically arranged lists of words that include spellings, pronunciations, definitions, and synonyms. The entries in desk dictionaries include the words that are used in college subjects as well as idioms, abbreviations, affixes, and information about people, places, events, and other topics. This chapter explains these and other features of standard desk dictionaries.

The number of entry words in a dictionary is a guide to how complete it is. **Entry words** are the words printed in boldface type that serve as headings in dictionary entries. Following are the entries beginning with *jilt* and ending with *jimmy* in the desk and paperback editions of *The American Heritage Dictionary.*

Desk Edition

jilt (jĭlt) *tr.v.* **jilt·ed, jilt·ing, jilts.** To deceive or drop (a lover) suddenly or callously. —**jilt** *n.* One who discards a lover. [Possibly from obsolete *jilt,* harlot, alteration of *gillot,* diminutive of *gille,* woman, girl, from Middle English. See GILL⁴.]

Jim Crow or **jim crow** (jĭm′ krō′) *Slang. n.* The systematic practice of discriminating against and suppressing Black people. —*adj.* **1.** Upholding or practicing discrimination against and suppression of Black people: *Jim Crow laws; a Jim Crow town.* **2.** Reserved for a racial or ethnic group that is to be discriminated against: *"I told them I wouldn't take a Jim Crow job"* (Ralph Bunche). [From obsolete *Jim Crow,* derogatory name for a Black person, ultimately from the title of a 19th-century minstrel song, from CROW¹.] —**Jim′-Crow′ism** (jĭm′krō′iz′əm) *n.*

jim-dan·dy (jĭm′dăn′dē) *n., pl.* **-dies.** *Informal.* One that is very pleasing or excellent of its kind. [*Jim* (nickname for *James*) + DANDY.] —**jim′-dan′dy** *adj.*

Ji·mé·nez (hē-mě′něs, -něth), **Juan Ramón.** 1881–1958. Spanish poet who introduced modernism to Spanish verse. He won the 1956 Nobel Prize for literature.

Jiménez de Cis·ne·ros (dě sěs-ně′rôs, *thě* thěs-), **Francis-co.** 1436–1517. Spanish prelate and political leader. The confessor of Isabella I, he imposed conversion to Christianity on the Moors of Granada, leading to an uprising (1499–1500), and was appointed grand inquisitor (1507).

jim-jams (jĭm′jămz′) *pl.n. Slang.* **1.** The jitters. **2.** Delirium tremens. [Expressive of the trembling associated with delirium tremens.]

jim·mies (jĭm′ēz) *pl.n.* Small particles of chocolate or flavored candy sprinkled on ice cream as a topping. [Origin unknown.]

jim·my (jĭm′ē) *n., pl.* **-mies.** A short crowbar with curved ends. —**jimmy** *tr.v.* **-mied, -my·ing, -mies.** To pry (something) open with or as if with a jimmy: *jimmy a door.* [Probably from the name *Jimmy,* nickname for *James.*]

Paperback Edition

jilt (jĭlt) *v.* To cast aside (a lover). —*n.* One who discards a lover. [Orig. unknown.]
Jim Crow *n.* The practice of discriminating against and segregating black people. [< the title of a 19th-cent. song.] —**Jim′-Crow′** *adj.*
jim·my (jĭm′ē) *n., pl.* **-mies.** A short crowbar with curved ends. —*v.* **-mied, -my·ing.** To pry open with or as if with a jimmy. [< *Jimmy,* nickname for *James.*]

Notice that the desk edition gives many more definitions than the paperback edition and that the definitions in the desk edition are more complete. When desk dictionaries are condensed to fit on the pages of paperback books, a great deal is lost. Desk dictionaries list up to about 200,000 words, but paperback dictionaries usually list only about 50,000 words.

You should own a paperback dictionary to carry with you to classes and a desk dictionary to use where you study. Paperback dictionaries are handy reference sources, but they do not include sufficient information for a college student's needs.

Of several excellent dictionaries, I especially recommend *The American Heritage Dictionary of the English Language,* Third Edition. Other reputable dictionaries include *Webster's New World Dictionary of the American Language* and *The Random House Dictionary of the English Language.* If you do not own a good desk dictionary, compare dictionaries and buy the one with definitions written so they are easy for you to understand. It is essential that you own a dictionary that explains word meanings clearly; if you do not understand the definitions in your dictionary, you probably will not use it often.

Spellings

Dictionaries provide the answers to almost all questions about the correct spellings of words. For instance, the following entry indicates that the plural of *criterion* may be spelled *criteria* or *criterions.*

> **cri·te·ri·on** (krī-tîr′ē-ən) *n., pl.* **-te·ri·a** (-tîr′ē-ə) or **-te·ri·ons.** A standard, rule, or test on which a judgment or decision can be based. See Synonyms at **standard.** [Greek *kritērion,* from *kritēs,* judge, from *krinein,* to separate, judge. See **krei-** in Appendix.] —**cri·te′ri·al** (-əl) *adj.*

It is correct to use *criterion* in the phrase "the *criterion* is," but *criteria* in the phrase "the *criteria* are."

Chapter 21 gives detailed explanations about how to use a dictionary to find the correct spellings of words.

Pronunciations

Pronunciation spellings follow most words in desk dictionaries. The spelling enclosed in parentheses after *aegis* in the following entry indicates the correct pronunciation of the word.

> **ae·gis** also **e·gis** (ē′jĭs) *n.* **1.** Protection: *a child whose welfare is now under the aegis of the courts.* **2.** Sponsorship; patronage: *a concert held under the aegis of the parents' association.* **3.** *Greek Mythology.* The shield or breastplate of Zeus, later an attribute of Athena, carrying at its center the head of Medusa. [Latin, from Greek *aigis.*]

Chapter 5 explains how to interpret pronunciation spellings such as the one given for *aegis,* and most of the other chapters in *College Vocabulary Skills* provide practice in interpreting pronunciation spellings.

Parts of Speech

Parts of speech are indicated by italicized abbreviations that follow pronunciation spellings. The abbreviation *n.* following the pronunciation spelling of *coast* indicates the word is a noun.

> **coast** (kōst) *n.* **1.a.** Land next to the sea; the seashore. **b. Coast.** The Pacific Coast of the United States. **2.** A hill or other slope down which one may coast, as on a sled. **3.** The act of sliding or coasting; slide. **4.** *Obsolete.* The frontier or border of a country. **—coast** *v.* **coast·ed, coast·ing, coasts.** *—intr.* **1.a.** To slide down an incline through the effect of gravity. **b.** To move effortlessly and smoothly. See Synonyms at **slide. 2.** To move without further use of propelling power. **3.** To act or move aimlessly or with little effort: *coasted for a few weeks before applying for a job.* **4.** *Nautical.* To sail near or along a coast. *—tr. Nautical.* To sail or move along the coast or border of. [Middle English *coste,* from Old French, from Latin *costa,* side. See **kost-** in Appendix.] **—coast′al** (kō′stəl) *adj.*

Many words function in more than one part of speech. For example, *coast* can be both a noun (as in "a town on the *coast*") and a verb (as in "to *coast* down a hill"). In this entry for *coast,* four noun definitions are followed by four verb definitions. The first noun definition is "land next to the sea," and the first verb definition is "to slide down an incline through the effect of gravity."

The abbreviations used for the eight traditional parts of speech are *n.* (noun), *v.* (verb), *adj.* (adjective), *adv.* (adverb), *pron.* (pronoun), *conj.* (conjunction), *prep.* (preposition), and *interj.* (interjection). Verbs may be *tr.v.* (transitive verbs) or *intr.v.* (intransitive verbs). Transitive verbs take a direct object ("he *studied* math"), whereas intransitive verbs do not have direct objects ("she *studied*"). Most verbs may be used either transitively or intransitively.

Definition Sequences

Dictionary writers use two methods to sequence definitions. Sometimes they list definitions chronologically, with the oldest known meaning first, and other times they list the most common or general meaning first.

Webster's Ninth New Collegiate Dictionary lists definitions chronologically, with the oldest known meaning first.

> **sym·po·sium** \sim-'pō-zē-əm *also* -zh(ē-)əm\ *n, pl* **-sia** \-zē-ə, -zh(ē-)ə\ *or* **-siums** [L, fr. Gk *symposion,* fr. *sympinein* to drink together, fr. *syn-* + *pinein* to drink — more at POTABLE] (1603) **1 a :** a convivial party (as after a banquet in ancient Greece) with music and conversation   **b :** a social gathering at which there is free interchange of ideas   **2 a :** a formal meeting at which several specialists deliver short addresses on a topic or on related topics — compare COLLOQUIUM   **b :** a collection of opinions on a subject; *esp :* one published by a periodical   **c :** DISCUSSION
>
> ——— Oldest meaning
>
> ——— Most recent meaning

WEBSTER'S NINTH NEW COLLEGIATE DICTIONARY

Notice that *symposium* first referred to drinking parties in ancient Greece. Now, however, *symposium* also refers to a collection of published opinions or other writings about a topic.

The American Heritage Dictionary lists the most common or general meanings first.

> **sym·po·si·um** (sĭm-pō′zē-əm) *n., pl.* **-si·ums** or **-si·a** (-zē-ə). **1.** A meeting or conference for discussion of a topic, especially one in which the participants form an audience and make presentations. **2.** A collection of writings on a particular topic, as in a magazine. **3.** A convivial meeting for drinking, music, and intellectual discussion among the ancient Greeks. [Latin, drinking party, from Greek *symposion* : *sun-*, syn- + *posis*, drinking; see **pō(i)-** in Appendix.]
>
> — Most common meaning
>
> THE AMERICAN HERITAGE DICTIONARY

The editors of *The American Heritage Dictionary* have listed first the definition most commonly applied to *symposium* today.

Compare the sequences of definitions for *symposium* in the two dictionaries. You will find that it is easier to locate definitions in your dictionary when you know what method was used to list them.

Etymologies

An **etymology** is the information about the origin and development of a word; it is placed before the first definition of the word in dictionaries that list definitions chronologically. In the following entry from *Webster's Ninth New Collegiate Dictionary*, the etymology of *tuxedo* is enclosed in brackets just before the first definition.

> **tux·e·do** \ˌtək-'sēd-(ˌ)ō\ *n. pl* **-dos** or **-does** [*Tuxedo* Park, N.Y.] (1899) **1** : a single-breasted or double-breasted usu. black or blackish blue jacket   **2** : semiformal evening clothes for men — **tux·e·doed** \-(ˌ)ōd\ *adj*
>
> — An etymology
>
> WEBSTER'S NINTH NEW COLLEGIATE DICTIONARY

An etymology is placed after the last definition in dictionaries that list the most common or general meaning first. In the following entry from *The American Heritage Dictionary*, the etymology of *tuxedo* is enclosed in brackets at the end of the entry.

> **tux·e·do** (tŭk-sē′dō) *n., pl.* **-dos** or **-does**. **1.** A man's dress jacket, usually black with satin or grosgrain lapels, worn for formal or semiformal occasions. Also called *dinner jacket*. **2.** A complete outfit including this jacket, trousers usually with a silken stripe down the side, a bow tie, and often a cummerbund. [Short for *Tuxedo coat*, after a country club at *Tuxedo* Park, a village of southeast New York.] **—tux·e′doed** *adj*.
>
> — An etymology
>
> THE AMERICAN HERITAGE DICTIONARY

Both etymologies for *tuxedo* state that the word comes from the name Tuxedo Park, New York.

Subject Labels

Desk dictionaries provide subject labels to help you locate definitions that pertain to subjects you study in college. **Subject labels** are terms printed in italic type that indicate the fields of knowledge to which the definitions apply. The following entry for *regression* includes four subject labels: the italicized words *Psychology, Biology, Statistics,* and *Astronomy.*

> **re·gres·sion** (rĭ-grĕsh′ən) *n.* **1.** Reversion; retrogression. **2.** Relapse to a less perfect or developed state. **3.** *Psychology.* Reversion to an earlier or less mature pattern of feeling or behavior. **4.** *Biology.* The return of a population to an earlier or less complex physical type in successive generations. **5.** *Statistics.* The relationship between the mean value of a random variable and the corresponding values of one or more independent variables. **6.** *Astronomy.* Retrograde motion of a celestial body.

When you study psychology, the third definition will be of special interest to you, whereas when you study astronomy, the sixth definition will be the one you want.

Synonyms

Desk dictionaries are excellent sources of information about **synonyms**—words that have the same or nearly the same meaning. The following entry for *amiable* is accompanied by explanations of the synonyms *affable, good-natured, obliging, agreeable,* and *pleasant.*

> **a·mi·a·ble** (ā′mē-ə-bəl) *adj.* **1.** Friendly and agreeable in disposition; good-natured and likable. **2.** Cordial; sociable; congenial: *an amiable gathering.* [Middle English, from Old French, from Late Latin *amīcābilis.* See AMICABLE.] **—a′mi·a·bil′i·ty,** **a′mi·a·ble·ness** *n.* **—a′mi·a·bly** *adv.*
>
> **SYNONYMS:** *amiable, affable, good-natured, obliging, agreeable, pleasant.* These adjectives mean willing or showing a willingness to please. *Amiable* implies friendliness: *"an amiable villain with a cocky, sidelong grin"* (Hal Hinson). *Affable* especially fits a person who is easy to approach, responsive in conversation, and slow to anger: *She is affable enough when she is not preoccupied with business problems. Good-natured* suggests a tolerant, easygoing disposition; sometimes it also implies a docile nature: *You are too good-natured to resent a little criticism. Obliging* specifies willingness or eagerness to be of help to others or indulge their wishes: *The obliging waiter was in no hurry for us to pay the bill and leave. Agreeable* suggests being in accord with one's own feelings, nature, or tastes: *"My idea of an agreeable person . . . is a person who agrees with me"* (Benjamin Disraeli). *Pleasant* applies broadly to agreeable manner, behavior, or appearance: *"I couldn't handle it, I didn't enjoy it and it probably didn't make me a pleasant person to be around"* (James Caan).

Synonyms

Chapter 17 describes how to interpret dictionary discussions, such as the one above, that explain how synonyms differ in meaning and usage.

Idioms

An **idiom** is a phrase that has a meaning that is not clear from the common meanings of the words in the phrase; it is an accepted phrase that cannot be interpreted literally. For example, the common meanings of the words in the phrase *green thumb* suggest that it refers to a thumb the color of grass. However, idiomatically, *green thumb* refers to a special talent for growing plants.

> **green thumb**   *n.* An ability to make plants grow well.

Idioms are sometimes defined in entries for the principal words in them. For instance, since *worst* is the principal word in *if worst comes to worst,* the idiom is defined in the entry for *worst.* Locate the four idiomatic phrases printed in boldface in the following entry.

> **worst** (wûrst) *adj.* Superlative of **bad**[1], **ill.** **1.** Most inferior, as in quality, condition, or effect. **2.** Most severe or unfavorable. **3.** Being furthest from an ideal or a standard; least desirable or satisfactory. —**worst** *adv.* Superlative of **badly, ill.** In the worst manner or degree. —**worst** *tr.v.* **worst·ed, worst·ing, worsts.** To gain the advantage over; defeat. —**worst** *n.* Something that is worst. —*idioms.* **at (the) worst.** Under the most negative circumstances, estimation, or interpretation: *At worst, the storm will make us postpone the trip.* **get** (or **have) the worst of it.** To suffer a defeat or disadvantage. **if (the) worst comes to (the) worst.** If the very worst thing happens. **in the worst way.** *Informal.* Very much; a great deal: *wanted to be elected in the worst way.* [Middle English, from Old English *wyrsta.* See **wers-** in Appendix.]

— An idiom

The four idiomatic phrases defined in this entry are *at worst, get the worst of it, if worst comes to worst,* and *in the worst way.*

Some idioms you should know are listed on page 27.

Homographs

Homographs are words that have the same spelling but different meanings and etymologies. Entries for homographs are indicated by small raised numbers called *superscripts.* Notice the superscripts *1, 2,* and *3* after *husky* in the following three entries.

> **husk·y**[1] (hŭs′kē) *adj.* **-i·er, -i·est.** **1.** Hoarse or rough in quality: *a voice husky with emotion.* **2. a.** Resembling a husk. **b.** Containing husks. [From HUSK.] —**husk′i·ly** *adv.*
>
> **husk·y**[2] (hŭs′kē) *adj.* **-i·er, -i·est.** **1.** Strongly built; burly. **2.** Heavily built: *clothing sizes for husky boys.* —**husky** *n.,* *pl.* **-ies.** A husky person. [Perhaps from HUSK.]
>
> **hus·ky**[3] also **hus·kie** (hŭs′kē) *n.,* *pl.* **-kies.** **1.** Often **Husky** or **Huskie.** A dog of a breed developed in Siberia for pulling sleds and having a dense, variously colored coat. Also called *Siberian husky.* **2.** A similar dog of Arctic origin. [Probably from shortening and alteration of ESKIMO.]

The superscript numbers indicate that *husky*[1], *husky*[2], and *husky*[3] are homographs. When an entry word is followed by such numbers, you may need to consult more than one entry to locate the definition you want.

People, Places, and Other Topics

Desk dictionaries include entries for people, places, and many other topics. Entries for people range from famous historical figures to prominent individuals in politics, art, music, film, and sports.

> **King,** **Martin Luther, Jr.** 1929–1968. American cleric whose eloquence and commitment to nonviolent tactics formed the foundation of the civil rights movement of the 1950's and 1960's. He won the 1964 Nobel Peace Prize, four years before he was assassinated in Memphis, Tennessee.

Some Important Idioms

act of God *n., pl.* **acts of God.** An unusual, extraordinary, or unforeseeable manifestation of the forces of nature beyond the powers of human intervention, such as a tornado or a bolt of lightning.

alpha and omega *n.* **1.** The first and the last: *"I am Alpha and Omega, the beginning and the ending, saith the Lord"* (Revelation 1:8). **2.** The most important part.

birthday suit *n.* The state of being nude; nakedness.

brain trust *n.* **1.** A group of experts who serve, usually unofficially, as advisers and policy planners, especially in a government.

cold shoulder *n. Informal.* Deliberate coldness or disregard; a slight or a snub: *received the cold shoulder from several members of the club.*

cold turkey *n. Slang.* **1.** Immediate, complete withdrawal from something on which one has become dependent, such as an addictive drug. **2.** Blunt language or procedural method. **3.** A cold fish.

crocodile tears *pl.n.* An insincere display of grief; false tears. [From the belief that crocodiles weep either to attract a victim or when eating one.]

elbow grease *n. Informal.* Strenuous physical labor and effort.

eleventh hour *n.* The latest possible time: *turned in the report at the eleventh hour.*

four-let·ter word (fôr′lĕt′ər, fōr′-) *n.* Any of several short English words generally regarded as vulgar or obscene.

gravy train *n. Slang.* An occupation or other source of income that requires little effort while yielding considerable profit.

Indian summer *n.* **1.** A period of mild weather occurring in late autumn. **2.** A pleasant, tranquil, or flourishing period occurring near the end of something: *the Indian summer of the administration.*

ivory tower *n.* A place or an attitude of retreat, especially preoccupation with lofty, remote, or intellectual considerations rather than practical everyday life. [Translation of French *tour d'ivoire : tour,* tower + *d',* of + *ivoire,* ivory.]

lip service *n.* Verbal expression of agreement or allegiance, unsupported by real conviction or action; hypocritical respect: *"Lip service continues to be paid to resolving regional conflicts, but there is no sense of urgency"* (Henry A. Kissinger).

Mur·phy's Law (mûr′fēz) *n.* Any of certain humorous axioms stating that anything that can possibly go wrong, will go wrong. [From the name *Murphy.*]

primrose path *n.* **1.** A way of life of worldly ease or pleasure. **2.** A course of action that seems easy and appropriate but can actually end in calamity.

red herring *n.* **1.** A smoked herring having a reddish color. **2.** Something that draws attention away from the central issue. [From its use to distract hunting dogs from the trail.]

rule of thumb *n., pl.* **rules of thumb.** A useful principle having wide application but not intended to be strictly accurate or reliable in every situation.

sacred cow *n.* One that is immune from criticism, often unreasonably so: *"The need for widespread secrecy has become a sacred cow"* (Bulletin of the Atomic Scientists). [From the veneration of the cow by Hindus.]

sitting duck *n. Informal.* An easy target or victim.

soft-soap (sôft′sōp′, sŏft′-) *tr.v.* **-soaped, -soap·ing, -soaps.** *Informal.* To flatter in order to gain something; cajole. —**soft′-soap′er** *n.*

staff of life *n., pl.* **staves of life** or **staffs of life.** A staple or necessary food, especially bread.

stool pigeon *n.* **1.** *Slang.* A person acting as a decoy or as an informer, especially one who is a spy for the police. **2.** A pigeon used as a decoy. [From the practice of tying decoy pigeons to a stool to attract other pigeons.]

straw man *n.* **1.** A person who is set up as cover or a front for a questionable enterprise. **2.** An argument or opponent set up so as to be easily refuted or defeated. **3.** A bundle of straw made into the likeness of a man and often used as a scarecrow.

tit for tat *n.* Repayment in kind, as for an injury; retaliation. [Probably alteration of *tip for tap.*]

tongue-in-cheek (tŭng′ĭn-chēk′) *adj.* Meant or expressed ironically or facetiously.

touch-and-go (tŭch′ən-gō′) *adj.* Dangerous and uncertain in nature or outcome; precarious; delicate: *major surgery followed by a touch-and-go recovery.*

Ty·phoid Mar·y (tī′foid′ mâr′ē) *n.* A person from whom something undesirable or deadly spreads to those nearby. [After *Mary Mallon,* a carrier of typhoid.]

vicious circle *n.* **1.** A situation in which the apparent solution of one problem in a chain of circumstances creates a new problem and increases the difficulty of solving the original problem.

walking papers *pl.n. Slang.* A notice of discharge or dismissal.

wet blanket *n. Informal.* One that discourages enjoyment or enthusiasm.

Entries for places include cities, states, countries, bodies of water, mountains, deserts, and ancient places.

Ma·chu Pic·chu (mä′chōō pēk′chōō, pē′-). An ancient Inca fortress city in the Andes northwest of Cuzco, Peru. Its extensive ruins, including elaborate terraces, were discovered in 1911.

Desk dictionaries also list entries for a wide variety of other topics.

punk rock *n. Music.* A form of hard-driving rock music characterized by harsh lyrics attacking conventional society and popular culture and often expressing alienation and anger.

When you want basic facts about a topic, you are likely to find them in a modern desk dictionary.

Abbreviations

Abbreviations are shortened forms of words or phrases, such as *Mr.* for *Mister* and *NY* for *New York*. Desk dictionaries list entries for abbreviations.

CO *abbr.* **1.** Colorado. **2.** Or **C.O.** Commanding officer. **3.** Also
  C.O. Conscientious objector.
co. *abbr.* **1.** Or **co, Co.** Company. **2.** County.
c.o. *abbr.* **1.** *Accounting.* Carried over. **2.** Cash order.
c/o also **c.o.** *abbr.* Care of.

These four entries give the meanings for the abbreviations spelled *CO, C.O., Co., co, co., c.o.,* and *c/o.*
   Abbreviations may also be found in entries for words. The following entry for *Colorado* lists three abbreviations for the state.

Col·o·ra·do (kŏl′ə-răd′ō, -rä′dō). *Abbr.* **CO, Col., Colo.** A state of the west-central United States. It was admitted as the 38th state in 1876. First explored by the Spanish in the 16th and 17th centuries, the region was added to the United States through the Louisiana Purchase (1803) and a cession by Mexico (1848). Denver is the capital and the largest city. Population, 2,889,735. **—Col′o·ra′dan** *adj. & n.*

The abbreviation *CO* is the one to use following a zip code, as in "Denver, CO 80817."
   Some abbreviations that are important to know are listed below.

Some Important Abbreviations

A.D. *abbr.* Often **A.D.** Anno Domini.
a.k.a. or **aka** *abbr.* Also known as.
A.M. *abbr.* **1.** Airmail. **2.** Or **A.M.** *Latin.* Anno mundi (in the year of the world). **3.** Also **a.m.** or **A.M.** Ante meridiem. See Usage Note at **ante meridiem. 4.** *Latin.* Artium magister (Master of Arts).
an·no Dom·i·ni (ăn′ō dŏm′ə-nī′, dŏm′ə-nē) *adv.* *Abbr.* **A.D., A.D.** In a specified year of the Christian era. [Medieval Latin : *annō,* in the year + *Domini,* genitive of *Dominus,* Lord.]
an·te me·rid·i·em (ăn′tē mə-rĭd′ē-əm) *adv. & adj. Abbr.* **A.M., a.m., A.M.** Before noon. Used chiefly in the abbreviated form to specify the hour: *10:30 A.M.; an A.M. appointment.* [Latin *ante,* before + *meridiem,* accusative of *meridiēs,* noon.]
ASAP or **asap** *abbr.* As soon as possible.
B.C. *abbr.* **1.** Bachelor of Chemistry. **2.** Also **B.C.** Before Christ. **3.** Or **BC** British Columbia.
BYOB or **B.Y.O.B** *abbr.* Bring your own booze; bring your own bottle.
CEO or **C.E.O.** *abbr.* Chief executive officer.
CPA also **C.P.A.** *abbr.* Certified public accountant.
D.A. *abbr.* **1.** Also **DA.** *Law.* District attorney. **2.** Doctor of Arts.
DC or **D.C.** *abbr.* District of Columbia.
D.D.S. *abbr.* **1.** Doctor of Dental Science. **2.** Doctor of Dental Surgery.
DOA *abbr.* Dead on arrival.
e.g. *abbr.* Exempli gratia.
ESP (ē′ĕs-pē′) *n.* Communication or perception by means other than the physical senses. [*e(xtra)s(ensory) p(erception).*]

ex·em·pli gra·ti·a (ĭg-zĕm′plē grä′shē-ə, ĕk-sĕm′plē grä′tē-ä′) *adv. Abbr.* **e.g.** For example. [Latin *exemplī grātiā,* for the sake of example : *exemplī,* genitive of *exemplum,* example + *grātiā,* ablative of *grātia,* favor.]
FYI *abbr.* For your information.
GNP *abbr.* Gross national product.
gross national product *n. Abbr.* **GNP** The total market value of all the goods and services produced by a nation during a specified period.
i.e. *abbr. Latin.* Id est (that is).
IOU (ī′ō-yōō′) *n., pl.* **IOU's** or **IOUs.** A promise to pay a debt, especially a signed paper stating the specific amount owed and often bearing the letters IOU. [From the pronunciation of *I owe you.*]
Ms. also **Ms** (mĭz) *n., pl.* **Mses.** also **Mses** also **Mss.** or **Mss** (mĭz′ĭz). Used as a courtesy title before the surname or full name of a woman or girl: *Ms. Doe; Ms. Jane Doe.* [Blend of Miss and Mrs.]
P.M. also **p.m.** or **P.M.** *abbr.* Post meridiem. See Usage Note at **ante meridiem.**
R.S.V.P. or **r.s.v.p.** *abbr. French.* Répondez s'il vous plaît (please reply).
SASE *abbr.* Self-addressed stamped envelope.
SOP *abbr.* Standard operating procedure.
TGIF *abbr.* Thank God it's Friday.
VIP (vē′ī-pē′) *n., pl.* **VIPs.** *Informal.* A person of great importance or influence, especially a dignitary who commands special treatment. [*v(ery) i(mportant) p(erson).*]

Affixes

In addition to defining words, dictionaries define **affixes**—prefixes and suffixes of the kinds you will study in Chapters 10 and 11. Entries for prefixes are followed by a hyphen (-), as in the following entry for *ultra-*.

> **ultra—** *pref.* **1.** Beyond; on the other side of: *ultraviolet.* **2.** Beyond the range, scope, or limit of: *ultrasonic.* **3.** Beyond the normal or proper degree; excessively: *ultraconservative.* [Latin *ultrā-*, from *ultrā*, beyond. See **al-**¹ in Appendix.]

Similarly, entries for suffixes are preceded by a hyphen, as in the following entry for *-esque.*

> **—esque** *suff.* In the manner of; resembling: *Lincolnesque.* [French, from Italian *-esco*, from Vulgar Latin **-iscus*, of Germanic origin.]

Entries for combining forms are also followed or preceded by hyphens. On page 102 there are dictionary entries for the combining forms *astro-* and *-cyte.*

Illustrations

Some dictionaries include excellent illustrations to help in understanding the meanings of words. For instance, the following illustration helps readers understand the meanings of *concave* and *convex.*

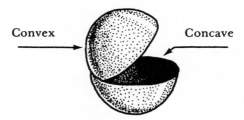

Convex   Concave

A *concave* object is hollow and curved like the inside of a basketball, while a *convex* object is curved outward like the outside surface of a ball.

Usages

Desk dictionaries also include a variety of information about the ways in which words are ordinarily used. The label *Vulgar Slang* in the following entry indicates that it is considered crude and impolite to refer to *nasal mucus* as *snot.*

> **snot** (snŏt) *n. Vulgar Slang.* **1.** Nasal mucus; phlegm. **2.** A person regarded as annoying, arrogant, or impertinent. [Middle English, from Old English *gesnot.*]

Chapter 19 explains how to use a dictionary for guidance in selecting words for expressing thoughts in papers you write for college credit.

EXERCISE 4.1   **Dictionary Checklist**

Use the following checklist to determine whether a dictionary that you own or are considering purchasing contains all the features you need in a dictionary. Write the title of the dictionary that you evaluate.

Title: _____

Yes   **No**

_____   _____   1. The dictionary was published no more than four years ago.

_____   _____   2. The definitions of words are easy to understand.

_____   _____   3. Biographical information is given (look up *Noah Webster*).

_____   _____   4. Geographical information is given (look up *New Mexico*).

_____   _____   5. Homographs are labeled with superscripts (look up *baker*[1], *baker*[2], and *baker*[3]).

_____   _____   6. Foreign phrases are defined (look up *bête noire*).

_____   _____   7. Prefixes, suffixes, and combining forms are defined (look up *retro-*, *-ish*, and *helio-*).

_____   _____   8. Abbreviations are defined (look up *P.S.*).

_____   _____   9. The dictionary has good illustrations and maps.

_____   _____   10. Some definitions have subject labels (look up *depression* to see whether some definitions are labeled *Economics*, *Astronomy*, or *Psychology*).

_____   _____   11. Some definitions have usage labels (look up *bug* to see whether a definition is labeled *Slang*, *Colloquial*, or *Informal*).

_____   _____   12. Meanings of synonyms are discussed (look up *old* to see whether its definitions are followed by a discussion of the meanings of words such as *ancient*, *antique*, and *archaic*).

EXERCISE 4.2 **Dictionary Entries**

Answer the following questions by referring to the entries that are listed at the bottom of this page.

1. Which is correct, "three *buffalo*," "three *buffaloes*," or "three *buffalos*"?

_____

2. What is the meaning of the prefix *contra-*?

_____

3. What is indicated by the numbers *1, 2,* and *3* that follow the entries for *gob*?

_____

4. In what year was *John F. Kennedy* assassinated?

_____

5. What is the meaning of *latent* in the study of psychology?

_____

6. Spell *love* in *pig Latin*.

_____

7. What is the meaning of the idiomatic phrase *make a stink*?

_____

8. What does the abbreviation *vol.* mean when it refers to publications?

buf·fa·lo (bŭf′ə-lō′) *n., pl.* **buffalo** or **-loes** or **-los. 1. a.** Any of several oxlike Old World mammals of the family Bovidae, such as the water buffalo and Cape buffalo. **b.** The North American bison, *Bison bison.* **2.** The buffalo fish.
contra— *pref.* **1.** Against; opposite; contrasting: *contraposition.* **2.** Lower in pitch: *contrabassoon.* [Middle English *contrā-*, from *contrā*, against. See **kom** in Appendix.]
gob¹ (gŏb) *n.* **1.** A small mass or lump. **2.** Often **gobs.** *Informal.* A large quantity: *a gob of money; gobs of time.* [Middle English *gobbe*, probably from Old French *gobe*, mouthful, from *gober*, to gulp, of Celtic origin.]
gob² (gŏb) *n. Slang.* The mouth. [Perhaps from Scottish and Irish Gaelic.]
gob³ (gŏb) *n. Slang.* A sailor. [Origin unknown.]
Kennedy, John Fitzgerald. 1917–1963. The 35th President of the United States (1961–1963). A U.S. representative (1947–1953) and senator (1953–1960) from Massachusetts, he became the youngest man elected to the presidency (1960). Kennedy approved the failed invasion of the Bay of Pigs (1961) and forced Khrushchev to remove Soviet missiles from Cuba (1962). He also established the Peace Corps (1961). Kennedy was assassinated in Dallas, Texas, on November 22, 1963.

la·tent (lāt′nt) *adj.* **1.** Present or potential but not evident or active: *latent talent.* **2.** *Pathology.* In a dormant or hidden stage: *a latent infection.* **3.** *Biology.* Undeveloped but capable of normal growth under the proper conditions: *a latent bud.* **4.** *Psychology.* Present in the unconscious mind but not consciously expressed.
pig Latin *n.* A jargon systematically formed by the transposition of the initial consonant to the end of the word and the suffixation of an additional syllable, as *igpay atinlay* for *pig Latin.*
stink (stĭngk) *v.* **stank** (stăngk) or **stunk** (stŭngk), **stunk, stink·ing, stinks.** —*intr.* **1.** To emit a strong foul odor. **2. a.** To be highly offensive or abhorrent. **b.** To be in extremely bad repute. **3.** *Slang.* To have something to an extreme or offensive degree: *a family that stinks with money; a deed that stinks of treachery.* **4.** *Slang.* To be of an extremely low or bad quality: *This job stinks.* —*tr.* To cause to stink: *garbage that stinks up the yard.* —**stink** *n.* A strong offensive odor; a stench. See Synonyms at **stench.** —*idiom.* **make** (or **raise**) **a stink.** *Slang.* To make a great fuss. [Middle English *stinken*, from Old English *stincan*, to emit a smell.] —**stink′y** *adj.*
vol. *abbr.* **1.** Volcano. **2.** Volume. **3.** Volunteer.

EXERCISE 4.3   Idioms and Abbreviations

The following questions test your knowledge of some of the idioms that are listed on page 27. Check the box in front of the choice that best states the meaning of each idiom.

1. The **alpha and omega** are the
   - ☐ a. beginning and end.
   - ☐ b. top and bottom.
   - ☐ c. best and worst.
   - ☐ d. blessed and damned.

2. The **eleventh hour** is
   - ☐ a. with time to spare.
   - ☐ b. at the last minute.
   - ☐ c. an hour before midnight.
   - ☐ d. an hour before noon.

3. An **ivory tower** is a
   - ☐ a. retreat from reality.
   - ☐ b. center for research.
   - ☐ c. church or cathedral.
   - ☐ d. hospital or school.

4. **Lip service** is
   - ☐ a. rudeness.
   - ☐ b. kisses.
   - ☐ c. insincere agreement.
   - ☐ c. talk with no action.

5. A **red herring** is
   - ☐ a. distracting.
   - ☐ b. smelly.
   - ☐ c. colorful.
   - ☐ d. tasty.

6. A **sacred cow** is
   - ☐ a. large and religious.
   - ☐ b. immune from criticism.
   - ☐ c. worshiped devoutly.
   - ☐ d. a boring issue.

Write the meanings of the following abbreviations, referring to page 28 for the meaning of any abbreviation that you do not know.

7. ASAP _____

8. D.A. _____

9. e.g. _____

10. ESP _____

11. FYI _____

12. GNP _____

13. i.e. _____

14. R.S.V.P. _____

15. SASE _____

16. VIP _____

Learn Pronunciations

One reason we mispronounce words is that very often their pronunciations are different from their spellings. For example, words pronounced *laf, fraze,* and *rek* are spelled *laugh, phrase,* and *wreck.* We also sometimes mispronounce words because we learn incorrect pronunciations from people whom we assume pronounce words correctly.

Fortunately, you do not need to rely on the spellings of words or pronunciations you hear to decide how to pronounce them. If you study this chapter carefully, you will learn how to find correct pronunciations of words by referring to a dictionary.

Pronunciation Spellings

In dictionaries, pronunciations are indicated by pronunciation spellings, which are enclosed in parentheses and placed immediately after entry words. The following entry provides two pronunciations for *dour.*

> **dour** (do͞or, dour) *adj.* **dour·er, dour·est. 1.** Marked by sternness or harshness; forbidding: *a dour, self-sacrificing life.* **2.** Silently ill-humored; gloomy: *the proverbially dour New England Puritan.* See Synonyms at **glum. 3.** Sternly obstinate; unyielding: *a dour determination.* [Middle English, possibly from Middle Irish *dúr*, probably from Latin *dūrus*, hard. See **deru-** in Appendix.] **—dour′ly** *adv.* **—dour′ness** *n.*

The pronunciation spellings for *dour* are (do͞or) and (dour). When more than one pronunciation is given, the first is *presumed* to be more common, but all pronunciations listed are equally acceptable. Pronunciation spellings are interpreted with the aid of a pronunciation key, such as the key printed at the bottom of this page. By studying this pronunciation key, you can determine that (do͞or) rhymes with *lure* and that (dour) rhymes with *hour.*

ă pat	ĭ pit	oi boy	th thin
ā pay	ī pie	ou out	*th* this
âr care	îr pier	o͝o took	hw which
ä father	ŏ pot	o͞o boot	zh vision
ĕ pet	ō toe	ŭ cut	ə about, item
ē be	ô paw	ûr urge	♦ regionalism

Consonants and Vowels

Consonants are usually said to be all the letters of the alphabet except *a, e, i, o, u,* and *y,* which may function as a consonant or a vowel. This explanation pertains to letters of the alphabet when they are used to spell words.

When words are spoken, **consonants** are the speech sounds produced by stopping breath or by forcing breath through a loose or narrow passage, and **vowels** are the speech sounds produced by using a free flow of breath. To understand the basic differences between consonants and vowels, pronounce the word *dish.* You stop your breath for *d* (a consonant), use a free flow of breath for *i* (a vowel), and force breath through a narrow passage for *sh* (a consonant combination).

There are only twenty-six letters in the English alphabet, but there are approximately forty-five sounds used to pronounce English words. These sounds are listed in the pronunciation key of *The American Heritage Dictionary,* which is printed on the inside front cover of this book and on page 33.

Pronunciation keys differ slightly from dictionary to dictionary; however, when you know how to use the pronunciation key for one dictionary, you can quickly learn to use the key for any other dictionary.

Consonants

Consonant letters are used to represent consonant sounds in pronunciation spellings. For example, the letters *h* and *t* represent consonant sounds in *hit* (hit), and the letters *s, t, r,* and *p* represent consonant sounds in *strap* (strap).

However, the letters *c, q,* and *x* are not used in pronunciation spellings. The letter *c* is usually pronounced *k,* as in *can* (kan), or *s,* as in *cent* (sent); the letter *q* is usually pronounced *kw,* as in *quit* (kwit); and the letter *x* is usually pronounced *ks,* as in *tax* (taks).

The following four words illustrate that pronunciation spellings often look very different from correct English spellings:

wrap	(rap)
knit	(nit)
his	(hiz)
gin	(jin)

Compare the spellings and pronunciations of *wrap, knit, his,* and *gin* to observe the differences between them. Then do Exercise 5.1 on page 38.

Consonant Digraphs

Consonant digraphs are combinations of consonants that are pronounced as single sounds. There are five common consonant digraphs:

ch as in *chip*	(chip)
ng as in wi*ng*	(wing)
sh as in *ship*	(ship)
th as in *thin*	(thin)
th as in *this*	(*th*is)

Notice that *th* in the pronunciation spelling of *thin* (thin) is not italicized, but it is italicized in the pronunciation spelling of *this* (this). Pronounce *thin* and *this* to recognize the two ways in which *th* is pronounced. The *th* in (thin) is voiceless, which means that the vocal cords do not vibrate to pronounce it. On the other hand, the *th* in (this) is voiced—the vocal cords do vibrate to pronounce it.

The sixth consonant digraph is *zh,* which is heard in words such as *measure* but not in common short words of the type in Exercise 5.2 at the end of this chapter. Do Exercise 5.2 on page 39 before you read the following discussion about long and short vowels.

Long and Short Vowels

The letters *a, e, i, o,* and *u* are used for most vowel sounds in pronunciation spellings. However, since there are only five vowel letters to represent approximately twenty vowel sounds, marks are used above vowels to indicate how they are pronounced.

Long vowels are the sounds that rhyme with the letters *a, e, i, o,* and *u.* Say the letters *a, e, i, o,* and *u* aloud. The sounds you said when you named the vowels are their long sounds. The following pronunciation spellings illustrate that most long vowel sounds are indicated by a mark called a **macron** (¯).

hate	(hāt)
beat	(bēt)
kite	(kīt)
goat	(gōt)
cute	(kyo͞ot)

Notice that the long sound of *u* is indicated differently from the other long vowel sounds, because it begins with the consonant sound *y,* as in *you.*

Short vowels are the sounds that are usually heard in three-letter words that begin and end with a consonant. Say the words *hat, bet, kit, got,* and *cut* aloud. The vowel sounds in these words are the short vowels.

Some dictionaries use no mark to indicate short vowels; all the words in Exercises 5.1 and 5.2 on pages 38 and 39 have short vowels and no mark is used over them. Other dictionaries use a mark called a **breve** (˘) to indicate short vowel sounds.

hat	(hăt)
bet	(bĕt)
kit	(kĭt)
got	(gŏt)
cut	(kŭt)

If you have difficulty hearing the short sounds of vowels, memorize these words: *add, egg, it, odd,* and *up.* After you have memorized these words, learn the short vowels by saying only the sounds that begin the words. For instance, recall the short sound of *a* by saying the *a* in *add,* but not the *dd.*

Do Exercises 5.3 and 5.4 on pages 40 and 41 before you read the following discussion about the dieresis and circumflex vowels.

The Dieresis and Circumflex Vowels

In addition to its long and short sounds, *a* has a sound that is indicated by a mark called a **dieresis** (¨).

     a as in *a*rm   (ärm)

The vowels *a, i, o,* and *u* all have sounds that are indicated by a mark called a **circumflex** (ˆ).

     a as in h*ai*r   (hâr)
     i as in h*e*re   (hîr)
     o as in l*aw*   (lô)
     u as in v*e*rb   (vûrb)

In some parts of the country the *a* sound in *arm* (ärm) and the *o* sound in *law* (lô) are pronounced as though they are the same sound. If you pronounce the two sounds the same way, you may have difficulty distinguishing between them in Exercise 5.5 on page 42, which you should do before you read on.

Four More Vowel Sounds

The vowel *o* has two sounds in addition to the ones indicated by the macron (ō), breve (ŏ), and circumflex (ô).

     o͞o as in bl*ue*   (blo͞o)
     o͝o as in b*oo*k   (bo͝ok)

One way to remember these sounds is to visualize the pronunciation spelling of *blue book* (blo͞o bo͝ok).

    Finally, there are two diphthongs. A **diphthong** is two vowel sounds that are blended and pronounced together.

     oi as in b*oy*   (boi)
     ou as in sc*ou*t   (skout)

To understand the characteristics of diphthongs, pronounce *bow* (bō) and then very slowly pronounce *boy* (boi). If you listen carefully, you should hear that the vowel sound in *boy* is the sound of long *o* (ō) blended with the sound of long *e* (ē).

    You may remember the diphthongs *oi* and *ou* by visualizing the pronunciation spelling of *boy scout* (boi skout).

    Do Exercise 5.6 on page 43 before you read the following discussion.

Syllables, Stress, and the Schwa

A **syllable** is a word or a part of a word that is pronounced as one unit. *Big, red,* and *hat* are examples of one-syllable words; they are all pronounced as one unit. However, most words have more than one syllable. The following words are printed with spaces between their syllables.

beau ty
beau ti fy
beau ti fi ca tion

Say these words aloud to hear the two syllables in *beauty*, three syllables in *beautify*, and five syllables in *beautification*.

When words have more than one syllable, one of the syllables is spoken with more stress. **Stress** is a general term that refers to the force with which syllables are spoken. **Primary stress** refers to the greater force with which one syllable is spoken in comparison with another syllable or other syllables in a word; it is indicated by a **primary accent mark** ('). Primary accent marks in the following words indicate which syllables receive primary stress when they are spoken.

ga rage'
beau' ty

Say *garage* and *beauty* aloud, giving primary stress to the syllables with the primary accent marks.

Secondary stress is weaker than primary stress but stronger than the stress given to unstressed, or unaccented, syllables; it is indicated by a **secondary accent mark** ('). Primary and secondary accent marks in the following words indicate which syllables receive primary and secondary stress.

rec' og nize'
in' dis pen' sa ble

Say *recognize* and *indispensable* aloud, giving primary and secondary stress to the syllables with the primary and secondary accent marks.

The syllables with no accent marks in *recognize* and *indispensable* are unstressed syllables. The vowel sounds in unstressed syllables are often indicated by a symbol called a **schwa**. The schwa looks like the letter *e* printed upside down (ə); it has the vowel sound heard in *of* when the phrase "bag *of* candy" is said quickly (băg əv kăn'dē). The following pronunciation spellings illustrate how accent marks and the schwa are used.

recognize   (rĕk'əg-nīz')
indispensable   (ĭn'dĭs-pĕn'sə-bəl)

In *recognize* the schwa represents a sound spelled by the letter *o*, and in *indispensable* schwas represent sounds spelled by the letters *a* and *e*. The schwa may represent sounds that are spelled by any vowel and by combinations of vowels. For example, the schwa represents the sound spelled by the letters *ai* in *mountain* (moun'tən).

Exercise 5.7 on page 44 explains how to divide two-syllable words, and you will practice dividing words into prefixes, bases, suffixes, and other elements when you study Chapters 10 through 14. Exercises 5.8 and 5.9 on pages 45 and 46 provide practice in interpreting all the consonant and vowel sounds and primary and secondary accent marks. Most of the other chapters in *College Vocabulary Skills* include additional practice for interpreting pronunciation spellings.

EXERCISE 5.1   Consonants

Read about consonants on page 34. Then respell the following words using the consonant sounds you hear when you pronounce the words. The first two problems are done to illustrate what you are to do.

1. crumb _____krum_____   6. pass _____

2. cell _____sel_____   7. has _____

3. bell _____   8. half _____

4. quick _____   9. gem _____

5. kick _____   10. cab _____

Check your answers to items 1 through 10 before you respell the following words.

11. knob _____   24. is _____

12. wax _____   25. calf _____

13. wreck _____   26. knot _____

14. dance _____   27. fix _____

15. quill _____   28. wrist _____

16. knack _____   29. glance _____

17. laugh _____   30. crust _____

18. lamb _____   31. quit _____

19. cent _____   32. golf _____

20. quack _____   33. yell _____

21. glass _____   34. lock _____

22. scrimp _____   35. knock _____

23. lick _____   36. cram _____

EXERCISE 5.2 Consonant Digraphs

Read about consonant digraphs on pages 34–35 and then do this exercise in the same way you did Exercise 5.1. Indicate the voiced *th* by underlining it. For example, underline the *th* in a word such as *this* (*th*is), but do not underline *th* in a word such as *thin* (thin).

1. chill	_____	5. bath	_____
2. shall	_____	6. than	_____
3. thick	_____	7. dish	_____
4. bang	_____	8. pink	_____

Check your answers for items 1 through 8 before you respell the following words.

9. catch	_____	23. long	_____
10. this	_____	24. itch	_____
11. them	_____	25. then	_____
12. crotch	_____	26. crash	_____
13. chunk	_____	27. stink	_____
14. shank	_____	28. ditch	_____
15. thumb	_____	29. that	_____
16. fifth	_____	30. froth	_____
17. thing	_____	31. cling	_____
18. witch	_____	32. thatch	_____
19. check	_____	33. clash	_____
20. gnash	_____	34. wrath	_____
21. scorch	_____	35. cinch	_____
22. crush	_____	36. wring	_____

EXERCISE 5.3   Short and Long Vowels

The following words illustrate that when there is only one vowel in a one-syllable word, the vowel usually has the short sound. Examine the words, and think of other one-syllable words like these.

Short a	Short e	Short i	Short o	Short u
back	spell	lick	fond	bulk
hand	dent	limp	block	lung
plant	west	disk	blot	junk
black	self	kiss	clog	dust
raft	zest	hint	flop	fund
lamp	mess	zip	chops	scrub
tack	kept	wilt	prom	skull
cash	bless	fist	slob	snug
gasp	stench	brisk	stock	blunt
tramp	chess	chin	drop	blush
drank	fresh	grill	flock	stuff
glass	swell	shift	crop	stunt
smash	trench	shrimp	snob	flush
brand	trend	skim	throb	gruff
crack	stress	thick	shock	smug
shack	dwell	twist	lock	grunt
scan	shred	drill	plot	crush
slash	smell	stitch	crock	thump

The following words illustrate common spellings of long vowels in one-syllable words: long **a** (lake, rain, stay); long **e** (sleep, neat); long **i** (like); long **o** (home, road); long **u** (cube). Examine the words, and think of other one-syllable words like these.

Long a	Long e	Long i	Long o	Long u
face		ride	those	tune
blame		write	nose	nude
scrape		drive	joke	mute
shape		wife	vote	cute
slave		pride	cope	fume
chain	teeth		soap	
plain	glee		toast	
snail	bleed		float	
quaint	screech		roach	
pail	Greek		throat	
pray	least			
spray	peach			
stray	streak			
tray	freak			
sway	cream			

EXERCISE 5.4 Long and Short Vowels

The following pairs of pronunciation spellings are identical except that one word in each pair has a long vowel sound and the other word has a short vowel sound (see page 35). Write a word for each pronunciation spelling. The first problem is done to illustrate what you are to do.

1. (hōp) _hope_   (hŏp) _hop_

2. (plān) _____   (plăn) _____

3. (strĭp) _____   (strīp) _____

4. (spĕk) _____   (spēk) _____

5. (kyo͞ob) _____   (kŭb) _____

6. (glŏb) _____   (glōb) _____

Check your answers for items 1 through 6 before you write words for the following pronunciation spellings.

7. (răn) _____   (rān) _____

8. (fĭt) _____   (fīt) _____

9. (sēd) _____   (sĕd) _____

10. (făt) _____   (fāt) _____

11. (kyo͞ot) _____   (kŭt) _____

12. (tōst) _____   (tŏst) _____

13. (ĭz) _____   (īz) _____

14. (dyo͞oz) _____   (dŭz) _____

15. (sĕz) _____   (sēz) _____

16. (fōks) _____   (fŏks) _____

17. (kwĭt) _____   (kwīt) _____

18. (āks) _____   (ăks) _____

EXERCISE 5.5   The Dieresis and Circumflex Vowels

Read about the dieresis and circumflex vowels on page 36 before you write the words represented by the following pronunciation spellings.

1. (käm) _____   4. (chôk) _____

2. (âr) _____   5. (bîr) _____

3. (ûrth) _____   6. (gärd) _____

Check your answers for items 1 through 6 before you write the words represented by the following pronunciation spellings.

7. (fôls) _____   22. (châr) _____

8. (dîr) _____   23. (stärch) _____

9. (sô) _____   24. (hûr) _____

10. (klîr) _____   25. (smôl) _____

11. (säm) _____   26. (stîr) _____

12. (tôk) _____   27. (kärd) _____

13. (îr) _____   28. (skwûrt) _____

14. (päm) _____   29. (pâr) _____

15. (gûrl) _____   30. (tîr) _____

16. (skâr) _____   31. (skwâr) _____

17. (thûrd) _____   32. (wôk) _____

18. (vûrs) _____   33. (stâr) _____

19. (drô) _____   34. (färs) _____

20. (kâr) _____   35. (nîr) _____

21. (tûrm) _____   36. (ûrj) _____

__EXERCISE 5.6__ **Four More Vowel Sounds**

Read the discussion entitled "Four More Vowel Sounds" on page 36 before you write the words that are represented by the following pronunciation spellings.

1. (fyo͞o) _____   4. (ko͝ok) _____

2. (toun) _____   5. (pro͞on) _____

3. (koin) _____   6. (kloud) _____

Check your answers to items 1 through 6 before you write the words represented by the following pronunciation spellings.

7. (sho͝od) _____   22. (glo͞o) _____

8. (nou) _____   23. (toiz) _____

9. (noiz) _____   24. (skro͞o) _____

10. (ko͝od) _____   25. (kroud) _____

11. (fro͞ot) _____   26. (chois) _____

12. (broun) _____   27. (vyo͞o) _____

13. (klo͞o) _____   28. (froun) _____

14. (koil) _____   29. (po͞ot) _____

15. (wo͝od) _____   30. (bro͞ot) _____

16. (hou) _____   31. (poiz) _____

17. (joi) _____   32. (thro͞o) _____

18. (kloun) _____   33. (vois) _____

19. (kro͝ok) _____   34. (jo͞os) _____

20. (boiz) _____   35. (kro͞od) _____

21. (flo͞ot) _____   36. (plou) _____

EXERCISE 5.7   Syllabication

Short Vowels   The following two-syllable words have two consonants in the middle and a short vowel in the first syllable. Divide words of this type between the two consonants: *sham/ble* (shăm′bəl), *bel/low* (bĕl′ō), *win/ter* (wĭn′tər), *con/cert* (kŏn′sûrt), *cun/ning* (kŭn′ĭng). Divide the following words between the middle consonants and pronounce them to hear the short sounds of vowels in the first syllables.

permit	lantern	parka	tender
circus	garden	hammer	better
trumpet	murmur	command	husband
motto	victim	bigger	banner
rabbit	cellar	mustard	conduct
burden	chopper	master	canvas
basket	garment	pardon	slimmer
sister	butter	cotton	lumber
goblet	garter	yellow	carbon
ladder	mitten	bandit	carpet
pencil	fabric	rudder	content
rumba	consent	bitten	central
signal	cutting	barber	sadden
border	fellow	normal	summer

Long Vowels   The following two-syllable words have one consonant in the middle and a long vowel in the first syllable. Divide words of this type after the first vowel: *fa/vor* (fā′vər), *de/cay* (dē-kā′), *ti/ger* (tī′gər), *so/da* (sō′də) *tu/lip* (tyōo′ləp). Now divide the following words after the first vowel and pronounce them to hear the long sounds of the vowels in the first syllables.

depart	polo	vital	defend
spiral	recent	radar	saber
pupil	basin	solar	behold
vacant	final	razor	siren
solo	zero	return	chosen
cedar	open	item	demote
raven	even	fever	safer
spider	baby	frozen	sinus
molar	rival	navy	deform
evil	paper	halo	clover
pretend	totem	climate	lunar
human	Cupid	butane	preview
taper	recess	veto	miser
silent	debate	locate	recall

You will practice dividing words into prefixes, bases, suffixes, and other elements when you study Chapters 10 through 14.

_____ **EXERCISE 5.8** Syllables, Stress, and the Schwa

Read about syllables, stress, and the schwa on pages 36–37 before you write the words that are represented by the following pronunciation spellings. Refer to a dictionary for correct spellings when necessary.

1. (byo͞o′tə-fəl) _____

5. (ăk′shən) _____

2. (ôl-rĕd′ē) _____

6. (kŭm′pə-nē) _____

3. (fĭg′yər) _____

7. (ĭn-krēs′) _____

4. (hyo͞o′mən) _____

8. (kən-tĭn′yo͞o) _____

Check your answers to items 1 through 8 before you write the words that are represented by the following pronunciation spellings.

9. (năsh′ən-əl) _____

23. (ôl′wāz) _____

10. (pŏs′ə-bəl) _____

24. (kwĕs′chən) _____

11. (kwī′ĭt) _____

25. (sên′chə-rē) _____

12. (shə-kŏ′gō) _____

26. (kăp′tən) _____

13. (kŏl′ĭj) _____

27. (dô′tər) _____

14. (ĭng′glənd) _____

28. (êk-spĭr′ē-əns) _____

15. (jĕn′ər-əl) _____

29. (ī′lənd) _____

16. (mĕzh′ər) _____

30. (mĭl′yən) _____

17. (nā′bər) _____

31. (pär′shəl) _____

18. (fə-mĭl′yər) _____

32. (pĭ-kyo͞ol′yər) _____

19. (sĭ-gär′) _____

33. (tro͞o′lē) _____

20. (ə-dĭsh′ən) _____

34. (kən-dĭsh′ən) _____

21. (kăr′ĭk-tər) _____

35. (ĭn′dē-ən) _____

22. (năch′ər-əl) _____

36. (po͝osch′ō′vər) _____

EXERCISE 5.9   Pronunciation Spellings

The following are examples of words for which you might need to consult a dictionary in order to determine their pronunciations. Study the pronunciation spellings of the words so you are able to read them aloud in class.

Part 1

1. acclimation (ăk′lə-mā′shən)
2. accouterment (ə-kōō′tər-mənt)
3. acerbity (ə-sûr′bə-tē)
4. acumen (ə-kyōō′mən)
5. adenoid (ăd′n-oid′)
6. albino (ăl-bī′nō)
7. ambidextrous (ăm′bĭ-děk′strəs)
8. anesthetist (ə-něs′thə-tĭst)
9. anomalous (ə-nŏm′ə-ləs)
10. apropos (ăp′rə-pō′)
11. archipelago (är′kə-pěl′ə-gō)
12. arduous (är′jōō-əs)
13. aspirant (ăs′-pər-ənt)
14. bisque (bĭsk)
15. cache (kăsh)
16. chamois (shăm′ē)
17. chauvinism (shō′vən-ĭz′əm)
18. chiropodist (kə-rŏp′ə-dĭst)
19. clientele (klī′ən-těl)
20. coccyx (kŏk′sĭks)

Part 2

1. comatose (kō′mə-tōs)
2. concerto (kən-chěr′tō)
3. connoisseur (kŏn′ə-sûr′)
4. cornucopia (kôr′nə-kō′pē-ə)
5. cuisine (kwĭ-zēn′)
6. debauch (dĭ-bôch′)
7. decorous (děk′ər-əs)
8. deleterious (děl′ə-tĭr′ē-əs)
9. diarrhea (dī′ə-rē′ə)
10. dubious (dōō′bē-əs)
11. entrepreneur (än′trə-prə-nûr′)
12. erudite (ěr′yōō-dīt)
13. exigency (ěk′sə-jən-sē)
14. facetious (fə-sē′shəs)
15. flaccid (flăk′sĭd)
16. funereal (fyōō-nîr′ē-əl)
17. geisha (gē′shə)
18. gubernatorial (gōō′bər-nə-tôr′ē-əl)
19. guillotine (gē′ə-tēn)
20. heinous (hā′nəs)

Part 3

1. hierarchy (hī′ə-rär′kē)
2. idiosyncrasy (ĭd′ē-ō-sĭng′krə-sē)
3. ignoramus (ĭg′nə-rā′məs)
4. impious (ĭm-pī′əs)
5. inamorata (ĭn-ăm′ə-rä′tə)
6. indefatigable (ĭn′dĭ-făt′ə-gə-bəl)
7. infantile (ĭn′fən-tīl)
8. ingenuous (ĭn-jěn′yōō-əs)
9. intrigue (ĭn′trēg′)
10. inveigle (ĭn-vē′gəl)
11. jeopardize (jěp′ər-dīz)
12. lackadaisical (lăk′ə-dā′zĭ-kəl)
13. libertine (lĭb′ər-tēn)
14. loge (lōzh)
15. lorgnette (lôrn-yět′)
16. lucrative (lōō′krə-tĭv)
17. malign (mə-līn′)
18. mediocre (mē′dē-ō′kər)
19. minuet (mĭn′yōō-ět′)
20. mnemonics (nĭ-mŏn′ĭks)

Understand Word Origins

Words come into English from many sources. For instance, the information enclosed in brackets at the end of the following entry, explains how *peeping Tom* came into English.

> **peep·ing Tom** (pē′pĭng tŏm) *n.* A person who gets pleasure, especially sexual pleasure, from secretly watching others; a voyeur. [After the legendary *Peeping Tom* of Coventry, England, who was the only person to see the naked Lady Godiva.]

The information enclosed in brackets at the end of this entry is an **etymology**, which is information about the origin and development of a word. The etymology for *peeping Tom* states that this phrase comes from the name of the only person who watched as Lady Godiva rode nude through the streets of Coventry, England.

Since interesting etymologies help in learning and remembering words, this chapter explains how to interpret etymologies in dictionaries.

Borrowing

Borrowing is the act of taking words from other languages to use as English words. For example, *tobacco* was borrowed from Spanish to name a plant and a product for which there was no English word, and *perish* was borrowed from French to use as a synonym for the word *die*. Through invasions, trade, exploration, and colonization, English speakers came in contact with most languages of the world. Thus English borrowed thousands of words including *gas* from Dutch, *etiquette* from French, *shampoo* from Hindi, *balcony* from Italian, *tattoo* from Polynesian, and *moccasin* from North American Indian.

Many words passed through two or more languages before they entered English. The following etymology states that English borrowed *assassin* from French, that French borrowed it from Medieval Latin, and that Medieval Latin borrowed it from an Arabic word that means "hashish user."

> **as·sas·sin** (ə-săs′ĭn) *n.* **1.** One who murders by surprise attack, especially one who carries out a plot to kill a prominent person. **2. Assassin.** A member of a secret order of Moslem fanatics who terrorized and killed Christian Crusaders and others. [French, from Medieval Latin *assassīnus*, from Arabic *ḥaššāšīn*, pl. of *ḥaššāš*, hashish user, from *ḥašīš*, hashish.]

When an etymology lists more than one language, English borrowed the word from the language that is listed first.

47

Some Important Latin Phases

ad hoc (ăd hŏk′, hōk′) *adv.* For the specific purpose, case, or situation at hand and for no other: *a committee formed ad hoc to address the issue of salaries.* —**ad hoc** *adj.* **1.** Formed for or concerned with one specific purpose: *an ad hoc compensation committee.* **2.** Improvised and often impromptu: *"On an ad hoc basis, Congress has . . . placed . . . ceilings on military aid to specific countries"* (New York Times). [Latin *ad,* to + *hoc,* this.]

ad in·fi·ni·tum (ăd ĭn′fə-nī′təm) *adv.* To infinity; having no end. [Latin *ad,* to + *īnfīnītum,* accusative of *īnfīnītus,* infinite.]

ad nau·se·am (ăd nô′zē-əm) *adv.* To a disgusting or ridiculous degree; to the point of nausea. [Latin *ad,* to + *nauseam,* accusative of *nausea,* sickness.]

al·ma ma·ter or **Al·ma Ma·ter** (ăl′mə mä′tər, äl′mə) *n.* **1.** The school, college, or university that one has attended. **2.** The anthem of an institution of higher learning. [Latin *alma,* nourishing + *mater,* mother.]

an·te·bel·lum (ăn′tē-bĕl′əm) *adj.* Belonging to the period before a war, especially the American Civil War. [Latin *ante bellum* : *ante,* before + *bellum,* war.]

bo·na fide (bō′nə fīd′, fī′dē, bŏn′ə) *adj.* **1.** Made or carried out in good faith; sincere: *a bona fide offer.* **2.** Authentic; genuine: *a bona fide Rembrandt.* See Synonyms at **authentic.** [Latin *bonā fidē* : *bonā,* feminine ablative of *bonus,* good + *fidē,* ablative of *fidēs,* faith.]

caveat emp·tor (ĕmp′tôr′) *n.* The axiom or principle in commerce that the buyer alone is responsible for assessing the quality of a purchase before buying. [From Latin, let the buyer beware : *caveat,* imperative of *cavēre,* to beware + *emptor,* buyer.]

corpus de·lic·ti (dĭ-lĭk′tī′) *n.* **1.** *Law.* The material evidence in a homicide, such as the discovered corpse of a murder victim, showing that a crime has been committed. **2.** A corpse. [New Latin : Latin *corpus,* body + Latin *delictī,* genitive of *delictum,* crime.]

et cet·er·a (ĕt sĕt′ər-ə, sĕt′rə). *Abbr.* **etc.** And other unspecified things of the same class; and so forth. —**et·cet·er·a** *n.* **1.** A number of unspecified persons or things. **2. etceteras.** Additional odds and ends; extras. [Latin : *et,* and + *cētera,* the rest, neuter pl. of *cēterus*; see **ko-** in Appendix.]

in me·mo·ri·am (ĭn′ mə-môr′ē-əm, -mōr′-) *prep.* In memory of; as a memorial to. Used especially in epitaphs. [From Latin *in memoriam,* to the memory (of) : *in,* in, into + *memoriam,* accusative of *memoria,* memory.]

in to·to (ĭn tō′tō) *adv.* Totally; altogether: *recommendations that were adopted in toto.* [Latin : *in,* in + *tōtō,* ablative of *tōtus,* all.]

mo·dus op·er·an·di (mō′dəs ŏp′ə-răn′dē, -dī′) *n.,* pl. **mo·di operandi** (mō′dē, -dī). *Abbr.* **m.o., M.O. 1.** A method of operating or functioning. **2.** A person's manner of working. [New Latin *modus operandī* : Latin *modus,* mode + Latin *operandī,* genitive sing. gerund of *operārī,* to work.]

non com·pos men·tis (nŏn kŏm′pəs mĕn′tĭs) *adj. Law.* Not of sound mind and hence not legally responsible; mentally incompetent. [Latin *nŏn compos mentis* : *nŏn,* not + *compos,* in control + *mentis,* genitive sing. of *mēns,* mind.]

non se·qui·tur (nŏn sĕk′wĭ-tər, -tŏor′) *n.* **1.** An inference or conclusion that does not follow from the premises or evidence. **2.** A statement that does not follow logically from what preceded it. [Latin *nŏn sequitur,* it does not follow : *nŏn,* not + *sequitur,* third person sing. present tense of *sequī,* to follow.]

per an·num (pər ăn′əm) *adv. Abbr.* **p.a.** By the year; annually: *A subscription costs 12 dollars per annum.* [Latin : *per,* per + *annum,* accusative of *annus,* year.]

per cap·i·ta (pər kăp′ĭ-tə) *adv. & adj.* **1.** Per unit of population; per person: *In that year, Americans earned $15,304 per capita. Among the states, Connecticut has a high per capita income.* **2.** Equally to each individual. [Medieval Latin, by heads : Latin *per,* per + Latin *capita,* accusative pl. of *caput,* head.]

per di·em (pər dē′əm, dī′əm) *adv. Abbr.* **p.d., P.D.** By the day; per day. —**per diem** *adj.* **1.** Reckoned on a daily basis; daily. **2.** Paid by the day. —**per diem** *n., pl.* **per diems.** An allowance for daily expenses. [Latin : *per,* per + *diem,* accusative of *diēs,* day.]

persona non gra·ta (nŏn grä′tə, grăt′ə) *adj.* Fully unacceptable or unwelcome, especially to a foreign government: *The diplomat was persona non grata.* [Latin *persōna,* person + *nŏn,* not + *grata,* acceptable.]

post·mor·tem (pōst-môr′təm) *adj. Abbr.* **p.m., P.M. 1.** Occurring or done after death. **2.** Of or relating to a medical examination of a dead body. —**postmortem** *n.* **1.** *Abbr.* **p.m., P.M.** See **autopsy** (sense 1). **2.** *Informal.* An analysis or review of a completed event. [Latin *post mortem* : *post,* afterward; see POST— + *mortem,* accusative of *mors,* death; see **mer-** in Appendix.] —**post mor′tem** *adv.*

pro for·ma (prō fôr′mə) *adj.* **1.** Done as a formality; perfunctory: *one-candidate, pro forma elections.* **2.** Provided in advance so as to prescribe form or describe items: *a pro forma copy of a document.* [New Latin *prō formā* : *prō,* for the sake of + *formā,* ablative of *forma,* form.]

quid pro quo (kwĭd′ prō kwō′) *n., pl.* **quid pro quos** or **quids pro quo.** An equal exchange or substitution. [Latin *quid prō quō* : *quid,* what + *prō,* for + *quō,* ablative of *quid,* what?]

status quo *n.* The existing condition or state of affairs. [Latin, state in which : *status,* state + *quō,* in which, ablative of *quī,* which.]

terra fir·ma (fûr′mə) *n.* Solid ground; dry land. [New Latin : Latin *terra,* earth + Latin *firmus,* solid.]

vi·ce ver·sa (vī′sə vûr′sə, vīs′) *adv. Abbr.* **v.v.** With the order or meaning reversed; conversely. [Latin *vice versā* : *vice,* ablative of **vix,* position + *versā,* feminine ablative of *versus,* past participle of *vertere,* to turn.]

English has borrowed more words and phrases from Latin and French than from other languages. Examine the Latin phrases above and the French phrases on page 49; they are examples of foreign expressions that you are likely to encounter in your college reading.

People and Places

Among the most interesting word origins are those that come from the names of people and places. The etymology for *derrick* explains that the word derives from a man named Derick, a 16th-century English hangman.

Some Important French Phrases

a·vant-garde (ä′vänt-gärd′, ăv′änt-) *n.* A group active in the invention and application of new techniques in a given field, especially in the arts. —**avant-garde** *adj.* Of, relating to, or being part of an innovative group, especially one in the arts: *avant-garde painters; an avant-garde theater piece.* [French, from Old French, vanguard. See VANGUARD.] —**a′vant-gard′ism** *n.* —**a′vant-gard′ist** *n.*

bête noire (bĕt nwär′) *n.* One that is particularly disliked or that is to be avoided: *"Tax shelters had long been the bête noire of reformers"* (Irwin Ross). [French : *bête,* beast + *noire,* black.]

bon vi·vant (bôn′ vē-vän′) *n., pl.* **bons vi·vants** (bôn′ vē-vän′). A person with refined taste, especially one who enjoys superb food and drink. [French : *bon,* good + *vivant,* present participle of *vivre,* to live.]

carte blanche (kärt blänsh′, kärts blänch′, blänch) *n., pl.* **cartes blanches** (kärt blänsh′, kärts blänch′, blänch′). Unrestricted power to act at one's own discretion; unconditional authority: *had given the interior decorator carte blanche and then detested the results.* [French : *carte,* ticket + *blanche,* blank.]

cause cé·lè·bre (kōz′ sā-lĕb′rə) *n., pl.* **causes cé·lè·bres** (kōz′ sā-lĕb′rə). **1.** An issue arousing widespread controversy or heated public debate. **2.** A celebrated legal case. [French : *cause,* case + *célèbre,* celebrated.]

crème de la crème (krĕm′ də lä krĕm′) *n.* **1.** Something superlative. **2.** People of the highest social level. [French : *crème,* cream + *de,* of + *la,* the + *crème,* cream.]

cul-de-sac (kŭl′dĭ-săk′, kōōl′-) *n., pl.* **culs-de-sac** (kŭlz′-, kōōlz′-) or **cul-de-sacs** (kŭl′-). **1.a.** A dead-end street.

dé·jà vu (dā′zhä vü′) *n.* **1.** *Psychology.* The illusion of having already experienced something actually being experienced for the first time. **2.a.** An impression of having seen or experienced something before: *Old-timers watched the stock-market crash with a distinct sense of déjà vu.* **b.** Dull familiarity; monotony: *the déjà vu of the tabloid headlines.* [French : *déjà,* already + *vu,* seen.]

dou·ble-en·ten·dre (dŭb′əl-än-tän′drə, dōō-blän-tän′drə) *n.* **1.** A word or phrase having a double meaning, especially when the second meaning is risqué. **2.** The use of such a word or phrase; ambiguity. [Obsolete French : *double,* double + *entendre,* meaning, interpretation.]

en masse (ŏn măs′) *adv.* In one group or body; all together: *The peace activists marched en masse to the capitol.* [French : *en,* in + *masse,* mass.]

fait ac·com·pli (fā′tä-kôn-plē′, fĕt′ä-) *n., pl.* **faits ac·com·plis** (fā′tä-kôn-plē′, -plēz′, fĕt′ä-). An accomplished, presumably irreversible deed or fact. [French : *fait,* fact + *accompli,* accomplished.]

faux pas (fō pä′) *n., pl.* **faux pas** (fō päz′). A social blunder. [French : *faux,* false + *pas,* step.]

femme fa·tale (fĕm′ fə-tăl′, -täl′, făm′) *n., pl.* **femmes fa·tales** (fĕm′ fə-tăl′, -tălz′, -täl′, -tälz′, făm′). **1.** A woman of great seductive charm who leads men into compromising or dangerous situations. **2.** An alluring and mysterious woman. [French : *femme,* woman + *fatale,* deadly.]

hors d'oeuvre (ôr dûrv′) *n., pl.* **hors d'oeuvres** (ôr dûrvz′) or **hors d'oeuvre.** An appetizer served before a meal. [French : *hors,* outside + *de,* of + *oeuvre,* (the main) work.]

joie de vi·vre (zhwä′ də vē′vrə) *n.* Hearty or carefree enjoyment of life. [French : *joie,* joy + *de,* of + *vivre,* to live, living.]

lais·sez faire also **lais·ser faire** (lĕs′ā fâr′) *n.* **1.** An economic doctrine that opposes governmental regulation of or interference in commerce beyond the minimum necessary for a free-enterprise system to operate according to its own economic laws. **2.** Noninterference in the affairs of others. [French : *laissez,* second person pl. imperative of *laisser,* to let, allow + *faire,* to do.] —**lais′sez-faire′** *adj.*

nom de plume (nŏm′ də plōōm′) *n., pl.* **noms de plume** (nŏm′). See **pen name.** [French : *nom,* name + *de,* of + *plume,* pen.]

nou·veau riche (nōō′vō rēsh′) *n., pl.* **nou·veaux riches** (nōō′vō rēsh′). One who has recently become rich, especially one who flaunts newly acquired wealth. [French : *nouveau,* new + *riche,* rich.]

ob·jet d'art (ôb′zhĕ där′) *n., pl.* **ob·jets d'art** (ôb′zhĕ där′). An object of artistic merit. [French : *objet,* object + *de,* of + *art,* art.]

par ex·cel·lence (pär ĕk-sə-läns′) *adj.* Being the best or truest of a kind; quintessential: *a diplomat par excellence.* [French : *par,* by + *excellence,* preeminence.]

rai·son d'ê·tre (rā′zōn dĕt′rə, rĕ-zôn) *n., pl.* **rai·sons d'ê·tre** (rā′zōn, rĕ-zôn). Reason or justification for existing. [French : *raison,* reason + *de,* of, for + *étre,* to be.]

ro·man à clef (rō-män′ ä klä′) *n., pl.* **ro·mans à clef** (rōmän′ zä klä′). A novel in which actual persons, places, or events are depicted in fictional guise. [French : *roman,* novel + *à,* with + *clef,* key.]

sa·voir-faire (săv′wär-fâr′) *n.* The ability to say or do the right or graceful thing. See Synonyms at **tact.** [French : *savoir,* to know how + *faire,* to do.]

tête-à-tête (tāt′ə-tāt′, tĕt′ə-tĕt′) *adv. & adj.* Without the intrusion of a third person; in intimate privacy: *talk tête-à-tête; a tête-à-tête supper.* —**tête-à-tête** *n.* **1.** A private conversation between two persons. **2.** A sofa for two, especially an S-shaped one allowing the occupants to face each other. [French : *tête,* head + *à,* to + *tête,* head.]

tour de force (tōōr′ də fôrs′, fôrs′) *n., pl.* **tours de force** (tōōr′). A feat requiring great virtuosity or strength, often deliberately undertaken for its difficulty: *"In an extraordinary structural tour de force the novel maintains a dual focus"* (Julian Moynahan). [French : *tour,* turn, feat + *de,* of + *force,* strength.]

vis-à-vis (vē′zə-vē′) *prep.* **1.** Face to face with; opposite to. **2.** Compared with. **3.** In relation to. —**vis-à-vis** *adv.* Face to face. —**vis-à-vis** *n., pl.* **vis-à-vis** (-vēz′, -vē′). **1.** One that is face to face with or opposite to another. **2.** A date or an escort, as at a party. **3.** One that has the same functions and characteristics as another; a counterpart. [French : *vis,* face + *à,* to.] —**vis′-à-vis′** *adj.*

der·rick (dĕr′ĭk) *n.* **1.** A machine for hoisting and moving heavy objects, consisting of a movable boom equipped with cables and pulleys and connected to the base of an upright stationary beam. **2.** A tall framework over a drilled hole, especially an oil well, used to support boring equipment or hoist and lower lengths of pipe. [Obsolete *derick,* hangman, gallows, after *Derick,* 16th-century English hangman.]

Other words derived from people's names include *nicotine* and *volt.* The word *jeans* has its origin in the name of a place.

> **jean** (jēn) *n.* **1.** A heavy, strong, twilled cotton, used in making uniforms and work clothes. **2. jeans.** Pants made of jean, denim, or another durable fabric. [Short for obsolete *jene (fustian),* Genoan (fustian), from Middle English *jene, gene,* from Old French *Genes,* Genoa.]

The etymology for *jean* states that the word derived from the name of the port city of Genoa, Italy, where the fabric from which jeans are made was first manufactured.

Other words derived from place names include *attic, tangerine, limousine,* and *academy.*

Fictitious People and Places

Some words have their origins in the names of fictitious people and places. For example, *quixotic,* which means "romantic but impractical," is derived from the name of a fictitious character.

> **quix·ot·ic** (kwĭk-sŏt′ĭk) also **quix·ot·i·cal** (-ĭ-kəl) *adj.* **1.** Caught up in the romance of noble deeds and the pursuit of unreachable goals; idealistic without regard to practicality. **2.** Capricious; impulsive: *"At worst his scruples must have been quixotic, not malicious"* (Louis Auchincloss). [From English *Quixote,* a visionary, after *Don Quixote,* hero of a romance by Miguel de Cervantes.] —**quix·ot′i·cal·ly** *adv.* —**quix′o·tism** (kwĭk′sətĭz′əm) *n.*

The etymology for *quixotic* states that the word is derived from *Don Quixote,* the fictitious hero of a romance by Miguel de Cervantes.

Similarly, *Shangri-la* is derived from literature.

> **Shan·gri-la** (shăng′grĭ-lä′) *n.* **1.** An imaginary, remote paradise on earth; utopia. **2.** A distant and secluded hideaway, usually of great beauty and peacefulness. [After *Shangri-La,* the imaginary land in the novel *Lost Horizon* by James Hilton.]

The etymology for *Shangri-la* states that it is an imaginary place created by James Hilton for his novel *Lost Horizon.*

Coinage

Coinages are invented words, such as *Jell-O, Vaseline, zipper, Kleenex,* and *nylon,* which were invented to name products.

> **ny·lon** (nī′lŏn′) *n.* **1.a.** Any of a family of high-strength, resilient synthetic polymers, the molecules of which contain the recurring amide group CONH. **b.** Cloth or yarn made from one of these synthetic materials. **2. nylons.** Stockings made of one of these synthetic materials. —*attributive.* Often used to modify another noun: *nylon stockings; a nylon curtain.* [Coined by its inventors, E.I. Du Pont de Nemours and Co., Inc.]

Etymologies usually state whether a word is coined.

Shortening

Shortenings are shortened forms of words, such as *phone* for *telephone, plane* for *airplane,* and *exam* for *examination.* The etymology for *fan,* meaning "admirer," states that the word was derived by shortening a longer word—*fanatic.*

fan² (făn) *n. Informal.* An ardent devotee; an enthusiast. [Short for FANATIC.]

The dozens of shortenings include *ad* (advertisement), *burger* (hamburger), *ref* (referee), *tux* (tuxedo), and *flu* (influenza).

Blending

A **blend** is a word formed by combining a part of one word with a part of another word, or part of one word with a complete other word. *Motel* was formed by combining the first two letters of *motor* and the last three letters of *hotel:* [MO(TOR) + (HO)TEL]. In this etymology, the letters *tor* and *ho* are enclosed in parentheses to indicate that they are not included in *motel.*

Medicare was formed by combining a part of one word with a complete other word.

Med·i·care also **med·i·care** (mĕd′ĭ-kâr′) *n.* A program under the U.S. Social Security Administration that reimburses hospitals and physicians for medical care provided to qualifying people over 65 years old. [MEDI(CAL) + CARE.]

In this etymology, the letters *cal* are enclosed in parentheses to indicate that they are not included in the word *medicare.*

Other blends include *smog* [SM(OKE) + (F)OG], *twirl* [TW(IST) + (WH)IRL], *hassle* [HA(GGLE) + (TU)SSLE], and *dumfound* [DUM(B) + (CON)FOUND].

Acronym

An **acronym** is a word made from the initial letters of other words. The etymology for *scuba* illustrates how the acronymic origins of words are indicated in dictionaries.

scu·ba (skōō′bə) *n.* A portable apparatus containing compressed air and used for breathing under water. [*s(elf) c(ontained) u(nderwater) b(reathing) a(pparatus).*]

In the etymology, the letters *elf* in *self* and other letters are enclosed in parentheses to indicate that they are not included in the word *scuba.*

Many acronyms are names of organizations, such as *CORE* (Congress of Racial Equality), *SWAT* (Special Weapons and Tactics), and *VISTA* (Volunteers in Service to America).

Imitation

Imitation is the formation of a word by imitating a sound that is associated with an animal, action, or object. Examples of imitation include *cock-a-doodle-doo, gargle,* and *wham.*

wham (hwăm, wăm) *n.* **1.** A forceful, resounding blow. **2.** The sound of such a blow; a thud. —**wham** *v.* **whammed, wham·ming, whams.** —*tr.* To strike or smash into with resounding impact. —*intr.* To smash with great force. [Imitative.]

Etymologies usually state when words are imitative.

Other imitative words include *bump, boom, bash, crunch, bang, pow, zip,* and *zing.*

Reduplication

Reduplication is the formation of a word by repeating it or by repeating a sound in it. *Tom-tom, mishmash, shilly-shally,* and *chitchat* are examples of reduplication.

> **chit·chat** (chĭt′chăt′) *n.* **1.** Casual conversation; small talk. **2.** Gossip. **—chitchat** *intr.v.* **-chat·ted, -chat·ting, -chats.** To engage in small talk or gossip. [Reduplication of CHAT.]

Etymologies usually state when words are formed by reduplication.

Derivation

Derivatives are words formed by joining prefixes or suffixes to bases or roots. For example, *kindness* is a derivative formed by joining the suffix *-ness* to the base word *kind,* whereas *revert* is a derivative formed by joining the prefix *re-* to the Latin root *vert,* which means "to turn."

Chapters 10 through 14 teach how to analyze the prefixes, suffixes, combining forms, and Latin roots in derivatives.

Compounding

Compounds are words formed by joining two or more words. There are thousands of compounds, including *drugstore, playboy, shortstop, brainwash, hitchhike,* and *earring.* Compounds of more than two words include *mother-in-law, hand-me-down,* and *merry-go-round.* Desk dictionaries usually do not state the etymologies of compounds.

Other Etymologies

The types of etymologies that are explained in this chapter account for the origins of at least 99 percent of all English words. However, there are other types of etymologies. For instance, a few words have their origins in customs that are no longer observed, such as the custom explained in the etymology for *baker's dozen.*

> **bak·er's dozen** (bā′kərz) *n.* A group of 13. [From the former custom among bakers of adding an extra roll as a safeguard against the possibility of 12 weighing light.]

The punishment for giving customers less bread than they were supposed to receive was so severe that bakers added a roll to make certain that customers received full measure.

The following exercises provide practice in interpreting etymological information to encourage you to read etymologies when you look up the meanings or spellings of words in a dictionary. If you acquire this habit, you will often be rewarded by learning something about a word that is helpful, interesting, or enjoyable to know.

EXERCISE 6.1 Borrowing

The words in this exercise were borrowed from foreign languages. Referring to the etymologies in the entries at the bottom of this page, fill in the name of the foreign language from which each word was borrowed and the meaning of the foreign word.

1. alfresco   _Italian_   "in the fresh air"

2. bravado   _____   _____

3. foible   _____   _____

4. kowtow   _____   _____

5. ostracize   _____   _____

6. robot   _____   _____

7. safari   _____   _____

8. saga   _____   _____

9. smorgasbord   _____   _____

10. stupendous   _____   _____

11. tundra   _____   _____

12. verboten   _____   _____

al·fres·co (ăl-frĕs′kō) _adv._ In the fresh air; outdoors: _dining alfresco._ —**alfresco** _adj._ Taking place outdoors; outdoor: _an alfresco conference._ [Italian _al fresco_, in the fresh (air) : _a il_, in the + _fresco_, fresh.]

bra·va·do (brə-vä′dō) _n., pl._ **-dos** or **-does. 1.a.** Defiant or swaggering behavior: _strove to prevent our courage from turning into bravado._ **b.** A pretense of courage; a false show of bravery. **2.** A disposition toward showy defiance or false expressions of courage. [Spanish _bravada_, from _bravo_, brave. See BRAVE.]

foi·ble (foi′bəl) _n._ **1.** A minor weakness or failing of character. See Synonyms at **fault. 2.** The weaker section of a sword blade, from the middle to the tip. [Obsolete French _foible_, weak point of a sword, weak, from Old French _feble_, weak. See FEEBLE.]

kow·tow (kou-tou′, kou′tou′) _intr.v._ **-towed, -tow·ing, -tows. 1.** To kneel and touch the forehead to the ground in expression of deep respect, worship, or submission, as formerly done in China. **2.** To show servile deference; fawn. See Synonyms at **fawn**[1]. —**kowtow** _n._ **1.** The act of kneeling and touching the forehead to the ground. **2.** An obsequious act. [From Chinese (Mandarin) _kòu tóu_, a kowtow : _kòu_, to knock + _tóu_, head.]

os·tra·cize (ŏs′trə-sīz′) _tr.v._ **-cized, -ciz·ing, -ciz·es. 1.** To exclude from a group. See Synonyms at **blackball. 2.** To banish by ostracism, as in ancient Greece. [Greek _ostrakizein_, from _ostrakon_, shell, potsherd (from the potsherds used as ballots in voting for ostracism). See **ost-** in Appendix.]

ro·bot (rō′bət, -bŏt′) _n._ **1.** A mechanical device that sometimes resembles a human being and is capable of performing a variety of often complex human tasks on command or by being programmed in advance. **2.** A machine or device that operates automatically or by remote control. **3.** A person who works mechanically without original thought, especially one who responds automatically to the commands of others. [Czech, from _robota_, drudgery. See **orbh-** in Appendix.] —**ro·bot′ic, ro′bot·is′tic** (-bə-tĭs′tĭk) _adj._

sa·fa·ri (sə-fär′ē) _n., pl._ **-ris. 1.** An overland expedition, especially one for hunting or exploring in eastern Africa. **2.** A journey or trip: _a sightseeing safari._ [Arabic _safarī_, journey, from _safara_, to travel, set out.]

sa·ga (sä′gə) _n._ **1.a.** A prose narrative usually written in Iceland between 1120 and 1400, dealing with the families that first settled Iceland and their descendants, with the histories of the kings of Norway, and with the myths and legends of early Germanic gods and heroes. **b.** A modern prose narrative that resembles a saga. **2.** A long, detailed report: _recounted the saga of their family problems._ [Old Norse. See sekʷ-[3] in Appendix.]

smor·gas·bord (smôr′gəs-bôrd′, -bōrd′) _n._ **1.** A buffet meal featuring a varied number of dishes. **2.** A varied collection: _"a smorgasbord of fashionable paranormal beliefs"_ (Martin Gardner). [Swedish _smörgåsbord_ : _smörgås_, bread and butter (_smör_, butter, from Old Norse + Swedish dialectal _gås_, lump of butter, from Old Norse _gås_, goose; see GOSLING) + _bord_, table (from Old Norse _bordh_).]

stu·pen·dous (stōō-pĕn′dəs, styōō-) _adj._ **1.** Of astounding force, volume, degree, or excellence; marvelous. **2.** Amazingly large or great; huge. See Synonyms at **enormous.** [From Late Latin _stupendus_, stunning, gerundive of Latin _stupēre_, to be stunned.] —**stu·pen′dous·ly** _adv._ —**stu·pen′dous·ness** _n._

tun·dra (tŭn′drə) _n._ A treeless area between the icecap and the tree line of Arctic regions, having a permanently frozen subsoil and supporting low-growing vegetation such as lichens, mosses, and stunted shrubs. [Russian, from Sami _tūndar_, flat-topped hill.]

ver·bo·ten (vər-bōt′n, fĕr-) _adj._ Forbidden; prohibited. [German, past participle of _verbieten_, to forbid, from Middle High German, from Old High German _farbiotan_. See **bheudh-** in Appendix.]

EXERCISE 6.2   Names of People and Places

The words in this exercise are from the names of people and places. Referring to the etymologies in the entries at the bottom of this page, fill in the name of the person from whom the word was derived and the country in which he lived.

1. boycott _____

2. chauvinism _____

3. martinet _____

4. maverick _____

5. sadism _____

Referring to the etymologies in the entries at the bottom of this page, fill in the place from which the word was derived.

6. bayonet _____

7. bikini _____

8. bunkum _____

9. denim _____

bay·o·net (bā′ə-nĭt, -nĕt′, bā′ə-nĕt′) *n.* A blade adapted to fit the muzzle end of a rifle and used as a weapon in close combat. **—bayonet** *tr.v.* **-net·ed, -net·ing, -nets** or **-net·ted, -net·ting, -nets.** To prod, stab, or kill with this weapon. [French *baïonnette*, after BAYONNE[1].]

Ba·yonne[1] (bā-ōn′, bä-yôn′). A town of southwest France near the Bay of Biscay and the Spanish border. French, Spanish, and Basque are all spoken here. Population, 41,381.

bi·ki·ni (bĭ-kē′nē) *n.* **1.a.** A very brief, close-fitting two-piece bathing suit worn by women. **b.** A very brief, close-fitting bathing suit worn by men. **2.** Often **bikinis.** Brief underpants that reach to the hips rather than to the waist. [French, after BIKINI.] **—bi·ki·′nied** (-nēd) *adj.*

Bi·ki·ni (bĭ-kē′nē). An atoll in the Ratak Chain of the Marshall Islands in the west-central Pacific Ocean. The area was the site of U.S. nuclear tests between 1946 and 1958, including the first aerial detonation of a hydrogen bomb (May 21, 1956).

boy·cott (boi′kŏt′) *tr.v.* **-cott·ed, -cott·ing, -cotts. 1.** To act together in abstaining from using, buying, or dealing with as an expression of protest or disfavor or as a means of coercion. See Synonyms at **blackball. 2.** To abstain from or unite with others in abstaining from using, buying, or dealing with. **—boycott** *n.* The act or an instance of boycotting. [After Charles C. *Boycott* (1832–1897), English land agent in Ireland.] **—boy′cott·er** *n.*

bun·kum also **bun·combe** (bŭng′kəm) *n.* Empty or insincere talk; claptrap. [After *Buncombe,* a county of western North Carolina, from a remark made around 1820 by its congressman, who felt obligated to give a dull speech "for Buncombe."]

chau·vin·ism (shō′və-nĭz′əm) *n.* **1.** Militant devotion to and glorification of one's country; fanatical patriotism. **2.** Prejudiced belief in the superiority of one's own gender, group, or kind: *"the chauvinism . . . of making extraterrestrial life in our own image"* (Henry S.F. Cooper, Jr.). [French *chauvinisme,* after Nicolas *Chauvin,* a legendary French soldier famous for his devotion to

Napoleon.] **—chau′vin·ist** *n.* **—chau′vin·is′tic** *adj.* **—chau′vin·is′ti·cal·ly** *adv.*

den·im (dĕn′ĭm) *n.* **1.a.** A coarse twilled cloth, usually cotton, used for jeans, overalls, and work uniforms. **b. denims.** Trousers or another garment made of this cloth. **2.** A similar but finer fabric used in draperies and upholstery. [French *(serge) de Nîmes,* (serge) of Nîmes, after NÎMES, France.]

mar·ti·net (mär′tn-ĕt′) *n.* **1.** A rigid military disciplinarian. **2.** One who demands absolute adherence to forms and rules. [After Jean *Martinet* (died 1672), French army officer.]

mav·er·ick (măv′ər-ĭk, măv′rĭk) *n.* **1.** An unbranded range animal, especially a calf that has become separated from its mother, traditionally considered the property of the first person who brands it. **2.** One that refuses to abide by the dictates of or resists adherence to a group; a dissenter. **—maverick** *adj.* Being independent in thought and action or exhibiting such independence: *maverick politicians; a maverick decision.* [Possibly after Samuel Augustus *Maverick* (1803–1870), American cattleman, or perhaps after Samuel *Maverick* (1602?–1676?), English-born colonist.]

Nîmes (nēm). A city of southern France northeast of Montpellier. Thought to have been founded by Greek colonists, it was one of the leading cities of Roman Gaul. Population, 124,220.

Sade (säd, săd), Comte **Donatien Alphonse François de.** Known as "Marquis de Sade." 1740–1814. French writer of novels, plays, and short stories characterized by a preoccupation with sexual violence.

sa·dism (sā′dĭz′əm, săd′ĭz′-) *n.* **1.** *Psychology.* **a.** The act or an instance of deriving sexual gratification from infliction of pain on others. **b.** A psychological disorder in which sexual gratification is derived from infliction of pain on others. **2.** Delight in cruelty. **3.** Extreme cruelty. [After Comte Donatien Alphonse François de SADE.] **—sa′dist** *n.* **—sa·dis′tic** (sə-dĭs′tĭk) *adj.* **—sa·dis′ti·cal·ly** *adv.*

EXERCISE 6.3 Fiction and Mythology

The words in this exercise are from the names of fictitious and mythological people and places. Referring to the etymologies in the entries at the bottom of this page, fill in the name of the author who invented the word and the book in which the word was introduced.

1. Lilliputian _____

2. malaprop _____

3. serendipity _____

4. utopia _____

5. yahoo _____

For the following items, fill in the name and mythical characters from whom the word was derived.

6. aphrodisiac _____

7. narcissism _____

8. nemesis _____

9. tantalize _____

aph·ro·dis·i·ac (ăf′rə-dĭz′ē-ăk′, -dē′zē-) *adj.* Arousing or intensifying sexual desire. —**aphrodisiac** *n.* Something, such as a drug or food, having such an effect. [Greek *aphrodisiakos,* from *aphrodisia,* sexual pleasures, from *Aphroditē,* Aphrodite.] —**aph′ro·di·si′a·cal** (-dĭ-zī′ĭ-kəl) *adj.*

Aph·ro·di·te (ăf′rə-dī′tē) *n. Greek Mythology.* The goddess of love and beauty. Also called *Cytherea.* [Greek *Aphroditē.*]

Lil·li·pu·tian also **lil·li·pu·tian** (lĭl′ə-pyōo′shən) —*n.* A very small person or being. —*adj.* **1.** Very small; diminutive. **2.** Trivial; petty. [After the *Lilliputians,* a people in *Gulliver's Travels* by Jonathan Swift.]

mal·a·prop (măl′ə-prŏp′) *n.* A malapropism. [After Mrs. *Malaprop,* a character in *The Rivals,* a play by Richard Brinsley Sheridan, from MALAPROPOS.]

mal·a·prop·ism (măl′ə-prŏp-ĭz′əm) *n.* **1.** Ludicrous misuse of a word, especially by confusion with one of similar sound. **2.** An example of such misuse. [From MALAPROP.] —**mal′a·prop′i·an** (-prŏp′ē-ən) *adj.*

nar·cis·sism (när′sĭ-sĭz′əm) also **nar·cism** (-sĭz′əm) *n.* **1.** Excessive love or admiration of oneself. See Synonyms at **conceit.** **2.** Erotic pleasure derived from contemplation or admiration of one's own body or self, especially as a fixation on or a regression to an infantile stage of development. [After NARCISSUS.] —**nar′cis·sist** *n.* —**nar′cis·sis′tic** *adj.*

Nar·cis·sus (när-sĭs′əs) *n. Greek Mythology.* A youth who pined away in love for his own image in a pool of water and was transformed into the flower that bears his name.

nem·e·sis (něm′ĭ-sĭs) *n., pl.* **-ses** (-sēz′). **1.** A source of harm or ruin: *Uncritical trust is my nemesis.* **2.** Retributive justice in its execution or outcome: *To follow the proposed course of action is to invite nemesis.* **3.** An opponent that cannot be beaten or overcome. **4.** One that inflicts retribution or vengeance. **5. Nemesis.** *Greek Mythology.* The goddess of retributive justice or vengeance. [Greek, retribution, the goddess Nemesis, from *nemein,* to allot. See **nem-** in Appendix.]

ser·en·dip·i·ty (sĕr′ən-dĭp′ĭ-tē) *n.* The faculty of making fortunate discoveries by accident. [From the characters in the Persian fairy tale *The Three Princes of Serendip,* who made such discoveries, from Persian *Sarandīp,* Sri Lanka, from Arabic *Sarandīb.*] —**ser′en·dip′i·tous** *adj.* —**ser′en·dip′i·tous·ly** *adv.*

tan·ta·lize (tăn′tə-līz′) *tr.v.* **-lized, -liz·ing, -liz·es.** To excite (another) by exposing something desirable while keeping it out of reach. [From Latin *Tantalus,* Tantalus. See TANTALUS.] —**tan′ta·li·za′tion** (-lĭ-zā′shən) *n.* —**tan′ta·liz′er** *n.* —**tan′ta·liz′ing·ly** *adv.*

Tan·ta·lus (tăn′tə-ləs) *n. Greek Mythology.* A king who for his crimes was condemned in Hades to stand in water that receded when he tried to drink, and with fruit hanging above him that receded when he reached for it. [Latin, from Greek *Tantalos.* See **tele-** in Appendix.]

u·to·pi·a (yōo-tō′pē-ə) *n.* **1.a.** Often **Utopia.** An ideally perfect place, especially in its social, political, and moral aspects. **b.** A work of fiction describing a utopia. **2.** An impractical, idealistic scheme for social and political reform. [New Latin *Ūtopia,* imaginary island in *Utopia* by Sir Thomas More : Greek *ou,* not, no + Greek *topos,* place.]

ya·hoo (yä′hōo, yā′-) *n., pl.* **-hoos.** A person regarded as crude or brutish. See Synonyms at **boor.** [From *Yahoo,* member of a race of brutes having human form in *Gulliver's Travels* by Jonathan Swift.] —**ya′hoo·ism** *n.*

EXERCISE 6.4   Other Etymologies

Referring to the etymologies in the entries at the bottom of this page, match the words listed below with the following etymological categories: (a) acronym, (b) blending, (c) coinage, (d), imitation, (e) reduplication, and (f) shortening.

_____   1. blurb

_____   2. boondoggle

_____   3. burp

_____   4. curio

_____   5. dink

_____   6. giggle

_____   7. hi-fi

_____   8. hoity-toity

_____   9. humongous

_____   10. informercial

_____   11. laser

_____   12. meow

_____   13. moped

_____   14. pant

_____   15. pooh-pooh

_____   16. WASP

_____   17. wishy-washy

_____   18. zoo

blurb (blûrb) *n.* A brief publicity notice, as on a book jacket. [Coined by Gelett Burgess (1866–1951), American humorist.] —**blurb** *v.*

boon·dog·gle (bōōn′dô′gəl, -dŏg′əl) *Informal. n.* Unnecessary, wasteful, and often counterproductive work. —**boondoggle** *intr.v.* **-gled, -gling, -gles.** To waste time or money on unnecessary and often counterproductive work. [From *boondoggle,* a plaited leather cord worn by Boy Scouts (coined by R.H. Link, 20th-century American scoutmaster).] —**boon′dog′gler** *n.*

burp (bûrp) *n.* A belch. —**burp** *v.* **burped, burp·ing, burps.** —*intr.* To belch. —*tr.* To cause (a baby) to expel gas from the stomach, as by patting the back after feeding. [Imitative.]

cu·ri·o (kyōōr′ē-ō′) *n., pl.* **-os.** A curious or unusual object of art or piece of bric-a-brac. [Short for CURIOSITY.]

DINK or **dink** (dĭnk) *n.* A two-career couple with no children. [*D(ual) I(ncome) N(o) K(ids).*]

gig·gle (gĭg′əl) *v.* **-gled, -gling, -gles.** —*intr.* To laugh with repeated short, spasmodic sounds. —*tr.* To utter while giggling. —**giggle** *n.* A short, spasmodic laugh. [Of imitative origin.] —**gig′gler** *n.* —**gig′gling·ly** *adv.* —**gig′gly** *adj.*

hi-fi (hī′fī′) *n., pl.* **-fis.** *Informal.* **1.** High fidelity. **2.** An electronic system for reproducing high-fidelity sound from radio or recordings. [HI(GH) + FI(DELITY).] —**hi′-fi′** *adj.*

hoi·ty-toi·ty (hoi′tē-toi′tē) *adj.* **1.** Pretentiously self-important; pompous. **2.** Given to frivolity or silliness. [From reduplication of dialectal *hoit,* to romp; perhaps akin to HOYDEN.]

hu·mon·gous (hyōō-mŏng′gəs, -mŭng′-) or **hu·mun·gous** (-mŭng′-) *adj. Slang.* Extremely large; enormous: *"humongous baked potatoes piled high with sour cream"* (Boston Globe). [Perhaps blend of HUGE and MONSTROUS or TREMENDOUS.]

in·for·mer·cial (ĭn′fər-mûr′shəl, -fə-) also **in·fo·mer·cial** (ĭn′fə-mûr′shəl, -fō-) *n.* A commercial television program or relatively long commercial segment offering consumer information, such as educational or instructional material, related to the sponsor's product or service. [INFOR(MATION) + (COM)MERCIAL.]

la·ser (lā′zər) *n.* **1.** Any of several devices that convert incident electromagnetic radiation of mixed frequencies to one or more discrete frequencies of highly amplified and coherent ultraviolet, visible, or infrared radiation. **2.** A device whose output is in an invisible region of the electromagnetic spectrum. [*l(ight) a(mplification by) s(timulated) e(mission of) r(adiation).*]

me·ow (mē-ou′) *n.* **1.** The cry of a cat. **2.** *Informal.* A malicious, spiteful comment. —**meow** *intr.v.* **-owed, -ow·ing, -ows.** To make the crying sound of a cat. [Imitative.]

mo·ped (mō′pĕd′) *n.* A lightweight motorized bicycle that can be pedaled as well as driven by a low-powered gasoline engine. [From MO(TOR) + PED(AL).]

pant² (pănt) *n.* **1.** Trousers. Often used in the plural. **2.** Underpants. Often used in the plural. —**idiom. with (one's) pants down.** *Slang.* In an embarrassing position. [Short for *pantaloon.*]

pooh-pooh (pōō′pōō′) *tr.v.* **-poohed, -pooh·ing, -poohs.** *Informal.* To express contempt for or impatience about; make light of: *"British actors have long pooh-poohed the Method"* (Stephen Schiff). [Reduplication of POOH.]

Wasp or **WASP** (wŏsp, wôsp) *n.* A white Protestant of Anglo-Saxon ancestry. [W(HITE) + A(NGLO-)S(AXON) + P(ROTESTANT).]

wish·y-wash·y (wĭsh′ē-wŏsh′ē, -wô′shē) *adj.* **-i·er, -i·est.** *Informal.* **1.** Thin and watery, as tea or soup; insipid. **2.** Lacking in strength of character or purpose; ineffective. [Reduplication of *washy,* thin, watery, from WASH.] —**wish′y-wash′i·ness** *n.*

zoo (zōō) *n., pl.* **zoos. 1.** A park or an institution in which living animals are kept and usually exhibited to the public. Also called *zoological garden.* **2.** *Slang.* A place or situation marked by confusion or disorder: *The bus station is a zoo on Fridays.* [Short for ZOOLOGICAL GARDEN.]

Unit One Review

REVIEW 1.1 Basic Word List

Your instructor may give you a test on the meanings of these words. If so, learn the meanings of any of the words that you do not know. Items 1 through 40 are followed by the page numbers on which dictionary entries for them are located, and items 41 through 50 are followed by the numbers of the exercises in which they are introduced.

1. act of God, 27
2. birthday suit, 27
3. cold shoulder, 27
4. elbow grease, 27
5. Indian summer, 27
6. ivory tower, 27
7. rule of thumb, 27
8. soft-soap, 27
9. staff of life, 27
10. tongue-in-cheek, 27
11. ASAP, 28
12. D.A., 29
13. D.C., 29
14. e.g., 29
15. ESP, 29
16. FYI, 29
17. GNP, 29
18. i.e., 29
19. R.S.V.P., 29
20. SASE, 29
21. ad infinitum, 48
22. bona fide, 48
23. et cetera, 48
24. in memoriam, 48
25. modus operandi, 48
26. per capita, 48
27. per diem, 48
28. status quo, 48
29. terra firma, 48
30. vice versa, 48
31. bon vivant, 49
32. cause célèbre, 49
33. cul-de-sac, 49
34. déjà vu, 49
35. double-entendre, 49
36. joie de vivre, 49
37. nom de plume, 49
38. nouveau riche, 49
39. savoir-faire, 49
40. tour de force, 49
41. foible, 6.1
42. ostracize, 6.1
43. stupendous, 6.1
44. verboten, 6.1
45. boycott, 6.2
46. maverick, 6.2
47. sadism, 6.2
48. Lilliputian, 6.3
49. utopia, 6.3
50. narcissism, 6.3

REVIEW 1.2 Advanced Word List

Your instructor may give you a test on the meanings of these words. If so, learn the meanings of any of the words that you do not know. Items 1 through 35 are followed by the page numbers on which dictionary entries for them are located and items 36 through 50 are followed by the numbers of the exercises in which they are introduced.

1. alpha and omega, 27
2. brain trust, 27
3. crocodile tears, 27
4. eleventh hour, 27
5. lip service, 27
6. red herring, 27
7. sacred cow, 27
8. straw man, 27
9. tit for tat, 27
10. touch-and-go, 27

11. Typhoid Mary, 27	31. par excellence, 49
12. vicious circle, 27	32. raison d'être, 49
13. walking papers, 27	33. roman à clef, 49
14. wet blanket, 27	34. tête-à-tête, 49
15. ad nauseum, 48	35. vis-à-vis, 49
16. antebellum, 48	36. alfresco, 6.1
17. caveat emptor, 48	37. bravado, 6.1
18. in toto, 48	38. kowtow, 6.1
19. non compos mentis, 48	39. bunkum, 6.2
20. non sequitur, 48	40. chauvinism, 6.2
21. persona non grata, 48	41. martinet, 6.2
22. postmortem, 48	42. malaprop, 6.3
23. pro forma, 48	43. serendipity, 6.3
24. quid pro quo, 48	44. yahoo, 6.3
25. avant-garde, 49	45. aphrodisiac, 6.3
26. bête noire, 49	46. nemesis, 6.3
27. carte blanche, 49	47. tantalize, 6.3
28. fait accompli, 49	48. boondoggle, 6.4
29. faux pas, 49	49. hoity-toity, 6.4
30. femme fatale, 49	50. pooh-pooh, 6.4

REVIEW 1.3   Sentence Completion

Complete the following sentences using words that make it clear that you know the meanings of the words or phrases that are printed in **boldface**.

1. We used **elbow grease** to ___wash our car after we drove___ ___over muddy mountain roads.___

2. If you ever go to **D.C.** _____

_____

3. I think she has **ESP** because _____

_____

4. One **SOP** in the classroom is _____

_____

5. The painting was proven to be a **bona fide** _____

_____

6. They **ostracized** him from the group because _____

_____

7. A **wet blanket** at a party is likely to _____

_____

8. He became **persona non grata** because _____

_____

9. A **martinet** is likely to _____

_____

10. My idea of **utopia** includes _____

_____

REVIEW 1.4 Writing Applications

Your instructor may assign one or more of the following writing activities.

1. Write six sentences, each of which includes a word or phrase from the Basic Word List on page 57 or the Advanced Word List on pages 57–58. Underline the six words and phrases in your sentences.

2. Write six sentences, each of which includes one of the following words and phrases specified by your instructor. Underline the six words and phrases in your sentences.

   a. _____   d. _____

   b. _____   e. _____

   c. _____   f. _____

3. Write a paragraph on a topic of your choice using six of the words and phrases from the Basic Word List on page 57 or the Advanced Word List on pages 57–58. Underline the six words and phrases in your paragraph.

4. Write a paragraph on a topic of your choice that includes the following six words and phrases specified by your instructor. Underline the six words and phrases in your paragraph.

   a. _____   d. _____

   b. _____   e. _____

   c. _____   f. _____

<u>***REVIEW 1.5***</u>   **Fill-in Questions**

Write on the lines the words that have been deleted from the following definitions of terminology introduced in Chapters 2 through 6.

1. An _____ is information about the origin and development of a word.

2. An _____ is a phrase such as "caught my eye," which has a meaning that is not clear from the meanings of the separate words in the phrase.

3. The _____ is a symbol used to indicate the sounds of vowels in unstressed syllables.

4. An _____ is a word such as *scuba*, which is made from the first letters of other words.

<u>***REVIEW 1.6***</u>   **Short-Answer Questions**

Refer to Chapter 4 to write the answers to the following questions.

1. What is the basic procedure you should use to determine which desk dictionary is the most appropriate one for you to purchase?

_____

_____

_____

_____

2. What help do dictionaries provide for locating the definitions of words that pertain to college subjects?

_____

3. How can you determine whether definitions in a dictionary are listed chronologically, beginning with the oldest known definition, or with the most common or general definition first?

_____

_____

_____

_____

Two

Study the Context

Learning Goals for Unit Two

In studying Chapters 7, 8, and 9 you will learn:

- That a *context* is a sentence, paragraph, or longer unit of writing that surrounds a word (Chapter 7).

- That the meanings of words may be stated in or suggested by context (Chapters 7 and 8).

- How to find the meanings of words when they are stated in context (Chapter 7).

- How to figure out the meanings of words when they are suggested or implied by context (Chapter 8).

- How to find or figure out the meanings of words that are stated in or hinted at in books you study for your college courses (Chapter 9).

Stated Meanings

A **context** is a sentence, paragraph, or longer unit of writing that surrounds a word. The meaning of *surrogate* (sûr′ə-gĭt) is stated in the following context.

> Psychologists have learned that infant monkeys will use any object, even a glove, as a **surrogate** mother—substitute parent.

The meaning of *surrogate* is set off in this sentence with a dash—it means "substitute."

Methods of Stating Meanings

Writers often give straightforward definitions of words. Underline the definition of *metamemory* (mĕt′ə-mĕm′ər-ē) that is directly stated in the following sentence from a psychology textbook.

> *Metamemory* is the name for knowledge about how your own memory works.

You should have underlined "knowledge about how your own memory works."
   Word meanings are also frequently set off with punctuation such as parentheses, commas, and dashes. Underline the meanings of *progeny* (prŏj′ə-nē), *orthography* (ôr-thŏg′rə-fē), and *plagiarize* (plā′jə-rīz′) that are set off by punctuation in the following sentences.

- **Parentheses:** The *progeny* (offspring) of one insect can number in the thousands, but most of them do not live long.
- **Commas:** Learn the rules of *orthography*, or spelling, that are explained in Chapter 22 of this book.
- **A Dash:** When you write papers for your college courses, take care that you do not *plagiarize*—present the words or ideas of others as though they were your own.

You should have underlined "offspring," "spelling," and "present the words or ideas of others as though they were your own."

Sometimes writers state the meaning of a word but do not set it off with punctuation. Underline the meaning of *devastated* (dĕv′ə-stāt′əd), which is given in the following sentence.

> When the storm hit town, it destroyed a hotel on the ocean, and it also **devastated** many homes inland.

In presenting facts about a storm, the sentence also gives the meaning of *devastated*; you should have underlined "destroyed."

Limitation of Context

Using context to determine word meanings has an important limitation: When a word has more than one meaning, a context reveals only one of the meanings.

> When females reach puberty, they are able to *conceive*—to become pregnant.

This sentence states that *conceive* (kən-sēv′) means "to become pregnant." However, *conceive* has other meanings, including "to develop in the mind," as in "Who first *conceived* of television?"

Problems with Stated Meanings

When you try to locate the meanings of words stated in contexts, keep in mind that punctuation may be used for purposes other that those illustrated in this chapter. For example, writers may use a dash to introduce the definition of a word, but they may also use it for other reasons.

> George is an artist, a scholar, an entrepreneur—a very bright guy.

Here the dash is used to emphasize that what follows sums up the writer's opinion of George. *Entrepreneur* (ŏn′trə-prə-nûr′) is not defined in the sentence; it means "one who organizes a business, risking potential loss for potential profits."

Also, do not mistake examples for definitions. Underline the definition of *soft goods* in the following sentence.

> Clothes, sheets, and towels are *soft goods*—products made out of cloth.

A **definition** is a statement of the meaning of a word; you should have underlined "products made out of cloth." An **example** is something selected to show the general characteristics of whatever is denoted by a term; clothes, sheets, and towels are examples of *soft goods* but they are not definitions of this term.

EXERCISE 7.1 Stated Meanings

Underline the synonyms or definitions of the **boldface** words.

1. He understood his mother's frown to be **adverse,** or unfavorable, criticism.

2. Casandra can't decide whether she wants to stay in college, and she is also **ambivalent** about getting married.

3. Kaspar's first step in gaining **autonomy** (independence) was to get a job that made it possible for him to pay all of his own expenses.

4. He has no **conception** of what is ethical—no idea of what is right and wrong.

5. Some people do not **condone** smoking in their homes, but others forgive, or overlook, their guests' smoking.

6. My biology professor gives lectures that confuse me and tests that **confound** me.

7. We have **contempt** for terrorists, and we also have a total lack of respect for nations that give them support.

8. Some people **contend** that the death penalty should be abolished, and others argue that there are times when death is the only appropriate penalty.

9. Our thoughts are **covert;** they are concealed, or hidden, from others until we share them.

10. **Criteria** are standards by which something is judged, such as the standards teachers use when they evaluate students' writing.

11. When you go from bright daylight into a darkened room, the pupils of your eyes **dilate** (enlarge) to compensate for the loss of light.

12. The library is the most prominent **edifice** on campus; it towers above all the other buildings.

Pronunciations

1. adverse (ăd-vûrs′) adj.
2. ambivalent (ăm-bĭv′ə-lənt) adj.
3. autonomy (ô-tŏn′ə-mē) n.
4. conception (kən-sĕp′shən) n.
5. condone (kən-dōn′) v.
6. confound (kən-found′) v.
7. contempt (kən-tĕmpt′) n.
8. contend (kən-tĕnd′) v.
9. covert (kō′vərt) adj.
10. criteria (krī-tîr′ē-ə) n. pl.
11. dilate (dī-lāt′) v.
12. edifice (ĕd′ə-fĭs) n.

EXERCISE 7.2   Stated Meanings

Underline the synonyms or definitions of the **boldface** words.

1. When new evidence is brought forward, those found guilty of crimes are sometimes **exonerated**—declared innocent and free of blame.

2. If I say, "Please call me Jim," it is **explicit** (or clearly stated) that I want you to call me "Jim."

3. Some people are **gullible**—easily cheated or tricked because they believe everything that others say.

4. Combat is a **harrowing** experience—it causes great mental anguish for most soldiers.

5. If I introduce myself to you as "Jim," it is **implicit**—suggested, though not directly stated—that I want you to call me "Jim."

6. The death sentence is sometimes carried out by **lethal** injection—a shot in the arm with a deadly chemical.

7. He was **maligned** by the spread of untrue and vicious rumors that he was a rapist.

8. Life is filled with **mundane** activities, such as the commonplace and day-to-day chores of washing dishes and cleaning the bathroom.

9. The mayor was severely criticized for showing favoritism to his relatives by hiring them for highly paid jobs and for engaging in other types of **nepotism.**

10. Please erase completely from your mind all worry that you may fail; **obliterate** such self-defeating thoughts.

11. He is **oblivious** to what others think; he is totally unaware that his stupid jokes are annoying.

12. As supervisor, one of her jobs is to familiarize new workers with company rules and to **orient** them to their responsibilities.

Pronunciations
1. exonerate (ĭg-zŏn′ə-rāt′) v.
2. explicit (ĭk-splĭs′ĭt) adj.
3. gullible (gŭl′ə-bəl) adj.
4. harrowing (hăr′ō-ĭng) adj.
5. implicit (ĭm-plĭs′ĭt) adj.
6. lethal (lē′thəl) adj.
7. malign (mə-līn′) v.
8. mundane (mŭn-dān′) adj.
9. nepotism (nĕp′ə-tĭz′əm) n.
10. obliterate (ə-blĭt′ə-rāt′) v.
11. oblivious (ə-blĭv′ē-əs) adj.
12. orient (ôr′ē-ənt) v.

_____ **EXERCISE 7.3** **Stated Meanings**

Underline the synonyms or definitions of the **boldface** words.

1. When we laugh, our thoughts become **overt;** laughter makes it apparent, or clear, that we are amused.

2. After her divorce, Laura moved to Denver, hoping that the move would be a remedy for her problems; however, Denver was not a **panacea** for her difficulties.

3. The notion that it is sophisticated to smoke is **passé**—it's as old-fashioned and out-of-date as greasy hair.

4. Your **peers** are your equals—your classmates, for instance.

5. I **perceive** that you are displeased with me; I am very much aware that I have made you unhappy for some reason.

6. When the going gets tough, the tough get going; they continue in spite of difficulty—they **persevere.**

7. The speaker's jokes were amusing and **pertinent;** they were directly related to the points she made in her speech.

8. It is **pretentious,** or showy, to wear a mink coat to a college class.

9. The doctor's **prognosis** (prediction about recovery) is that Luis will be strong enough to go back to work in three days.

10. A **protégé** is a person who is guided and helped by a more influential person.

11. A famine in Africa has resulted in widespread starvation and **rampant** disease.

12. Establish good **rapport** (a warm relationship) with your college teachers.

Pronunciations

1. overt (ō-vûrt′) adj.
2. panacea (păn′ə-sē′ə) n.
3. passé (pă-sā′) adj.
4. peer (pîr) n.
5. perceive (pər-sēv′) v.
6. persevere (pûr′sə-vîr′) v.
7. pertinent (pûr′tə-nənt) adj.
8. pretentious (prĭ-tĕn′shəs) adj.
9. prognosis (prŏg-nō′sĭs) n.
10. protégé (prō′tə-zhā′) n.
11. rampant (răm′pənt) adj.
12. rapport (rə-pôr′) n.

EXERCISE 7.4   Stated Meanings

Underline the synonyms or definitions of the **boldface** words.

1. Attorneys for defendants attempt to **refute** (disprove) claims of guilt.

2. Anthony owns a **replica** of the Venus de Milo—a copy of the famous armless statue housed in a museum in Paris.

3. Most office jobs are **sedentary**—they require workers to sit much of the time.

4. I have a brother and sister, but my best friend has no **sibling.**

5. When Sandra needs comfort, she turns to her husband for **solace.**

6. My English teacher claims that the argument in my paper is **specious**—it seems true, but it is false.

7. The contract specifies the number of hours we will work each week and it **stipulates** the pay we will receive for each hour's work.

8. I can give evidence to prove that I paid the bill; my canceled check will **substantiate** my claim.

9. A circle is **symmetrical;** when it is divided in half, it has an identical form on either side of the dividing line.

10. For an eighty-year-old person, a twenty year prison term is **tantamount** to (equivalent to) life in prison.

11. Those who want careers as motion picture actors must be **tenacious**—persistent and stubbornly determined to succeed.

12. Erika does many things well; she is an extremely **versatile** young woman.

Pronunciations

1. refute (rĭ-fyōot′) v.
2. replica (rĕp′lĭ-kə) n.
3. sedentary (sĕd′n-tĕr′ē) adj.
4. sibling (sĭb′lĭng) n.
5. solace (sŏl′ĭs) n.
6. specious (spē′shəs) adj.
7. stipulate (stĭp′yə-lāt′) v.
8. substantiate (səb-stăn′shē-āt′) v.
9. symmetrical (sĭ-mĕt′rĭ-kəl) adj.
10. tantamount (tăn′tə-mount′) adj.
11. tenacious (tə-nā′shəs) adj.
12. versatile (vûr′sə-təl) adj.

Implied Meanings

When the meaning of a word is not stated in a context, it may be suggested, or **implied.** You may infer the meaning of a word that is implied by a context. To **infer** is to use reasoning to arrive at a conclusion or decision. Infer the meaning of *satiated* (sā'shē-āt'ĭd) that is implied by the context of the following sentence.

> After eating a huge Thanksgiving dinner, I was *satiated*; I swore that I wouldn't eat again for a week.

If you have ever eaten so much that you swore you would not eat again for a long while, you should be able to infer the meaning of *satiated*. What causes you to swear that you will not eat again for a week? No doubt the feeling of being so filled up that you have no desire to eat or to think about food. If you reasoned in this way, you inferred the meaning of *satiated*; it means "having had enough or more than enough, especially more than enough food."

This chapter explains the three ways in which word meanings are usually implied by context: general sense, examples, and contrasts.

General Sense

Infer the meaning of *incarcerated* (ĭn-kär'sə-rāt'əd) that is implied by the general sense of the following context.

> Murderers are usually *incarcerated* for longer periods of time than robbers.

Since you know that those found guilty of murder and robbery are usually sentenced to serve time in prison, this context implies that *incarcerated* means "locked up in a jail, prison, or penitentiary."

Examples

When the meaning of a word is not implied by the general sense of a context, it may be implied by examples. Infer the meaning of *discipline* (dĭs'ə-plĭn) that is implied by examples in the following context.

> My history professor is an expert in three *disciplines*—history, architecture, and philosophy.

Since history, architecture, and philosophy are three branches of knowledge, this context implies that a *discipline* is a "branch of knowledge, learning, or study."

Contrasts

When the meaning of a word is not implied by the general sense of a context or by examples, it may be implied by a contrasting thought in a context. Infer the meaning of *credence* (krēd'ns) that is implied by a contrast in the following context.

> Dad gave *credence* to my story, but Mom's reaction was one of total disbelief.

Since this sentence contrasts Dad's reaction of *credence* with Mom's reaction of "total disbelief," it implies that *credence* is very different from "total disbelief." *Credence* means "belief."

Inferring Word Meanings

As you do the following exercises, keep in mind that when a sentence contains an unfamiliar word, it is sometimes possible to infer the general meaning of the sentence without inferring the exact meaning of the unknown word. Read the following sentence.

> After we have had the Martins over for dinner, they do not invite us to their home for dinner; however, when we have the Hoseys to dinner, they always *reciprocate.*

In reading this sentence, you may infer that the Hoseys are more desirable dinner guests than the Martins without inferring the exact meaning of *reciprocate* (rĭ-sĭp'rə-kāt'). On the other hand, you may have concluded that the Hoseys differ from the Martins in that they do something in return when they are invited for dinner, and decided correctly that *reciprocate* means "to do in return."

The following exercises provide practice in inferring the general meanings of sentences and the exact meanings of unfamiliar words.

EXERCISE 8.1   Implied Meanings

Infer the meanings of the **boldface** words and write them in the space below each item.

1. Vegetarians **abstain** from eating meat.

2. Both of them stood trial, but one was found guilty and sent to prison, and the other was **acquitted.**

3. Aspirin, fresh air, or something to eat will often **alleviate** a minor headache.

4. He **aspired** to be president, but he was elected secretary instead.

5. He was an **astute** lawyer—always to be found on the winning side.

6. She took a job during the summer to **augment** the salary she earns as a teacher.

7. Her job is selling real estate, but her **avocation** is photography.

8. My brother can make almost any automobile repair, and he is also a **competent** electrician and plumber.

9. We were assigned to write a **concise,** one-page summary of a five-hundred-page book.

10. The students reached a **consensus** that they would rather write a research paper than take a final examination.

Pronunciations

1. abstain (ăb-stān′) v.
2. acquit (ə-kwĭt′) v.
3. alleviate (ə-lē′vē-āt′) v.
4. aspire (ə-spīr′) v.
5. astute (ə-sto͞ot′) adj.

6. augment (ôg-měnt′) v.
7. avocation (ăv′ō-kā′shən) n.
8. competent (kŏm′pə-tənt) adj.
9. concise (kən-sīs′) adj.
10. consensus (kən-sěn′səs) n.

EXERCISE 8.2   Implied Meanings

Infer the meanings of the **boldface** words and write them in the space below each item.

1. After attending a concert, the students of music appreciation had to write a **critique** of the orchestra's performance.

2. Eating in restaurants became so expensive that we had to **curtail** dining out from once a week to once a month.

3. The presence of a traffic officer tends to **deter** motorists from violating traffic laws.

4. The neighborhood in which I grew up has **deteriorated;** the fine old houses are falling apart and the once beautiful gardens are overgrown with weeds.

5. He is having his teeth straightened in the hope that his smile will be **enhanced.**

6. My English teacher read us an **excerpt** from a play written by Shakespeare.

7. The photograph shows that the building has eight Greek columns on its **façade** and a huge dome on top.

8. Microwave ovens **facilitate** the quick preparation of meals.

9. Some of us expect physicians always to be correct, forgetting that they, like us, are **fallible.**

10. It is not **feasible** to drive from New York to Los Angeles in two days.

Pronunciations

1. critique (krĭ-tēk') n.
2. curtail (kər-tāl') v.
3. deter (dĭ-tûr') v.
4. deteriorate (dĭ-tîr'ē-ə-rāt') v.
5. enhance (ĕn-hăns') v.
6. excerpt (ĕk-sûrpt') n.
7. façade (fə-säd') n.
8. facilitate (fə-sĭl'ĭ-tāt') v.
9. fallible (făl'ə-bəl) adj.
10. feasible (fē'zə-bəl) adj.

EXERCISE 8.3   **Implied Meanings**

Infer the meanings of the **boldface** words and write them in the space below each item.

1. Only a few new businesses are successes—most are **fiascoes.**

2. We left the waitress a $5.00 **gratuity** because she was pleasant and gave us excellent service.

3. When Joe learned that his wife had been injured, he told his employer that it was **imperative** for him to leave work immediately.

4. I assure you that the error was **inadvertent;** we never intend to overcharge our customers.

5. When he totaled his debts, he realized that he must get a more **lucrative** job in order to pay them.

6. Few people have the **means** to purchase new homes nowadays.

7. In comparison to the other costs of owning and maintaining an automobile, the cost of gasoline is **negligible.**

8. Each **novice** mountain climber was guided by two people who had been climbing mountains for many years.

9. He does not need to study physics, but it is **obligatory** for him to study some physical science.

10. The jury found him guilty because they decided that his alibi was not **plausible.**

Pronunciations

1. fiasco (fē-ăs′kō) n.
2. gratuity (grə-tōo′ĭ-tē) n.
3. imperative (ĭm-pĕr′ə-tĭv) adj.
4. inadvertent (ĭn′əd-vûr′tənt) adj.
5. lucrative (lōo′krə-tĭv) adj.
6. means (mēnz) n.
7. negligible (nĕg′lĭ-jə-bəl) adj.
8. novice (nŏv′ĭs) n.
9. obligatory (ə-blĭg′ə-tôr′ē) adj.
10. plausible (plô′zə-bəl) adj.

EXERCISE 8.4 Implied Meanings

Infer the meanings of the **boldface** words and write them in the space below each item.

1. If there is something you must do that you can do today, do it today—don't **procrastinate.**

2. It is **prudent** to purchase paper towels, light bulbs, laundry soap, and other household essentials when they are on sale.

3. His **rationale** for taking large doses of vitamin C is that this practice will prevent him from catching a cold.

4. We **reimbursed** her for the gasoline she purchased to drive us to the party.

5. My psychology professor sometimes shows us films that are **relevant** to topics that we study in her class.

6. He **scrutinized** the dinner bill, which came to $72.37, to make certain that he had not been overcharged.

7. As she spoke in French, the interpreter gave us a **simultaneous** translation in English.

8. She doesn't **squander** her money on poorly made clothing that she can wear for only one season.

9. She had a C average her first semester, but a B average in all **subsequent** semesters.

10. His given name is John, and his **surname** is Smith.

Pronunciations

1. procrastinate (prō-krăs′tə-nāt′) v.
2. prudent (prood′ənt) adj.
3. rationale (răsh′ə-năl′) n.
4. reimburse (rē′ĭm-bûrs′) v.
5. relevant (rĕl′ə-vənt) adj.
6. scrutinize (skroot′n-īz′) v.
7. simultaneous (sī′məl-tā′nē-əs) adj.
8. squander (skwŏn′dər) v.
9. subsequent (sŭb′sĭ-kwənt′) adj.
10. surname (sûr′nām′) n.

Using the Context

This chapter explains how to apply what you learned about context in Chapters 7 and 8 to locate or infer the meanings of words in your college textbooks.

Stated Meanings

Locate the meanings of words that are stated in your college books, such as the meaning of *recidivism* that is stated in the following textbook excerpt.

> Originally, imprisonment was intended to provide the convict with the opportunity for solitary reflection and thus for penitence and rehabilitation, but this goal has certainly not been achieved in practice. In fact, the rate of **recidivism,** or repeated crime by those who have been convicted before, seems alarmingly high. Nearly three-quarters of all offenders released after serving prison time are rearrested within four years—sometimes for the same crimes. Since other released prisoners presumably also return to crime but are not arrested, the actual crime rate among released convicts is even greater.

Did you underline "repeated crime by those who have been convicted before?"

Implied Meanings

Infer word meanings that are implied by your books, such as the meanings of *fraught, elation,* and *dejection* that are implied by the following.

> In Western cultures, early adolescence, from twelve to sixteen or so, is **fraught** with ups and downs. Moods swing wildly from one extreme to the other: from **elation** at a girlfriend's kiss to **dejection** at a failed exam (Csikszentmihalyi & Larson, 1984).

1. *Fraught* means _____.

2. *Elation* means _____.

3. *Dejection* means _____.

You may have inferred that *fraught* means "filled," that *elation* means "joy or happiness," and that *dejection* means "depression or unhappiness."

EXERCISE 9.1   **Stated or Implied: History**

The meanings of the **boldface** words in this exercise are stated in or implied by context. Underline stated meanings and write implied meanings on the lines provided. The excerpts are from *A People and a Nation*, third edition, by Mary Beth Norton and others.

These many societies exhibited basic economic differences. Some were **nomadic,** surviving by moving continually in search of wild animals and edible plants; others combined regular seasonal movements with a limited reliance on agriculture. (p. 4)

1. **nomadic** (nō-măd′ĭk) adj. _____

Since the earliest known humanlike remains, about 3 million years old, have been found in what is now Ethiopia, it is likely that human beings originated on the continent of Africa. During many millennia, the growing human population slowly **dispersed** to other continents. (p. 5)

2. **disperse** (dĭ-spûrs′) v. _____

Indians' religious beliefs varied even more than did their political systems. Yet they were all **polytheistic,** involving a multitude of gods. (p. 9)

3. **subsist** (səb-sĭst′) v. _____

The English were an **ethnocentric** people—they believed firmly in the superiority of their values and civilization, especially when compared with the native cultures of Africa and North America. (p. 48, adapted)

4. **ethnocentric** (ĕth′nō-sĕn′trĭk) adj. _____

The relative lack of men increased the work demands on women and simultaneously encouraged **polygyny** (the practice of one man having several wives). (p. 49)

5. **polygyny** (pə-lĭj′ə-nē) n. _____

Given the economic importance of the slave trade, it is hardly surprising that European nations fought bitterly over control of it. The Portuguese, who initially dominated the trade, were **supplanted** by the Dutch in the middle of the seventeenth century. (p. 51)

6. **supplant** (sə-plănt′) v. _____

In the seventeenth century, some European thinkers began to analyze nature in an effort to determine the laws that govern the universe. They employed experimentation and abstract reasoning to discover general principles behind such everyday **phenomena** as the motions of the planets and stars, the behavior of falling objects, and the characteristics of light and sound. (pp. 93–94)

7. **phenomena** (fĭ-nŏm′ə-nə) n.pl. _____

The committee tried to **intimidate** him by sending armed men to his church to beat drums and practice the manual of arms during services. (p. 134)

8. **intimidate** (ĭn-tĭm′ĭ-dāt′) v. _____

Slaves faced a **dilemma** at the beginning of the Revolution: how could they best achieve their goal of escaping perpetual servitude? Should they fight with or against their white masters? (p. 137)

9. **dilemma** (dĭ-lĕm′ə) n. _____

His **stamina** was remarkable: in more than eight years of war Washington never had a serious illness and took only one brief leave of absence. Moreover, he both looked and acted like a leader. Six feet tall in an era when most men were five inches shorter, his presence was stately and commanding. (p. 142)

10. **stamina** (stăm′ə-nə) n. _____

She further contended that girls should be taught to support themselves by their own efforts: "Independence should be placed within their grasp." Because she rejected the **prevailing** notion that a young woman's chief goal in life should be in finding a husband, Judith Sargent Murray deserves the title of the first American feminist. (p. 162)

11. **prevailing** (prĭ-vā′lĭng) adj. _____

By far the fastest-spreading technological advance of the era was the magnetic telegraph. Samuel F. B. Morse's invention freed long-distance messages from the **restraint** of traveling no faster than the messenger; instantaneous communication became possible even over long distances. (pp. 248–249)

12. **restraint** (rĭ-strānt′) n. _____

For entertainment slaves made musical instruments with carved **motifs** that resembled some African stringed instruments. (p. 294)

13. **motif** (mō-tēf′) n. _____

The son of an African woman who passionately hated her enslavement, Nat was a **precocious** child who learned to read very young. (p. 297)

14. **precocious** (prĭ-kō′shəs) adj. _____

EXERCISE 9.2   Stated or Implied: Sociology

The meanings of the **boldface** words in this exercise are stated in or implied by context. Underline stated meanings and write implied meanings on the lines provided. The excerpts are from *Sociology*, third edition, by Ian Robertson.

"What a piece of work is man!" exclaims Hamlet in Shakespeare's play. "How noble in reason! How infinite in faculty! In form, and moving, how express and admirable! In action, how like an angel! In apprehension, how like a god! The beauty of the world! The **paragon** of animals!" (p. 56)

1. **paragon** (păr′ə-gŏn′) n. _____

Most modern psychologists agree that human beings do not have any "instincts." An **instinct** is a behavior pattern with three essential features: it is complex, it is unlearned, and it appears in all normal members of the species under identical conditions. For example, all members of some bird or insect species will build complex nests of exactly the same type, even if they have never seen such nests built before, as soon as the nesting season begins. (p. 60)

2. instinct (ĭn′stĭngkt′) n. _____

Some violations of mores are made almost unthinkable by a **taboo**—a powerful social belief that some specific act is utterly **loathsome.** In the United States, for example, there is a strong taboo against eating human flesh, a taboo so effective that most of the states do not even have laws prohibiting the practice. (p. 62)

3. **taboo** (tă-boo′) n. _____

4. **loathsome** (lōth′səm) adj. _____

Equally important, language enables us to give meaning to the world. Events in themselves have no meaning; we impose meaning on them by interpreting the evidence of our senses. Without language, all but the most **rudimentary** forms of thought are impossible. With language, we can apply reason to the world. (p. 78)

5. **rudimentary** (roo′də-mĕn′tə-rē) adj. _____

Until about a hundred years ago, Americans' favorite sports were such activities as foot racing, boat racing, cockfighting, hunting, and fishing; the large-scale spectator sports of football, baseball, hockey, and basketball were **virtually** unknown, and became popular only as the nation was transformed from a **predominantly** rural, agricultural society into an urban, industrial one. (p. 96)

6. **virtually** (vûr′choo-ə-lē) adv. _____

7. **predominantly** (prĭ-dŏm′ə-nənt′lē) adv. _____

Societies in which the clock is commonplace tend to think of time not in a cyclical but in a **linear** way—as a straight line from the past to the future on which we travel, at a constant speed, in the present. It is impossible to imagine modern industrialized society without the clock and the socially constructed time that it implies. (p. 163)

8. **linear** (lĭn′ē-ər) adj. _____

Today the social landscape is dominated by large, impersonal organizations that influence our lives from the moment of birth. Some of these organizations are *voluntary*, in the sense that people may freely join them or withdraw from them. Examples include religious movements, political parties, and professional organizations. Some are **coercive,** in the sense that people are forced to join them—for example, prisons or elementary schools. (p. 175)

9. **coercive** (kō-ûr′sĭv) adj. _____

Why, then, does the United States permit such widespread access to handguns? One reason is the persistent belief that, since criminals have guns, law-abiding people need them for self-protection. A second reason for the **proliferation** of handguns is the belief, deeply held by many Americans, that gun ownership is an individual right. (p. 202, adapted)

10. **proliferation** (prə-lĭf′ə-rā′shən) n. _____

Obesity provides a case in point. Until a few years ago, people who deviated from the ideal physical form by being overweight were held to have a personal problem of eating too much or exercising too little. Gradually, however, physicians have succeeded in defining **obesity** as a disease, to be cured by such means as scientific diets, psychotherapy, or even surgery. (p. 214)

11. **obesity** (ō-bē′sĭ-tē) n. _____

Most societies frown on extramarital sex: about two-thirds of the societies in the cross-cultural samples forbid **adultery,** or sexual relations involving partners at least one of whom is married to someone else. (p. 225)

12. **adultery** (ə-dŭl′trē) n. _____

Millions of American adults and children live in poverty. For these **impoverished** people, life may be marked by illiteracy and ignorance, insecurity and homelessness, disease and early death, the stunting of human lives and potential. Yet many Americans, accustomed to life in a generally **affluent,** optimistic society, tend to ignore the existence of poverty or even to blame the poor themselves for their **plight.** (p. 276)

13. **impoverished** (ĭm-pŏv′ər-ĭsht) adj. _____

14. **affluent** (ăf′lōō-ənt) adj. _____

15. **plight** (plīt) n. _____

EXERCISE 9.3   Stated or Implied: Government

The meanings of the **boldface** words in this exercise are stated in or implied by context. Underline stated meanings and write implied meanings on the lines provided. The excerpts are from *The Challenge of Democracy*, third edition, by Kenneth Janda and others.

> People hold different opinions about the merits of government policies. Sometimes their views are based on self-interest. For example, senior citizens **vociferously** oppose increasing their contributions to Medicare, the government program that **defrays** medical costs for the elderly. (p. 21, adapted)

1. **vociferous** (vō-sĭf'ər-əs) adj. _____

2. **defray** (dĭ-frā') v. _____

> The first **objective** of paid political advertising is name recognition. The next is to promote the candidate by **extolling** his or her virtues. (p. 318, adapted)

3. **objective** (əb-jĕk'tĭv) n. _____

4. **extol** (ĭk-stōl') v. _____

> Once appointed to a committee, a representative or senator has great **incentive** to remain on it and to gain increasing expertise over the years. That incentive can be translated as influence in Congress, and the influence increases as a member's level of expertise grows. Influence also grows in a more formal way, with **seniority**, or years of consecutive service on a committee. In the **quest** for expertise and seniority, members tend to stay on the same committees. (p. 392)

5. **incentive** (ĭn-sĕn'tĭv) n. _____

6. **seniority** (sēn-yôr'ĭ-tē) n. _____

7. **quest** (kwĕst) n. _____

> One early use of the inherent power of the presidency occurred during George Washington's **tenure** in office. The British and French were at war, and Washington was under some pressure from members of his own administration to show favoritism toward the French. Instead, he issued a proclamation of strict neutrality, angering many who harbored anti-British sentiments; the **ensuing** controversy provoked a constitutional debate. (p. 422–423)

Reference
Richard M. Pious, *The American Presidency* (New York: Basic Books, 1979), pp. 51–52.

8. **tenure** (tĕn'yər) n. _____

9. **ensuing** (ĕn-sōo'ĭng) adj. _____

Unit Two Review

REVIEW 2.1 Basic Word List

Your instructor may give you a test on the meanings of these words. If so, learn the meanings of any of the words that you do not know. The words are followed by the numbers of the exercises in which they are introduced.

1. adverse, 7.1	26. consensus, 8.1
2. conception, 7.1	27. curtail, 8.2
3. condone, 7.1	28. excerpt, 8.2
4. contempt, 7.1	29. facilitate, 8.2
5. criteria, 7.1	30. fallible, 8.2
6. dilate, 7.1	31. feasible, 8.2
7. explicit, 7.2	32. fiasco, 8.3
8. gullible, 7.2	33. imperative, 8.3
9. harrowing, 7.2	34. inadvertent, 8.3
10. lethal, 7.2	35. negligible, 8.3
11. obliterate, 7.2	36. obligatory, 8.3
12. oblivious, 7.2	37. plausible, 8.3
13. orient, 7.2	38. prudent, 8.4
14. peer, 7.3	39. relevant, 8.4
15. perceive, 7.3	40. scrutinize, 8.4
16. persevere, 7.3	41. subsequent, 8.4
17. sibling, 7.4	42. dilemma, 9.1
18. stipulate, 7.4	43. intimidate, 9.1
19. substantiate, 7.4	44. phenomena, 9.1
20. abstain, 8.1	45. precocious, 9.1
21. acquit, 8.1	46. prevailing, 9.1
22. alleviate, 8.1	47. loathsome, 9.2
23. astute, 8.1	48. predominantly, 9.2
24. competent, 8.1	49. virtually, 9.2
25. concise, 8.1	50. incentive, 9.3

REVIEW 2.2 Advanced Word List

Your instructor may give you a test on the meanings of these words. If so, learn the meanings of any of the words that you do not know. The words are followed by the numbers of the exercises in which they are introduced.

1. confound, 7.1	10. prognosis, 7.3
2. covert, 7.1	11. protégé, 7.3
3. edifice, 7.1	12. rampant, 7.3
4. implicit, 7.2	13. rapport, 7.3
5. nepotism, 7.2	14. refute, 7.4
6. overt, 7.3	15. sedentary, 7.4
7. passé, 7.3	16. solace, 7.4
8. pertinent, 7.3	17. specious, 7.4
9. pretentious, 7.3	18. tenacious, 7.4

19. aspire, 8.1
20. augment, 8.1
21. avocation, 8.1
22. critique, 8.2
23. deter, 8.2
24. deteriorate, 8.2
25. enhance, 8.2
26. façade, 8.2
27. gratuity, 8.3
28. lucrative, 8.3
29. means, 8.3
30. novice, 8.3
31. rationale, 8.4
32. reimburse, 8.4
33. simultaneous, 8.4
34. squander, 8.4

35. surname, 8.4
36. disperse, 9.1
37. motif, 9.1
38. restraint, 9.1
39. stamina, 9.1
40. subsist, 9.1
41. supplant, 9.1
42. affluent, 9.2
43. coercive, 9.2
44. plight, 9.2
45. proliferation, 9.2
46. rudimentary, 9.2
47. defray, 9.3
48. ensuing, 9.3
49. extol, 9.3
50. vociferous, 9.3

REVIEW 2.3 Sentence Completion

Complete the following sentences using words that make it clear that you know the meanings of the words that are printed in **boldface.**

1. One of my high school teachers did not **condone** *illegible homework — she insisted that we write clearly.*

2. Suicide is sometimes committed using a **lethal** _____

3. My **peers** include _____

4. I am **competent** at _____

5. It is **prudent** to _____

6. My favorite **edifice** is _____

7. It is **pretentious** to _____

8. I **aspire** to _____

9. I am a **novice** when it comes to _____

_____

10. A **loathsome** _____

_____

___**REVIEW 2.4**   **Writing Applications**

Your instructor may assign one or more of the following writing activities.

1. Write six sentences, each of which includes a word from the Basic Word List on page 81 or Advanced Word List on pages 81–82. Underline the six words in your sentences.

2. Write six sentences, each of which includes one of the following words specified by your instructor. Underline the six words in your sentences.

   a. _____   d. _____

   b. _____   e. _____

   c. _____   f. _____

3. Write a paragraph on a topic of your choice using six of the words from the Basic Word List on page 81 or the Advanced Word List on pages 81–82. Underline the six words in your paragraph.

4. Write a paragraph on a topic of your choice which includes the following six words specified by your instructor. Underline the six words in your paragraph.

   a. _____   d. _____

   b. _____   e. _____

   c. _____   f. _____

5. Describe a **harrowing** experience you have had.

6. Explain what your college has done to **orient** you to college life.

7. Tell about an instance when you were **gullible.**

8. Explain how to establish good **rapport** with college teachers.

9. What are some of your **criteria** for selecting your friends?

10. Describe the **façade** of one of the buildings on your campus.

REVIEW 2.5   Fill-in Questions

Write on the lines the words that are missing from the following definitions of terminology introduced in Chapters 7 and 8.

1. A _____ is a sentence, paragraph, or longer unit of writing that surrounds a word.

2. A _____ is a statement of the meaning of a word.

3. An _____ is something selected to show the general characteristics of whatever is denoted by a term.

4. To _____ is to suggest or hint.

5. To _____ is to use reasoning to arrive at a conclusion or decision.

REVIEW 2.6   Short-Answer Questions

Refer to Chapters 7 and 8 to write answers to the following questions.

1. What three types of punctuation are frequently used to set off the meanings of words in context

    a. _____

    b. _____

    c. _____

2. What is a limitation of using context to determine a word meaning?

    _____

    _____

3. What is a problem with using context to determine a word meaning?

    _____

    _____

4. What are the three ways in which word meanings are usually implied by context?

    a. _____

    b. _____

    c. _____

Three

Analyze Word Structure

Learning Goals for Unit Three

In studying Chapters 10 through 14 you will learn:

- How to analyze words such as *inclusive,* which contains the base *include* and the suffix *-ive* (Chapter 10).

- How to analyze words such as *illegality,* which contains the prefix *il-,* the base *legal,* and the suffix *-ity* (Chapter 11).

- How to analyze words such as *pathology,* which contains the combining forms *patho-* and *-logy* (Chapter 12).

- How to recognize words that are derived from Latin roots, such as *contradict,* which is derived from the Latin root *dicere* (Chapter 13).

- How to figure out the meanings of words in your college books by analyzing them for bases, suffixes, prefixes, combining forms, and Latin roots (Chapter 14).

Suffixes

When the meaning of a word is not stated in or implied by a context, you may be able to determine the meaning by analyzing the unfamiliar word's base word and suffix.

A **suffix** is a letter or group of letters that is added to the end of a base word. For example, in *truthful*, the base is *truth* and the suffix is *-ful*. Words you have never seen in print before may sometimes consist of a base word you know and an added suffix.

> How many years was her *mayoralty?*

Mayoralty (mā'ər-əl-tē) is a word that does not appear very often in print; it may be unfamiliar to you. However, by locating the base word in *mayoralty* you can easily understand that the question is "For how many years was she mayor?"

Words you know may be the base words for five, ten, fifteen, or more other words that you do not read or hear often. For example:

*adapt*able	*adapt*ation	*adapt*er
*adapt*ableness	*adapt*ational	*adapt*ive
*adapt*ability	*adapt*ationally	*adapt*iveness

If you know that *adapt* means "to make suitable," you know the essential meaning of these nine words, even if you have never seen some of them in print before. Notice that some of the words contain two suffixes. For instance, *adaptableness* contains the suffixes *-able* and *-ness.*

Suffixes and Parts of Speech

A suffix usually identifies the part of speech of a word without giving important information about the word's meaning. For instance, *adapt* is a verb, *adaptable* is an adjective, and *adaptation* is a noun. *Adapt, adaptable,* and *adaptation* represent different parts of speech, but they have similar meanings. Since they are different parts of speech, they cannot be used correctly in identical grammatical constructions.

> She can *adapt* to difficult situations.
> She is *adaptable* to difficult situations.
> She can make *adaptations* to difficult situations.

Though *adapt* is a verb, *adaptable* is an adjective, and *adaptation* is a noun, all three of these sentences have very similar meanings.

The most common adjective, noun, verb, and adverb suffixes are italicized in the following words.

- **Adjective suffixes:** approach*able*, crit*ical*, depend*ent*, fear*ful*, angel*ic*, child*ish*, life*less*, danger*ous*, sleep*y*.
- **Noun suffixes:** annoy*ance*, differ*ence*, preven*tion*, novel*ist*, real*ity*, punish*ment*, great*ness*.
- **Verb suffixes:** fals*ify*, social*ize*.
- **Adverb suffixes:** quick*ly*, after*ward*.

Suffixes and Word Meanings

Of the more than one hundred suffixes, only three are fairly reliable indicators of the meanings of words.

1. *-er*, which indicates "a person," as in *builder*.

2. *-ist*, which indicates "a person," as in *organist*.

3. *-less*, which indicates "without," as in *armless*.

The suffixes *-er*, *-ist*, and *-less* all have other meanings, but they do not have as many different meanings as other suffixes. For example, the suffix *-ful*, which usually indicates "full" in such words as *armful*, has forty other meanings as well, and the suffix *-ant*, which indicates "a person" in such words as *accountant*, has fifty-nine additional meanings.[1]

Locating Base Words

It is sometimes difficult to locate base words because their spellings frequently change when suffixes are added to them.

- If a base word ends in *e*, the *e* may be dropped when a suffix is added to it: *mature + -ity = maturity*.
- If a base word ends in *y*, the *y* may be changed to *i* when a suffix is added to it: *harmony + -ous = harmonious*.
- Base words may undergo other spelling changes when suffixes are added to them: *reclaim + -ation = reclamation* (the *i* in *reclaim* is dropped).

Keep this information in mind as you do the following exercises.

[1]Edward L. Thorndike, *The Teaching of English Suffixes* (New York: Teachers College Press, 1941), pp. 1–15, 25.

EXERCISE 10.1 Suffixes

Locate the base words in the **boldface** words and write them on the lines provided. Pronunciations for these words are at the bottom of this page.

1. The rest room is an **accommodation** for customers.

   It is provided to _____ customers.

2. He overcame the **adversity** of poverty to succeed.

   He overcame _____ conditions to succeed.

3. She studied **amply** for the test.

   She did _____ study for the test.

4. We established the **authenticity** of our antique chair.

   We have an _____ antique chair.

5. The flood was a **calamitous** event.

   The flood was a _____.

6. The automobile accident left her **comatose.**

   The accident left her in a _____.

7. He had **comparative** good luck.

   If you _____ his luck to her luck, his luck was good.

8. Please prepare a **compilation** of the facts.

   Please _____ the facts.

9. The stages of life are **cyclical.**

   The stages of life occur in a _____.

10. Traffic laws are a **deterrent** to reckless driving.

    Traffic laws _____ reckless driving.

Pronunciations
1. accommodation (ə-kŏm′ə-dā′shən) n.
2. adversity (ăd-vûr′sə-tē) n.
3. amply (ăm′plē) adv.
4. authenticity (ô′thĕn-tĭs′ə-tē) n.
5. calamitous (kə-lăm′ə-təs) adj.
6. comatose (kō′mə-tōs′) adj.
7. comparative (kəm-păr′ə-tĭv) adj.
8. compilation (kŏm′pə-lā′shən) n.
9. cyclical (sĭk′lĭ-kəl) adj.
10. deterrent (dĭ-tûr′ənt) n.

EXERCISE 10.2   Suffixes

Locate the base words in the **boldface** words and write them on the lines provided. Pronunciations for these words are at the bottom of this page.

1. Can you **differentiate** between the twins?

   Can you see how the twins _____?

2. Who were the **disputants?**

   Who engaged in the _____?

3. She has a **distinctive** way of speaking.

   Her speech is _____ from others' speech.

4. We selected children's furniture for its **durability.**

   We selected _____ children's furniture.

5. We find his good humor **enviable.**

   We _____ his good humor.

6. Illness necessitated an unexpected **expenditure.**

   We had to _____ money unexpectedly.

7. Its **expiration** date is December 31, 1999.

   It will _____ on December 31, 1999.

8. We experienced many **familial** difficulties.

   We experienced many difficulties in our _____.

9. We thank you for your **leniency.**

   We thank you for being _____.

10. He has a **maniacal** laugh.

    He laughs like a _____.

Pronunciations

1. differentiate (dĭf′ə-rĕn′shē-āt′) v.
2. disputant (dĭs-pyoo′tənt) n.
3. distinctive (dĭs-tĭngk′tĭv) adj.
4. durability (door′ə-bĭl′ə-tē) n.
5. enviable (ĕn′vē-ə-bəl) adj.
6. expenditure (ĕk-spĕn′də-chər) n.
7. expiration (ĕk′spə-rā′shən) n.
8. familial (fə-mĭl′yəl) adj.
9. leniency (lē′nē′ən-sē) n.
10. maniacal (mə-nī′ə-kəl) adj.

EXERCISE 10.3 Suffixes

Locate the base words in the **boldface** words and write them on the lines provided. Pronunciations for these words are at the bottom of this page.

1. Your work is **meritorious.**

   Your work has _____.

2. Make a **methodical** search for base words.

   Use a good _____ to search for base words.

3. This machine has a **multiplicity** of parts.

   This machine has _____ parts.

4. The rain forest was not **penetrable.**

   They could not _____ the rain forest.

5. Donnamarie is a **perfectionist.**

   She wants to be _____ in every way.

6. They give the elderly **preferential** treatment.

   They show a _____ for the elderly.

7. Reginald does all things with **propriety.**

   He does all things in a _____ manner.

8. What **provocation** does he need to leave forever?

   What will _____ him to leave forever?

9. The problem is **remediable.**

   There is a _____ to the problem.

10. Please send your **remittance** of $19.99 for the book.

    Please _____ $19.99 for the book.

Pronunciations

1. meritorious (mĕr′ə-tôr′ē-əs) adj.
2. methodical (mə-thŏd′ĭ-kəl) adj.
3. multiplicity (mŭl′tə-plĭs′ə-tē) n.
4. penetrable (pĕn′ə-trə-bəl) adj.
5. perfectionist (pər-fĕk′shən-ĭst) n.
6. preferential (prĕf′ə-rĕn′shəl) adj.
7. propriety (prə-prī′ə-tē) n.
8. provocation (prŏv′ə-kā′shən) n.
9. remediable (rĭ-mē′dē-ə-bəl) adj.
10. remittance (rĭ-mĭt′əns) n.

EXERCISE 10.4   Suffixes

Locate the base words in the **boldface** words and write them on the lines provided. Pronunciations for these words are at the bottom of this page.

1. The plumber said that the damage is **reparable.**

   The plumber can _____ the damage.

2. We strive for the **retention** of high standards.

   We strive to _____ high standards.

3. Sight is **sensory.**

   Sight is a _____.

4. He has a **servile** manner.

   He has the manner of those who _____.

5. Drive only in a state of **sobriety.**

   Drive only when you are _____.

6. My **supposition** is that he is innocent.

   I _____ that he is innocent.

7. The numbers are in **tabular** form.

   The numbers are arranged in a _____.

8. They told **variant** stories about the accident.

   Their stories about the accident _____.

9. Did they **victimize** you?

   Did they make you their _____?

10. The records of the long murder trial are **voluminous.**

    There is a great _____ of records for the trial.

Pronunciations
1. reparable (rĕp′ər-ə-bəl) adj.
2. retention (rĭ-tĕn′shən) n.
3. sensory (sĕn′sər-ē) adj.
4. servile (sûr′vīl) adj.
5. sobriety (sō′brī′ə-tē) n.
6. supposition (sŭp′ə-zĭsh′ən) n.
7. tabular (tăb′yə-lər) adj.
8. variant (vâr′ē-ənt) adj.
9. victimize (vĭk′tə-mīz) v.
10. voluminous (və-lōo′mə-nəs) adj.

EXERCISE 10.5 **Base Words**

Locate the base words in the following fifty words and write them on the lines provided.

1. accentuate   _accent_   26. grievous   _____

2. adversary   _____   27. habituate   _____

3. angularity   _____   28. hardiness   _____

4. civility   _____   29. hindrance   _____

5. climatic   _____   30. icily   _____

6. collegiate   _____   31. inclusive   _____

7. combative   _____   32. lyricist   _____

8. commutation   _____   33. mobilize   _____

9. compliance   _____   34. motivate   _____

10. conical   _____   35. muscly   _____

11. continual   _____   36. notably   _____

12. contractual _____   37. phraseology   _____

13. conveyance   _____   38. picturesque   _____

14. corruption   _____   39. porosity   _____

15. curative   _____   40. reclamation   _____

16. demonstrable _____   41. renunciation   _____

17. devastation _____   42. satanic   _____

18. dictatorial _____   43. sensual   _____

19. electorate   _____   44. singly   _____

20. embodiment   _____   45. slavish   _____

21. equatorial   _____   46. sobriety   _____

22. erroneous   _____   47. solidify   _____

23. expertise   _____   48. torturous   _____

24. fluidity   _____   49. victimize   _____

25. fragmentary _____   50. witticism   _____

EXERCISE 10.6   Parts of Speech

Make grammatically correct sentences by writing the appropriate nouns, verbs, or adjectives on the lines.

1. consumption (n.), consume (v.), consumable (adj.)

   How can I reduce my _____ of calories?

   Simply _____ less sweets and fats.

2. inclusion (n.), include (v.), inclusive (adj.)

   Did you _____ everything on the list?

   Yes, this is an _____ list.

3. scandal (n.), scandalize (v.), scandalous (adj.)

   Did he tell you his _____ story?

   Yes, but it didn't _____ me.

4. commendation (n.), commend (v.), commendable (adj.)

   Why was she given a _____ by her employer?

   Because her work is _____.

5. intrusion (n.), intrude (v.), intrusive (adj.)

   Do you find my questions to be _____?

   No, they do not _____ on my privacy.

6. motive (n.), motivate (v), motivational (adj.)

   What do they do to _____ workers?

   They give _____ pay increases.

7. demonstration (n.), demonstrate (v.), demonstrable (adj.)

   Did she _____ how to deal with customers?

   No, she will give me a _____ tomorrow.

8. grief (n.), grieve (v.), grievous (adj.)

   What did they do to cause you _____?

   They have done many _____ things.

Prefixes

A **prefix** is a letter or group of letters that is added to the beginning of a base word. For example, in *untrue* the prefix is *un-* and the base word is *true*. Words that are unfamiliar to you may sometimes consist of a base word you know and an added prefix. For instance:

> We were shocked to learn of the *illimitability* of the dictator's power.

Illimitability (ĭ-lĭm′ĭ-tə-bĭ′l′ə-tē) is a word that does not appear very often in print; it may be unfamiliar to you. However, you can probably locate its base word, *limit,* which means "to restrict." If you also know that the prefix *il-* means "not," you should be able to determine that *illimitability* refers to that which has no limits or restrictions. The sentence means, "We were shocked to learn that there is no limit to the dictator's power."

Chapter 10 includes a list of nine words in which *adapt* is the base word. Following are fifteen of the more than thirty words in which *adapt* is preceded by a prefix.

mal*adapt*ation	non*adapt*ive	re*adapt*ation
mal*adapt*ed	pre*adapt*	un*adapt*able
mis*adapt*ation	pre*adapt*ation	un*adapt*ableness
non*adapt*able	re*adapt*ability	un*adapt*ively
non*adapt*ation	re*adapt*able	un*adapt*iveness

If you know that *adapt* means "to make suitable" and you also know the meanings of the prefixes *mal-, mis-, non-, pre-, re-,* and *un-,* you know the essential meanings of these fifteen words, even if you have not read or heard them before.

Prefixes and Word Meanings

Unabridged dictionaries (the very large ones) list thousands of derivatives that begin with the common prefixes. For example, most unabridged dictionaries list more than 10,000 words that begin with *non-* and more than 400 words that begin with *pseudo-*. If you know the meanings of *non-* and *pseudo-*, you know something important about the meanings of more than 10,400 words.

By mastering the meanings of twenty prefixes and by using the skills that you learned in Chapter 10, you can increase the words you know by hundreds, or even thousands, in a very short time.

Following are the most useful meanings of the common English prefixes.

Prefix	Meaning	Example
1. un-	not; no	*un*happy means *not* happy
2. non-	not; no	*non*living means *not* living
3. dis-	not; no	to *dis*trust is *not* to trust
4. in-	not; no	*in*direct means *not* direct
5. im-	not; no	*im*perfect means *not* perfect
6. ir-	not; no	*ir*rational means *not* rational
7. il-	not; no	*il*legal means *not* legal
8. a-	not; without	*a*typical means *not* typical
9. de-	remove	to *de*frost is to *remove* frost
10. pre-	before	*pre*war means *before* a war
11. post-	after	*post*war means *after* a war
12. anti-	opposing	*anti*war means *opposing* war
13. pro-	favor(ing)	*pro*war means *favoring* war
14. inter-	between	*inter*state means *between* states
15. hyper-	excessive(ly)	*hyper*active means *excessively* active
16. mal-	bad(ly)	*mal*nutrition is *bad* nutrition
17. mis-	incorrect(ly)	to *mis*spell is to spell *incorrectly*
18. pseudo-	false(ly)	a *pseudo*science is a *false* science
19. semi-	partly	*semi*public means *partly* public
20. re-	again	to *re*write is to write *again*

This is not a complete list of English prefixes. Exercise 11.4 on page 100 provides an opportunity for you to learn the meanings of additional prefixes.

Defining Words with Prefixes

Dictionary definitions of words that begin with prefixes usually include the base word and the meaning of the prefix. For instance, most dictionaries give "to *write again*" as the definition of *rewrite*. You may use the same method that dictionary writers use for defining words with prefixes. For example, you may define *pseudoscience* by using the meaning of the prefix ("false") and the base word ("science"); *pseudoscience* means "a false science." Exercises at the end of this chapter provide practice so you can learn to define words with prefixes in the way that dictionaries define them.

EXERCISE 11.1 **Prefixes**

Write the meanings of the prefixes and the base words in the **boldface** words.

1. A lawyer **maladministered** the money she inherited.

   Meaning of *mal-:* _badly_   Base word: _administer_

2. It is **atypical** for short men to be professional basketball players.

   Meaning of *a-:* _____   Base word: _____

3. He **invariably** eats lunch at noon.

   Meaning of *in-:* _____   Base word: _____

4. I was offended by his **hypercritical** remarks.

   Meaning of *hyper-:* _____   Base word: _____

5. Her doctor advised her to drink **decaffeinated** coffee.

   Meaning of *de-:* _____   Base word: _____

6. His testimony was a **misrepresentation** of the facts.

   Meaning of *mis-:* _____   Base word: _____

7. Negotiators must often be **noncommittal.**

   Meaning of *non-:* _____   Base word: _____

8. The story is **pseudobiographical.**

   Meaning of *pseudo-:* _____   Base word: _____

9. Many well-groomed people use an **antiperspirant** when the weather is hot and humid.

   Meaning of *anti-:* _____   Base word: _____

10. The paper was written in **illegible** handwriting.

   Meaning of *il-:* _____   Base word: _____

Pronunciations

1. maladminister (măl′əd-mĭn′ĭs-tər) v.
2. atypical (ā-tĭp′ĭ-kəl) adj.
3. invariably (ĭn-vâr′ē-ə-blē) adv.
4. hypercritical (hī′pər-krĭt′ĭ-kəl) adj.
5. decaffeinated (dē-kăf′ə-nāt′ĭd) adj.
6. misrepresentation (mĭs′rĕp-rĭ-zĕn-tā′shən) n.
7. noncommittal (nŏn′kə-mĭt′l) adj.
8. pseudobiographical (soo′dō-bī-ə-grăf′ĭ-kəl) adj.
9. antiperspirant (ăn′tē-pûr′spər-ənt) n.
10. illegible (ĭ-lĕj′ə-bəl) adj.

EXERCISE 11.2   Prefixes

Write the meanings of the prefixes and the base words in the **boldface** words.

1. After a long sea voyage, we had to **reorient** ourselves to walking on land.

   Meaning of *re-:* _____   Base word: _____

2. The patient was **semiconscious** a few hours after the operation.

   Meaning of *semi-:* _____   Base word: _____

3. Our team is **prequalified** to run in the marathon.

   Meaning of *pre-:* _____   Base word: _____

4. His mother's death left him **disconsolate.**

   Meaning of *dis-:* _____   Base word: _____

5. The laws of nature are **unalterable.**

   Meaning of *un-:* _____   Base word: _____

6. The jurors were **proacquittal** after only an hour of deliberation.

   Meaning of *pro-:* _____   Base word: _____

7. Hermits are **asocial** people.

   Meaning of *a-:* _____   Base word: _____

8. It is **imprudent** to drive a car with faulty brakes.

   Meaning of *im-:* _____   Base word: _____

9. We watched a motion picture during an **intercontinental** flight.

   Meaning of *inter-:* _____   Base word: _____

10. My algebra teacher sometimes tells jokes that are **irrelevant** to the study of mathematics.

    Meaning of *ir-:* _____   Base word: _____

Pronunciations

1. reorient (rē-ôr′ē-ənt) v.
2. semiconscious (sĕm′ē-kŏn′shəs) adj.
3. prequalified (prē-kwŏl′ə-fīd′) adj.
4. disconsolate (dĭs′kŏn′sə-lĭt) adj.
5. unalterable (ŭn′ôl′tər-ə-bəl) adj.
6. proacquittal (prō-ə-kwĭt′l) adj.
7. asocial (ā-sō′shəl) adj.
8. imprudent (ĭm-pro͞od′ənt) adj.
9. intercontinental (ĭn′tər-kŏn′tə-nĕn′təl) adj.
10. irrelevant (ĭ-rĕl′ə-vənt) adj.

EXERCISE 11.3 Prefixes

Write the meanings of the prefixes and the base words in the **boldface** words.

1. Life in prison is a **dehumanizing** experience.

   Meaning of *de-:* _____ Base word: _____

2. Talking while chewing food is an **impropriety** in polite company.

   Meaning of *im-:* _____ Base word: _____

3. Garbage is **malodorous** on hot, summer days.

   Meaning of *mal-:* _____ Base word: _____

4. It was wise of her to select a **noncontroversial** topic for her speech.

   Meaning of *non-:* _____ Base word: _____

5. After she earns a college degree, she will do **postgraduate** study in England.

   Meaning of *post-:* _____ Base word: _____

6. She gave a thoughtful and **dispassionate** speech.

   Meaning of *dis-:* _____ Base word: _____

7. Many actors are **hypersensitive** to adverse criticism of their work.

   Meaning of *hyper-:* _____ Base word: _____

8. He has an insane and **inimitable** laugh.

   Meaning of *in-:* _____ Base word: _____

9. The fire in the museum did **irreparable** damage to several priceless paintings.

   Meaning of *ir-:* _____ Base word: _____

10. Many people believe that the death penalty is **amoral.**

    Meaning of *a-:* _____ Base word: _____

Pronunciations

1. dehumanize (dē-hyoō′mə-nīz′) v.
2. impropriety (ĭm′prə-prī′ĭ-tē) n.
3. malodorous (măl-ō′dər-əs) adj.
4. noncontroversial (nŏn′-kŏn′trə-vûr′shəl) adj.
5. postgraduate (pōst′grăj′oō-ĭt) adj.

6. dispassionate (dĭs-păsh′ə-nĭt) adj.
7. hypersensitive (hī′pər-sĕn′sĭ-tĭv) adj.
8. inimitable (ĭn-ĭm′ĭ-tə-bəl) adj.
9. irreparable (ĭ-rĕp′ər-ə-bəl) adj.
10. amoral (ā-môr′əl) adj.

EXERCISE 11.4   Prefixes in Dictionaries

This exercise is about prefixes that are not introduced in this chapter. Use a standard desk dictionary to locate the meanings of the following prefixes and two words that begin with each prefix. Write your answers on notebook paper.

1. ante-
2. auto-
3. circum-
4. co-
5. counter-
6. extra-
7. hypo-
8. intra-
9. retro-
10. sub-
11. super-
12. trans-

EXERCISE 11.5   Negative Prefixes

The negative prefixes are *un-*, *in-*, and *non-* and the other prefixes that mean "not or no." Sometimes more than one negative prefix may be used with a word. *Atypical, untypical,* and *nontypical* are words, but *intypical* is not a word. Unfortunately, there is no rule that explains which negative prefix to use with a word. **Add the prefix *un-*, *in-*, or *non-* to the following words.** Refer to a dictionary if necessary. Write your answers on notebook paper.

1. user
2. accurate
3. sure
4. fatal
5. equal
6. equality
7. thawed
8. capable
9. delivery

EXERCISE 11.6   Assimilation

The negative prefixes *il-*, *im-*, and *ir-* are assimilations of the prefix *in-*. In language, **assimilation** is a process whereby a sound in a word, influenced by a neighboring sound, tends to become like the neighboring sound. The prefix *in-* has been assimilated to *il-* before words that begin with *l (illegal)*, to *ir-* before words that begin with *r (irrational)*, and to *im-* before words that begin with *b, m,* or *p (imperfect,* for example). Use this information to **add the prefix *il-*, *im-*, *in-*, or *ir-* to the following words.** Write your answers on notebook paper and refer to a dictionary if necessary.

1. effective
2. responsible
3. mature
4. literate
5. regular
6. personal
7. complete
8. balance
9. religious

Combining Forms

Combining forms are Greek and Latin word parts that are joined with other combining forms or base words. For example, the combining forms *graph-* and *-ology* may be combined to form *graphology* (grǎ-fŏl′ə-jē), and the base word *Egypt* may be combined with *-ology* to form *Egyptology* (ē′jĭp-tŏl′ə-jē). *Graphology* is the study of handwriting—specifically, the study of handwriting to discover clues about personality, and *Egyptology* refers to the study of Egypt, especially the study of the civilization of ancient Egypt.

The principal way in which combining forms differ from prefixes and suffixes is that combining forms may be joined, or combined, to create words; however, prefixes and suffixes cannot be combined to create words. For example, the combining form *biblio-* (which indicates "books") and *-phile* (which indicates "love") can be combined to create the word *bibliophile* (bĭb′lē-ə-fĭl′), which refers to one who loves books. On the other hand, the prefix in *unkind (un-)* and the suffix in *kindness (-ness)* cannot be combined to create a word (*unness* is not a word).

Combining Forms and Word Meanings

Chapter 10 states that suffixes such as *-able* and *-ation* do not convey important information about the specific meanings of words. Combining forms are very different in this regard. For example, if you know that *-ology*, or *-logy*, indicates "study" or "science of," you can use this information to determine that words such as *osteology* (ŏs′tē-ŏl′ə-jē) and *ecology* (ĭ-kŏl′ə-jē) refer to the study or science of a subject. If you also know that *osteo-* indicates "bone or bones" and that *eco-* indicates "environment or habitat," you may make good inferences about the meanings of *osteology* and *ecology*. Write the meanings you infer for these words on the following lines.

1. *Osteology* is _____

   _____

2. *Ecology* is _____

   _____

You may have inferred that *osteology* is the study of the structure and functions of the bones and that *ecology* is the science that studies living organisms and their environments.

Learning Combining Forms

Learn the meanings of combining forms by making logical associations rather than by memorizing them. For instance, you probably know that *hypnosis* (hĭp-nō′sĭs) refers to a sleeplike state (*hypno-* indicates "sleep"). Thus, if you study about *manias* (abnormal cravings) in a psychology course, use what you know about the word *hypnosis* to infer that *hypnomania* (hĭp′-nə-mān′ē-ə) refers to the abnormal craving for sleep.

It is worthwhile to learn the meanings of the combining forms that are introduced in the exercises in this chapter. In addition, learn the meanings of combining forms that appear in the terminology of your college courses. For instance, if you study biology, you will learn the meaning of *astrocyte*, a word that is created from the combining forms *astro-* and *-cyte*. Compare the following definitions of *astrocyte*, *astro-*, and *-cyte*.

> **as·tro·cyte** (ăs′trə-sīt′) *n.* A star-shaped cell, especially a neuroglial cell of nervous tissue. —**as′tro·cyt′ic** (-sĭt′ĭk) *adj.*
> **astro—** or **astr—** *pref.* **1.a.** Star: *astrophysics.* **b.** Celestial body: *astrometry.* **c.** Outer space: *astronaut.* **2.** The aster of a cell: *astrosphere.* [Greek, from *astron*, star. See **ster-**³ in Appendix.]
> **—cyte** *suff.* Cell: *leukocyte.* [New Latin *-cyta*, from Greek *kutos*, hollow vessel. See **(s)keu-** in Appendix.]

With your knowledge of the meaning of *astrocyte*, you may infer that *leukocyte* (loo′kə-sīt′), *phagocyte* (făg′ə-sīt′), and other words ending in *-cyte* also refer to specific types of cells.

EXERCISE 12.1 ## Combining Forms in Dictionaries

Use a standard desk dictionary to locate the meanings of the following combining forms and two words that begin with each combining form. Write your answers on notebook paper.

1. ambi-	6. necro-	11. sex-
2. chromo-	7. omni-	12. somato-
3. frater-	8. para-	13. soro-
4. helio-	9. patri-	14. syn-
5. matri-	10. poly-	15. tele-

Thirty-five more combining forms are introduced in the following exercises.

EXERCISE 12.2   **Numbers**

Fill in the missing words in the following sentences by referring to the meanings of the combining forms listed below.

Combining Form	Meaning	Combining Form	Meaning
mono-, uni-	one	sept-	seven
bi-	two	octo-	eight
tri-	three	deca-, deci-	ten
quadri-	four	multi-	more than two

1. A **monolingual** person knows only _____*one*_____ language.

2. A _____ person uses two languages.

3. A _____ person uses more than two languages.

4. A **unilateral** decision is made by _____ person or country.

5. A _____ decision is made by two people or countries.

6. If a thing is **unique,** it is the only _____ like it.

7. A **bicentennial** is a _____ hundredth anniversary celebration.

8. A _____ is a four-hundredth anniversary celebration.

9. A **biennial** event occurs every _____ years.

10. A _____ event occurs every three years.

11. A **quadruped** is an animal with _____ feet.

12. A _____ is an animal with two feet.

13. To **decimate** an army is to kill every _____ man.

14. There are _____ events in the **decathlon.**

15. **Septuagenarians** are people 70 to _____ years old.

16. **Octogenarians** are people _____ to _____ years old.

The pronunciations of these words are listed in Exercise 12.7 on page 108.

EXERCISE 12.3   **Branches of Learning**

Use the meanings of the following combining forms to fill in the missing words in the following sentences. The missing words in sentences 1 through 11 end in -logy, which indicates "science" or "study of," and the missing words in sentences 12 through 14 end in -ist, which indicates "one who practices."

Combining Form	Meaning	Combining Form	Meaning
anthropo-	human	gyneco-	woman
archaeo-	ancient times	patho-	disease
audio-	hearing	psycho-	mind
bio-	life	seismo-	earthquake
chrono-	time	theo-	God or gods
geo-	earth		

1. ___Anthropology___ is the study of the origin and development of humankind.

2. _____ is the study of dates and the sequences of events in time.

3. _____ is the scientific study of disease.

4. _____ is the study of objects left from life and culture in ancient times.

5. _____ is the medical science of women's health.

6. _____ is the study of hearing.

7. _____ is the study of the origin and structure of the earth.

8. _____ is the scientific study of behavior and the processes of the mind.

9. _____ is the scientific study of earthquakes.

10. _____ is the study of living things.

11. _____ is the study of religious truth and the nature of God.

12. An ___anthropologist___ is a student of anthropology.

13. A _____ is a student of gynecology.

14. A _____ is a student of pathology.

The pronunciations of these words are listed in Exercise 12.7 on page 108.

NAME _____   DATE _____   **105**

EXERCISE 12.4   Using What You Have Learned

Use what you learned when you did Exercises 12.2 and 12.3 to fill in the missing words in the following sentences.

1. That which is **archaic** belongs to ____*ancient*____ times.

2. A **chronic** headache lasts for a long _____.

3. A **psychic** has extraordinary _____ abilities.

4. **Seismic** activity is caused by an _____.

5. The **biotic** elements of nature are the _____ elements.

6. The **abiotic** elements of nature are _____ living.

7. A **theist** is a person who believes in _____.

8. An **atheist** is a person who does _____ believe in

   _____.

9. **Polytheism** is the belief in more than one _____.

10. **Monotheism** is the belief in _____

    _____.

11. A **chronometer** measures _____ precisely.

12. An **audiometer** measures _____.

13. A **seismometer** records _____.

14. **Geophysics** is the science of the physics of the _____.

15. **Biochemistry** is the chemistry of _____ things.

16. A **gynecocracy** is the rule of a state by _____.

17. A **theocracy** is _____ of a state by _____.

18. A **pathogen** is an agent that can cause _____.

19. A **chronological** sequence is a _____ sequence.

20. A **monologue** is a long speech by _____ speaker.

The pronunciations of these words are listed in Exercise 12.7 on page 108.

EXERCISE 12.5 **Good, Bad, and Marriage**

Fill in the missing words in the following sentences by referring to the meanings of the combining forms listed below and in Exercise 12.2.

Combining
Form   **Meaning**
bene-   good or well
gam-, gamo-   marriage or sexual union
hetero-   different or other
homo-   same, like, or similar
mal-   bad, wrong, or ill

1. **Monogamy** is marriage to _____*one*_____ person at a time.

2. **Polygamy** is _____ to more than one person at the same time.

3. **Bigamy** is illegal marriage to _____ people at the same time.

4. **Heterogeneous** means "having _____ elements or parts."

5. **Homogeneous** means "having _____ elements or parts."

6. **Heterosexuals** are attracted to members of the _____ sex.

7. **Homosexuals** are attracted to people of the _____ sex.

8. A **benevolent** person treats others _____.

9. A **malevolent** person treats others _____.

10. Your **benefactor** treats you _____.

11. A **malefactor** wishes you _____.

12. A **benign** tumor is not _____; it will not cause death.

13. A **malignant** tumor is _____; it is likely to cause death.

14. **Malicious** statements are _____ or evil.

15. That which is **beneficial** is _____.

The pronunciations of these words are listed in Exercise 12.7 on page 108.

EXERCISE 12.6 **Fears and Cravings**

The combining form -*phobia* indicates "a strong abnormal or irrational fear." For instance, *zoophobia* is the abnormal or irrational fear of animals. Referring to the meanings of the combining forms listed below and in Exercise 12.3, match the words and definitions.

Combining Form	Meaning	Combining Form	Meaning
acro-	height	ego-	self
biblio-	books	nycto-	night or darkness
claustro-	closed places	nympho-	bride
dipso-	thirst	pyro-	fire

_____ 1. **acrophobia**   a. abnormal fear of darkness

_____ 2. **bibliophobia**   b. abnormal fear of closed places

_____ 3. **claustrophobia**   c. abnormal fear of disease

_____ 4. **gynephobia**   d. abnormal fear of people

_____ 5. **anthrophobia**   e. abnormal fear of height

_____ 6. **nyctophobia**   f. abnormal fear of fire

_____ 7. **pathophobia**   g. abnormal fear of books

_____ 8. **pyrophobia**   h. abnormal fear of women

The combining form -*mania* indicates "a mental illness characterized by a strong abnormal craving for a particular object." For instance, *klep*- indicates "to steal," and *kleptomania* is the abnormal desire to steal. Match the following words and definitions.

_____ 9. **bibliomania**   a. abnormal craving for alcoholic drink

_____ 10. **theomania**   b. abnormal craving for God's attention

_____ 11. **dipsomania**   c. abnormal craving for sexual activity

_____ 12. **nymphomania**   d. abnormal craving for books

_____ 13. **pyromania**   e. abnormal craving for oneself

_____ 14. **egomania**   f. abnormal craving for fire

The pronunciations of these words are listed in Exercise 12.7 on page 108.

EXERCISE 12.7   Pronunciations

Learn these pronunciations for words from Exercises 12.1 through 12.6.

abiotic (ā-bī-ŏt′ĭk) adj.
acrophobia (ăk′rə-fō′bē-ə) n.
anthrophobia (ăn′thrə-fō′bē-ə) n.
anthropologist (ăn′thrə-pŏl′ə-jĭst) n.
anthropology (ăn′thrə-pŏl′ə-jē) n.
archaeology (är′kē-ŏl′ə-jē) n.
archaic (är-kā′ĭk) adj.
atheist (ā′thē-ĭst) n.
audiology (ô′dē-ŏl′ə-jē) n.
audiometer (ô′dē-ŏm′ĭ-tər) n.
benefactor (běn′ə-făk′tər) n.
beneficial (běn′ə-fĭsh′əl) adj.
benevolent (bə-něv′ə-lənt) adj.
benign (bĭ-nīn′) adj.
bibliomania (bĭb′lē-ə-mā′nē-ə) n.
bibliophobia (bĭb′lē-ə-fō′bē-ə) n.
bicentennial (bī′sěn-těn′ē-əl) n.
biennial (bī-ěn′ē-əl) adj.
bigamy (bĭg′ə-mē) n.
bilateral (bī-lăt′ər-əl) adj.
bilingual (bī-lĭng′gwəl) adj.
biochemistry (bī′ō-kěm′ĭ-strē) n.
biology (bī-ŏl′ə-jē) n.
biotic (bī-ŏt′ĭk) adj.
biped (bī′pěd′) n.
chronic (krŏn′ĭk) adj.
chronological (krŏn′ə-lŏj′ĭ-kəl) adj.
chronology (krə-nŏl′ə-jē) n.
chronometer (krə-nŏm′ĭ-tər) n.
claustrophobia (klô′strə-fō′bē-ə) n.
decathlon (dĭ-kăth′lŏn′) n.
decimate (děs′ə-māt′) v.
dipsomania (dĭp′sə-mā′nē-ə) n.
egomania (ē′gō-mā′nē-ə) n.
geology (jē-ŏl′ə-jē) n.
geophysics (jē′ō-fĭz′ĭks) n.
gynecocracy (jĭn′ĭ-kŏk′rə-sē) n.
gynecologist (gī′nĭ-kŏl′ə-jĭst) n.
gynecology (gī′nĭ-kŏl′ə-jē) n.
gynephobia (gī′nə-fō′bē-ə) n.
heterogeneous
   (hět′ər-ĕ-jē′nē-əs) adj.
heterosexual
   (hět′ə-rō-sěk′shoo-əl) adj.

homogeneous (hō′mə-jē′nē-əs) adj.
homosexual
   (hō′mō-sěk′shoo-əl) adj.
malefactor (măl′ə-făk′tər) n.
malevolent (mə-lěv′ə-lənt) adj.
malicious (mə-lĭsh′əs) adj.
malignant (mə-lĭg′nənt) adj.
monogamy (mə-nŏg′ə-mē) n.
monolingual
   (mŏn′ə-lĭng′gwəl) adj.
monologue (mŏn′ə-lŏg′) n.
monotheism (mŏn′ə-thē-ĭz′əm) n.
multilingual (mŭl′tē-lĭng′gwəl) adj.
nyctophobia (nĭk′tə-fō′bē-ə) n.
nymphomania (nĭm′fə-mā′nē-ə) n.
octogenarian (ŏk′tə-jə-nâr′ē-ən) n.
pathogen (păth′ə-jən) n.
pathologist (pă-thŏl′ə-jĭst) n.
pathology (pă-thŏl′ə-jē) n.
pathophobia (păth′ə-fō′bē-ə) n.
polygamy (pə-lĭg′ə-mē) n.
polytheism (pŏl′ē-thē-ĭz′əm) n.
psychic (sī′kĭk) adj.
psychology (sī-kŏl′ə-jē) n.
pyromania (pī′rō-mā′nē-ə) n.
pyrophobia (pī′rō-fō′bē-ə) n.
quadricentennial
   (kwŏd′rĭ-sěn-těn′ē-əl) n.
quadruped (kwŏd′rə-pěd′) n.
seismic (sīz′mĭk) adj.
seismology (sīz-mŏl′ə-jē) n.
seismometer (sīz-mŏm′ĭ-tər) n.
septuagenarian
   (sěp′too-ə-jə-nâr′ē-ən) n.
theist (thē′ĭst) n.
theocracy (thē-ŏk′rə-sē) n.
theology (thē-ŏl′ə-jē) n.
theomania (thē′ō-mā′nē-ə) n.
triennial (trī-ěn′ē-əl) adj.
unilateral (yoo′nə-lăt′ər-əl) adj.
unique (yoo-nēk′) adj.

Latin Roots

A **root** is an element from which a word is derived. For instance, *specere,* a Latin word that means "to look," is the root of English words such as *spectacular.* Since roots are sometimes confused with the combining forms explained in Chapter 12, the following discussions explain important differences between them.

Combining Forms vs. Latin Roots

There are three important differences between combining forms and Latin roots.

   1. **Combining forms have consistent spellings in English words but Latin roots do not.** For instance, the combining form *biblio-,* which means "book," is always spelled *biblio* as in *bibliography.* On the other hand, the Latin root *specere,* which means "to look," has various spellings, including *spect* in *spectacular, spise* in *despise, pect* in *expect,* and *spec* in *specimen.*

   2. **The meaning of a combining form is usually an essential part of the definitions of words that contain it, but the same is not true of Latin roots.** For instance, *book* is an essential part of the definitions of *bibliography, bibliophile, bibliotherapy,* and other words that contain the combining form *biblio-.* On the other hand, *to look* is not an essential part of the definitions of *circumspect, prospective, spectacular,* and most other words that contain the root *specere. Circumspect* means "cautious or careful," *prospective* means "likely to become," and *spectacular* means "strikingly unusual."

   3. **Combining forms are entry words in dictionaries but Latin roots are not.** For instance, dictionaries include an entry for the combining form *biblio-,* as in *bibliography,* but they do not include an entry for the Latin word *specere* or any of its spellings, such as the *spect* in *spectacular.* Latin roots are not entry words in dictionaries because they do not have consistent spellings and meanings in their various occurrences in English words.

Some English Words from Latin Roots

Latin Root	Meaning	Examples
am	love	amateur, amiable, amorous
ann	year	annual, annuity, semiannual
aqua	water	aquamarine, aquarium, aquatic, aqueous
aud	hear	audience, audiovisual, auditorium
cap	head	capital, captain, decapitate
cord	heart	accord, concord, cordial, discord
cur	run	concur, current, excursion, recur
dent	tooth	dental, dentist, indent, trident
duct	lead	aqueduct, conduct, educate, induct
form	shape	conform, reform, transform, uniform
homo	man	homage, hombre, homicide
ject	throw	eject, inject, project, reject
lab	work	collaborate, elaborate, labor
liber	free	liberal, liberate, liberty
lust	shine	illustrate, lackluster, luster
man	hand	manipulate, manufacture, manuscript
miss	send	dismiss, missile, missionary
mit	send	admit, remit, submit, transmit
mort	death	immortal, mortal, mortuary
nat	born	natal, nation, native, nativity
ped	foot	biped, pedal, pedestrian, pedestal
pel	drive	compel, expel, propel, repel
pop	people	populace, popular, population
port	carry	export, import, portable, transport
rupt	break	abrupt, bankrupt, erupt, interrupt
sect	cut	dissect, intersection, section, sector
tract	pull	attraction, subtract, traction
vac	empty	evacuate, vacant, vacate, vacuum
ver	turn	convert, introvert, invert, reverse

Importance of Latin Roots

English vocabulary includes thousands of words that are derived from Latin roots, including the ones listed in "Some English Words from Latin Roots" above. When you know the meaning of a Latin root, you can often use the information as a hint to the meanings of several words. The exercises in this chapter provide information about seven Latin words that are the roots of many English words.

EXERCISE 13.1 To Trust or Believe *(Cred)*

The Latin word *credere*, which means "to trust or believe," is spelled *cred* in the following six derivatives. Other words derived from *credere* include *grant* and *miscreant*.

credence (krēd'ns) *n.* The acceptance of what others say as true; belief [to give *credence* to an excuse].
credible (krěd'ə-bəl) *adj.* Can be believed; believable [a *credible* explanation].
credo (krē'dō) *n.* A statement of belief on any subject [Her *credo* is "Be kind to all."].
credulous (krěj'ə-ləs) *adj.* Ready to believe; easily convinced [to deceive a *credulous* child].
discredit (dĭs-krěd'ĭt) *v.* To cause to be doubted or distrusted; disgrace, dishonor [to *discredit* testimony given during a trial].
incredulous (ĭn-krěj'ə-ləs) *adj.* Unable or unwilling to believe; disbelieving, doubting, skeptical [*incredulous* of a story about a ghost].

The words *credence, credible, credo, credulous, discredit,* and *incredulous* are deleted from the following sentences. Write the missing words on the lines.

1. The jury found him innocent because he had a _____ alibi.

2. A _____ shopper might easily become the victim of a dishonest salesperson.

3. We were _____ when we were told that our home had burned to the ground.

4. Mom didn't believe me, but Dad gave _____ to my story.

5. "In God we trust" is the _____ engraved on United States coins.

6. They tried to _____ the mayor by spreading the rumor that he was a drug addict and sexual pervert.

EXERCISE 13.2 To Say or Speak *(Dict)*

The Latin word *dicere*, which means "to say or speak," is spelled *dic* and *dict* in the following six derivatives. Other words derived from *dicere* include *condition, ditto,* and *indite*.

abdicate (ăb'dĭ-kāt') *v.* To give up an office or responsibility; surrender [to *abdicate* responsibility for a child by putting it up for adoption].
contradict (kŏn'trə-dĭkt') *v.* To state the opposite of what someone else has said; disagree with; oppose [Facts *contradict* the theory that earth is flat.].
dictatorial (dĭk'tə-tôr'ē-əl) *adj.* Ordering others about in a domineering manner; highhanded [a *dictatorial* prison guard].

diction (dĭk′shən) *n.* The use of words in writing and speech; wording [to use good *diction* when writing papers for college credit].

edict (ē′dĭkt′) *n.* A command or order that has the force of law [the *edict* that there is to be no smoking on domestic flights in Argentina].

verdict (vûr′dĭkt) *n.* The finding of a judge or jury in a trial; judgment [the *verdict* of guilty or not guilty].

The words *abdicate, contradict, dictatorial, diction, edict,* and *verdict* are deleted from the following sentences. Write the missing words on the lines.

1. Argentina and Chile are among the South American countries that have

   been ruled by leaders who assumed absolute _____ powers.

2. In 313 A.D. the Roman emperor Constantine the Great issued the

   _____ of Milan, which legalized Christianity.

3. Edward VIII, who was king of England in 1936, _____ his throne to marry a divorced woman.

4. Statements made by a witness for the prosecution _____ testimony that was given by the defendant.

5. "Those guys don't know nothing," is an example of _____ to be avoided during an interview for professional employment.

6. Empty theaters indicate that the public's _____ is that a film is not worth the price of admission.

EXERCISE 13.3   Even or Equal *(Equi)*

The Latin word *aequus,* which means "even or equal," is spelled *equi* in the following six derivatives. Other words derived from *aequus* include *adequate* and *equalize.*

equilibrium (ē′kwə-lĭb′rē-əm) *n.* Intellectual, or emotional balance; balance between opposing forces [the *equilibrium* of influence between Democrats and Republicans].

equitable (ĕk′wĭ-tə-bəl) *adj.* Fair, just, or impartial [the *equitable* distribution of their parents' estate].

equivalent (ĭ-kwĭv′ə-lənt) *adj.* Essentially equal [a sneer *equivalent* to a statement of disapproval].

equivocal (ĭ-kwĭv′ə-kəl) *adj.* Allowing for more than one interpretation often for the purpose of misleading or confusing; ambiguous [an *equivocal* answer].

inequitable (ĭn′ĕk′wĭ-tə-bəl) *adj.* Unfair or unjust [*inequitable* pay for women].

unequivocal (ŭn′ĭ-kwĭv′ə-kəl) *adj.* Allowing for only one interpretation; unambiguous, plain, or clear [*unequivocal* evidence recorded by a video camera].

The words *equilibrium, equitable, equivalent, equivocal, inequitable,* and *unequivocal* are deleted from the following sentences. Write the missing words on the lines.

1. My doctor did not prescribe the operation for me because its effectiveness

   in treating my condition is _____.

2. The results of the vote are _____; a vast majority of the
   employees are ready to strike for better working conditions.

3. Good mental health includes establishing _____ between
   work and social life.

4. Ten dimes are _____ to one dollar.

5. Our ideal is _____ treatment for all people, regardless of
   their race, religion, or sex.

6. There is an _____ distribution of wealth in the United
   States; more than seventy-five percent of our society's wealth is owned by
   the richest twenty percent of American households.

EXERCISE 13.4   To Trust *(Fid)*

The Latin word *fidere,* which means "to trust," is spelled *fid* in the following
six derivatives. Other words derived from *fidere* include *defy* and *fiance.*

confidant (kŏn'fĭ-dänt') *n.* A trusted friend with whom one shares secrets [to
   discuss controversial opinions with a *confidant*].
confide (kən-fīd') *v.* To share secrets with a trusted person; reveal; disclose
   [to *confide* in one's spouse].
confident (kŏn'fĭ-dənt) *adj.* Believing or trusting in a person or thing; certain;
   positive; sure [players who are *confident* that their team will win].
diffident (dĭf'ĭ-dənt) *adj.* Lacking confidence in one's self; shy; timid [too
   diffident to be an effective leader].
fidelity (fĭ-dĕl'ĭ-tē) *n.* Faithfulness; loyalty [to act in *fidelity* to one's family].
infidelity (ĭn'fĭ-dĕl'ĭ-tē) *n.* Unfaithfulness to a sexual partner; disloyalty [a
   divorce caused by *infidelity*].

The words *confidant, confide, confident, diffident, fidelity,* and *infidelity*
are deleted from the following sentences. Write the missing words on the lines.

1. We are _____ that our candidate will win the election.

2. Adultery and fornication are two types of _____.

3. Her husband is her _____.

4. A _____ person is not likely to become a successful motion picture actor.

5. We are expected not to reveal the secrets that others _____ in us.

6. He always votes for Republican candidates out of _____ to that political party.

EXERCISE 13.5   To Speak *(Loqu)*

The Latin word *loqui,* which means "to speak," is spelled *loq* and *loqu* in the following six derivatives. Other words derived from *loqui* include *elocution* and *ventriloquist.*

colloquial (kə-lō′kwē-əl) *adj.* Characteristic of spoken language; casual style of speaking or writing; informal ["Out of line" is a colloquial expression used to mean "improper."].

colloquium (kə-lō′kwē-əm) *n.* An organized meeting for the exchange of ideas on a specific subject; seminar [to attend a *colloquium* about dictionary preparation].

eloquence (ĕl′ə-kwəns) *n.* Powerful, fluent, and persuasive speech or writing [the *eloquence* of Dr. Martin Luther King].

eloquent (ĕl′ə-kwənt) *adj.* Marked by powerful, fluent, or persuasive expression [an *eloquent* speech].

loquacious (lō′kwā′shəs) *adj.* Maintaining a constant flow of talk; talkative [a *loquacious* salesperson].

soliloquy (sə-lĭl′ə-kwē) *n.* An act of talking to oneself; a speech given by a character in a drama that reveals thoughts to an audience but not to other characters in the drama; monologue [Hamlet's *soliloquy,* which starts, "To be, or not to be"].

The words *colloquial, colloquium, eloquence, eloquent, loquacious,* and *soliloquy* are deleted from the following sentences. Write the missing words on the lines.

1. I have a friend who is so _____ that he seldom gives me a chance to say anything.

2. The psychology department offers a _____ to help students in writing research reports.

3. If an actor in a drama speaks directly to the audience, unheard by other characters in the play, the actor is giving a _____.

4. Abraham Lincoln's speeches are remembered for their _____.

5. Shakespeare is generally considered the most _____ of English writers.

6. Everyday conversation is _____ rather than formal.

EXERCISE 13.6 ## To Look (Spect)

The Latin word *specere,* which means "to look," is spelled *spect* in the following six derivatives. Other words derived from *specere* include *despise, expect, specimen,* and *spy.*

circumspect (sûr′kəm-spĕkt′) *adj.* Careful to consider all related circumstances and possible consequences; cautious, careful, watchful [to be *circumspect* about changing jobs].
introspection (ĭn′trə-spĕk′shən) *n.* The act of examining one's own thoughts and feelings; self-examination [using *introspection* to understand one's motives].
perspective (pər-spĕk′tĭv) *n.* A position from which something is viewed or evaluated; a point of view [the varying *perspectives* of students and teachers].
prospective (prə-spĕk′tĭv) *adj.* Likely to be or become; expected, future [a *prospective* father].
retrospect (rĕt′rə-spĕkt′) *n.* A review of past events [to evaluate one's education in *retrospect*].
spectacular (spĕk-tăk′yə-lər) *adj.* Strikingly unusual; dramatically thrilling; impressive, sensational [*spectacular* fireworks].

The words *circumspect, introspection, perspective, prospective, retrospect,* and *spectacular* are deleted from the following sentences. Write the missing words on the lines.

1. It is wise to be _____ about statements made by a used car salesperson.

2. In _____, we know that we should have purchased a house ten years ago when they were much cheaper.

3. After much _____, she decided that she would not be happy working as a teacher.

4. Many popular motion pictures feature _____ special effects.

5. It is difficult to see things from another person's _____.

6. I don't want to be late for my interview with a _____ employer.

EXERCISE 13.7   To Call *(Voc, Vok)*

The Latin word *vocare*, which means "to call," is spelled *voc* and *vok* in the following six derivatives. Other words derived from *vocare* include *voice*, *vouch*, and *vowel*.

advocate (ăd′və-kāt′) *v.* To argue in favor of; speak, plead, support [to *advocate* harsh penalties for drunken driving].
evocative (ĭ-vŏk′ə-tĭv) *adj.* Having the power to call to mind [an aroma *evocative* of mother's cooking].
evoke (ĭ-vōk′) *v.* To call to mind [a song that *evokes* a happy summertime experience].
invoke (ĭn-vōk′) *v.* To call upon for help or support [to *invoke* God's blessing].
provoke (prə-vōk′) *v.* To excite, stir up, or call forth action or feeling; stimulate, rouse [insults that *provoke* anger].
revoke (rĭ-vōk′) *v.* To recall or take back; withdraw, cancel [to *revoke* a driver's license].

The words *advocate, evocative, evoke, invoke, provoke,* and *revoke* are deleted from the following sentences. Write the missing words on the lines.

1. Victims of earthquakes and other disasters often _____ the federal government for financial assistance.

2. Most doctors _____ a diet that is low in fat and salt.

3. Her husband's infidelity _____ her to seek a divorce.

4. The fragrance of roses _____ memories of his mother, who loved them.

5. When doctors are convicted of serious crimes, states _____ their licenses to practice medicine.

6. The hot, humid day was _____ of a summer she spent in New York City.

Analyzing Word Structure

This chapter explains how to apply the word structure skills you learned in Chapters 10–13 to figure out the meanings of unfamiliar words in your college textbooks. Exercises at the end of the chapter provide practice in refining these skills.

Suffixes

Locate the base words in derivatives that contain a base word and a suffix, such as the boldface words in the following textbook excerpt.

> The pollution problem is an **exceedingly** difficult one to solve, for several reasons. First, some people and governments see pollution as a **regrettable** but inevitable byproduct of desired economic **development**—"where there's smoke, there's jobs." Second, control of pollution sometimes requires international **coordination,** for one country's **emissions** or pesticides can end up in other countries' air or food. Third, the effect of pollution may not show up for many years, so severe **environmental** damage can occur with little public **awareness** that it is taking place.

You should have located the following base words: exceed, regret, develop, coordinate, emit, environment, and aware.

Prefixes

Also locate the prefixes in derivatives, such as the prefix in the boldface word in the following textbook passage.

> As the students progress through medical school, they also acquire a detachment in dealing with the human body, disease, and death. Lay people treat dead bodies with respect; medical students have to cut them to pieces, and often dispel the tension they experience by joking **irreverently** about cadavers—for example, by giving them nicknames.

117

Irreverently contains the prefix *ir-*, which means "not"; the base word *reverent*; and the adverbial suffix *-ly*. The passage states that medical students are not reverent about dead bodies.

Combining Forms

Be on the alert for combining forms, such as those in the boldface words in the following textbook passage.

> Where should newly married people live? The answer to that question depends very much on the norms of their society. Because marriage in traditional societies is essentially an alliance of kinship groups, the partners are usually expected to reside with their kin. **Patrilocal** residence is the custom in which marriage partners settle in or near the household of the husband's father; **matrilocal** residence is the custom in which married partners settle in or near the household of the wife's father. In modern societies, where marriage is conceived as a love-match between individuals, the predominant practice is **neolocal** residence, the custom in which marriage partners establish a new residence separate from the kin of either spouse.

The boldface words contain the combining forms **patri-** ("father"), **matri-** ("mother"), and **neo-** ("new").

Latin Roots

When you encounter an unfamiliar word, consider if it has the same Latin root as a word you know.

> The medical institution has grown steadily in size and social importance during this century, consuming an even greater share of society's resources and thus diverting them from other goals. The number of doctors, nurses, and hospital beds has continued to climb, far outpacing increases in population size. The **pharmaceutical** industry has now become one of the largest in the economy.

You are correct if you inferred that the adjective *pharmaceutical* has the same Latin root as the noun *pharmacy*, which refers to the preparation and dispensing of drugs.

EXERCISE 14.1 Word Structure: History

The excerpts in this exercise are from *A People and a Nation*, third edition, by Mary Beth Norton and others (Houghton Mifflin, 1990). Answer the questions that follow the selections.

> An English traveler several years later commented that the Indians had "died on heaps, as they lay in their houses," and that bones and skulls covered the remains of their villages. Because of this dramatic **depopulation** of the area, just a few years later English colonists were able to establish settlements virtually unopposed by native peoples. (p. 19)

1. **depopulation** (dē-pŏp′yə-lā′shən) n. The prefix **de-** means _____

   and the base word is _____.

> Both Luther and Calvin rejected Catholic rituals and denied the need for an elaborate church hierarchy. They also asserted that salvation came through faith alone, rather than—as Catholic teaching had it—through a combination of faith and good works. Calvin, though, went further than Luther in stressing God's absolute **omnipotence** and emphasizing the need for people to submit totally to His will. (p. 21)

2. **omnipotence** (ŏm-nĭp′ə-təns) n. The combining form **omni-** means "all"

   and the base word is _____, which means "powerful."

> After 1700, therefore, white southerners were **irrevocably** committed to black slavery as their chief source of labor. The same was not true of white northerners. (p. 55)

3. **irrevocably** (ĭ-rĕv′ə-kə-blē) adv. The prefix **ir-** means _____

   and the base word is _____.

> On other plantations, masters were more lenient and respectful of slaves' property and their desire to live with other members of their families. But even in households where whites and blacks displayed genuine affection for one another, there were **inescapable** tensions. (p. 91)

4. **inescapable** (ĭn′ĭ-skā′pə-bəl) adj. The prefix **in-** means _____

   and the base word is _____.

> The great victory over France had an **irreversible** impact on North America, the effects of which were felt first by the interior tribes. (p. 110)

5. **irreversible** (ĭr′ĭ-vûr′sə-bəl) adj. The prefix **ir-** means _____

and the base word is _____.

Women also took the lead in promoting **nonconsumption** of tea. In Boston more than three hundred matrons publicly promised not to drink tea, "Sickness excepted." (p. 121)

6. **nonconsumption** (nŏn′kən-sŭmp′shən) n. The prefix **non-** means _____

and the base word is _____.

Freed people quickly learned that if they were to survive and prosper they would have to rely on their own collective efforts rather than on the **benevolence** or goodwill of their white compatriots. (p. 167)

7. **benevolence** (bə-nĕv′ə-ləns) n. The combining form **bene-** means

_____; *benevolence* is the inclination to be kindly.

On June 15 Paterson presented an alternative scheme, the New Jersey Plan, calling for **modifications** in the Articles of Confederation rather than a complete overhaul of the government. (p. 178)

8. **modification** (mŏd′ə-fĭ-kā′shən) n. The base word is _____.

He conducted his election campaign from jail, winning an overwhelming majority. The fine, which he could not afford, was **ceremoniously** paid by contributions from leading Republicans around the country. (p. 201)

9. **ceremoniously** (sĕr′ə-mō′nē-əs-lē) adv. The base word is _____.

At revival meetings led by his brother Martin, a preacher, Gabriel recruited other blacks like himself—artisans who moved easily in both black and white circles and who lived in **semifreedom** under minimal white supervision. (p. 209)

10. **semifreedom** (sĕm-ē′frē′dəm) n. The prefix **semi-** means _____

and the base word is _____.

The president had a long-standing interest in Louisiana and the West. As early as 1782, as an American envoy in France, Jefferson had suggested sending an **exploratory** mission across the continent to California. (p. 219)

11. **exploratory** (ĭk-splôr′ə-tôr′ē) adj. The base word is _____.

The Monroe Doctrine proved popular at home as an anti-British, **anti-European** assertion of American nationalism, and it eventually became the foundation of American policy in the Western Hemisphere. (p. 237)

12. **anti-European** (ăn′tē-yoor′ə-pē′ən) adj. The prefix **anti-** means _____

and the base word is _____.

In defining **interstate** commerce broadly, the Marshall Court expanded federal powers over the economy while limiting the ability of states to control economic activity within their borders. (p. 252)

13. **interstate** (ĭn′tər-stāt′) adj. The prefix **inter-** means _____

and the base word is _____.

The **paternalistic** planter saw himself not as an oppressor, but as the benevolent guardian of an inferior race. (p. 286)

14. **paternalistic** (pə-tûr′nə-lĭs′ĭk) adj. The combining form **pater-** means

"father"; a *paternalistic* planter is a _____ person.

The family grew or produced all their necessities except for coffee, tea, and whiskey, which they got by sending butter or chickens to market. But until other settlers came to live near them, they lacked the human contact that a community offered. For their inexpensive land and **self-sufficiency** they paid the price of isolation and loneliness. (p. 307)

15. **self-sufficiency** (sĕlf′sə-fĭsh′ən-sē) n. The prefix is _____

and the base word is _____, which means "as much as is needed."

EXERCISE 14.2 **Word Structure: Sociology**

The excerpts in this exercise are from *Sociology*, third edition, by Ian Robertson (Worth Publishers, 1987). Answer the questions that follow the selections.

> Sometimes a component of the social system can be functional in one respect and **dysfunctional** in another. American industry, for example, is functional in that it provides the goods on which the society's way of life depends, but it is also dysfunctional in that it seriously pollutes the environment. (pp. 18–19)

1. **dysfunctional** (dĭs-fŭngk'shən-əl) adj. The prefix **dys-** means "impaired"

   and the base word is _____.

> Of course, different people age physically at very different rates; but ill-health becomes steadily more common until more than three-quarters of those aged sixty-five or over suffer from some chronic health condition. Yet the **infirmity** of some of the aged can have social as well as physical causes: if we offer the very old the role of an infirm person who has outlived any real usefulness to society, we must not be surprised that some of the elderly live up to these social expectations. (p. 136)

2. **infirmity** (ĭn-fûr'mĭ-tē) n. The prefix **in-** means _____ and

   the base word is _____, which means "strong."

> Socialization for death is almost **nonexistent** in the United States. In preindustrial societies, deaths usually took place at home in the context of the family, and young people grew up with a close understanding of the experience. In modern America, however, death is very much a taboo subject; we speak of it in hushed tones and use such euphemisms as "passed away." (p. 136)

3. **nonexistent** (nŏn'ĭg-zĭs'tənt) adj. The prefix **non-** means _____

   and the base word is _____.

> In principle, your social network can be depicted **diagrammatically** on a piece of paper, with a point to represent each acquaintance and a line between the points to represent a relationship. In practice, such a diagram would soon blunt your pencil in an illegible chaos of dots and crossing lines. (p. 174)

4. **diagrammatically** (dī'ə-grə-măt'ĭk-lē) adv. The base word is _____.

> Psychiatry, Szasz argues, is not really a medical science at all, but rather a **pseudoscience** like astrology and alchemy; its various diagnostic labels are just mumbo-jumbo that lends it a veneer of scientific respectability. (p. 212)

Reference
Thomas Szasz. *The Manufacture of Madness* (New York: Dell, 1970).

5. **pseudoscience** (sōō′dō-sī′əns) n. The prefix **pseudo-** means _____

and the base word is _____.

Pornography has become deeply controversial, largely because many people believe that it directly or indirectly causes sex crimes. Studies of the issue have generally produced **inconclusive** findings, for it is difficult in practice to prove or disprove a general causal link between the use of pornography and acts such as rape or incest. (p. 234)

6. **inconclusive** (ĭn′kən-klōō′sĭv) adj. The prefix **in-** means _____

and the base word is _____.

Unequal treatment (and not mere numbers) is an essential aspect of the sociological concept of a minority group. There are many numerical minorities in American society—such as blue-eyed people, people of Scottish extraction, or Episcopalians—but these are not minority groups, for they did not suffer group **deprivation.** (p. 287)

7. **deprivation** (dĕp′rə-vā′shən) n. The base word is _____.

In several parts of the world **genocide**—the extermination of entire populations—has been attempted and even achieved. The methods of genocide range from systematic slaughter by force of arms to the deliberate spreading of infectious diseases, particularly smallpox, among peoples who have no natural immunity to them. (p. 288)

8. **genocide** (jĕn′ə-sīd′) n. The Latin root **gene-** indicates "race" and the combining form **-cide** indicates "killing"; *genocide* means

_____.

Women are widely viewed as being in some sense the sexual property of men, and so are expected to be suitably **submissive** and deferential. (p. 321, adapted)

9. **submissive** (səb-mĭs′ĭv) adj. The base word is _____.

Despite the stereotype that women talk too much—that men "can't get a word in edgewise"—the fact is that when men and women are talking, men dominate the conversation. They not only speak for a **disproportionate** amount of time; they are also responsible, on the average, for more than 95 percent of the interruptions that occur. (p. 326)

10. **disproportionate** (dĭs′prə-pôr′shə-nĭt) adj. The prefix **dis-** means _____

and the base word is _____.

Social **gerontology** is the study of the social aspects of aging. This subdiscipline of sociology examines the influence of social forces on the aged and the aging processes, and the impact of the aged and their needs on society. (p. 335)

11. **gerontology** (jĕr′ən-tôl′ə-jē) n. The combining form **geronto-** means "old

    age" and the combining form **-logy** means _____.

Every society distinguishes between offspring born in wedlock and those born out of wedlock. *Legitimate* birth is birth to a mother and father who are married to each other; **illegitimate** birth is birth to a mother who is not married to the father. All societies encourage legitimacy, because it enables them to automatically allocate the social roles of mother and father to specific persons who are then responsible for the care and protection of the young. (p. 349)

12. **illegitimate** (ĭl′ĭ-jĭt′ə-mĭt) adj. The prefix **il-** means _____

    and the base word is _____.

Patterns of authority between husband and wife are always affected by the personalities of the spouses, but they generally follow the norms of the surroundings of society. In nearly all societies the prevailing pattern is **patriarchy,** a system in which the husband has the greater authority in family matters. No society has a **matriarchy,** a system in which the wife has the greater authority in family matters, although several societies give the wife more influence than the husband in some domestic areas. (pp. 354–355)

13. **patriarchy** (pā′trē-är′kē) n. The combining form **patri-** means "father" and the combining form **-archy** means "rule"; a *patriarchy* is a

    _____ by _____.

14. **matriarchy** (mā′trē-är′kē) n. The combining form **matri-** means "mother" and the combining form **-archy** means "rule"; a *matriarchy* is a

    _____ by _____.

In several modern societies, metropolitan areas have expanded to such an extent that they have merged with adjacent metropolises. The result in a **megalopolis,** a virtually unbroken urban tract consisting of two or more central cities and their surrounding suburbs. (p. 579)

15. **megalopolis** (mĕg′ə-lŏp′ə-lĭs) n. The combining form **megalo-** means "large" and the Greek root **polis** means "city"; a *megalopolis* is a

    _____.

EXERCISE 14.3 Word Structure: Government

The excerpts in this exercise are from *The Challenge of Democracy*, third edition, by Kenneth Janda and others (Houghton Mifflin, 1992). Answer the questions that follow the selections.

> The prevailing social order prescribes behavior in many different areas: how students should dress in school (neatly, no purple hair) and behave toward their teachers (respectfully); under what conditions people should have sexual relations (married, different sexes); what the press should not publish (sexually explicit photographs); and what the proper attitude toward religion and country should be **(reverential).** (pp. 13–15)

1. **reverential** (rĕv′ə-rĕn′shəl) adj. The base word is _____.

> In a centralized structure, decisions are made at one point, the top of the hierarchy. But a **decentralized,** complex government structure offers the access and openness necessary for pluralist democracy. (p. 47, adapted).

2. **decentralize** (dē-sĕn′trə-līz′) v. The prefix **de-** means _____

   and the base word is _____.

> The First Continental Congress had declared in 1774 that the colonists were entitled to "life, liberty, and property." Jefferson **reformulated** the objectives of government as "Life, Liberty, and the pursuit of Happiness." (p. 71)

3. **reformulate** (rē′fôr′myə-lāt) v. The prefix **re-** means _____

   and the base word is _____.

> The growth of government programs, the **hyperresponsiveness** of Congress, and the pressure of interest groups have created a federal system that critics describe as "overloaded and out of control." (p. 128)

4. **hyperresponsiveness** (hī′pər-rĭ-spŏn′sĭv-nĭs) n. The prefix **hyper-** means

   _____ and the base word is _____.

> Religious institutions recognize the value of socialization; they offer Sunday schools and other activities that are high on exposure, communication, and receptivity—reinforcing parental guidance. American political parties, on the other hand, sponsor few activities to win the hearts of little Democrats and Republicans, which leaves children open to **counterinfluences** in the school and community. (pp. 160–161, adapted)

5. **counterinfluence** (koun′tər-ĭn′flōō-əns) n. The prefix **counter-** means

   _____ and the base word is _____.

If many citizens view politics according to governing style, the role of political leadership becomes a more important **determinant** of public opinion than the leader's actual policies. (p. 181)

6. **determinant** (dĭ-tûr′mə-nənt) n. The base word is _____.

A study of stories on nuclear energy carried in the media over a period of ten years found that stories in the *New York Times* were well balanced between **pronuclear** and **antinuclear** sources. In contrast, the major news-magazines and television tended to favor antinuclear sources and to slant their stories against nuclear energy. (p. 218)

Reference

Stanley Rothman and S. Robert Lichter, "Elite Ideology and Risk Perception in Nuclear Energy Policy," *American Political Science Review* 81 (June 1987): 393.

7. **pronuclear** (prō′-noo′klē-ər) adj. The prefix **pro-** means _____

and the base word is _____.

8. **antinuclear** (ăn′tē-noo′klē-ər) adj. The prefix **anti-** means _____

and the base word is _____.

People with more education, higher incomes, and white-collar or professional occupations tend to be more aware of the impact of politics on their lives, to know what can be done to influence government actions, and to have the necessary resources (time, money) to take action. So they are more likely to participate in politics than are people of lower **socioeconomic** status. (p. 252)

Reference

Sidney Verba and Norman H. Nie. *Participation in America: Political Democracy and Social Equality* (New York: Harper & Row, 1972), p. 13.

9. **socioeconomic** (sō′sē-ō-ĕk′ə-nŏm′ĭk) adj. *Socioeconomic* status involves

both _____ and _____ factors.

Although Democrats and Republicans have issue-neutral names, many minor parties in the United States have used their names to advertise their policies: the Prohibition party, the Farmer-Labor party, and the Socialist party, for example. The neutrality of their names suggests that the two major parties are also **undifferentiated** in their politics. This is not true. They regularly adopt very different policies in their platforms. (p. 269, adapted)

10. **undifferentiated** (ŭn-dĭf′ə-rĕn′shē-āt′ĭd) adj. The prefix **un-** means _____

and the base word is _____.

Unit Three Review

REVIEW 3.1   Basic Word List

Your instructor may give you a test on the meanings of these words. If so, learn the meanings of any of the words that you do not know. The words are followed by the exercise numbers in which they are introduced.

1. adversity, 10.1
2. amply, 10.1
3. authenticity, 10.1
4. comparative, 10.1
5. deterrent, 10.1
6. durability, 10.2
7. expenditure, 10.2
8. leniency, 10.2
9. penetrable, 10.3
10. preferential, 10.3
11. provocation, 10.3
12. remittance, 10.3
13. sensory, 10.4
14. supposition, 10.4
15. variant, 10.4
16. voluminous, 10.4
17. atypical, 11.1
18. invariably, 11.1
19. misrepresentation, 11.1
20. noncommittal, 11.1
21. irrelevant, 11.2
22. semiconscious, 11.2
23. unalterable, 11.2
24. asocial, 11.2
25. dispassionate, 11.3
26. amoral, 11.3
27. bicentennial, 12.2
28. unique, 12.2
29. anthropology, 12.3
30. archaeology, 12.3
31. theology, 12.3
32. abiotic, 12.4
33. biotic, 12.4
34. chronic, 12.4
35. monotheism, 12.4
36. benevolent, 12.5
37. benign, 12.5
38. heterogeneous, 12.5
39. homogeneous, 12.5
40. malicious, 12.5
41. malignant, 12.5
42. polygamy, 12.5
43. credible, 13.1
44. confidant, 13.4
45. colloquial, 13.5
46. prospective, 13.6
47. revoke, 13.7
48. deprivation, 14.2
49. infirmity, 14.2
50. submissive, 14.2

REVIEW 3.2   Advanced Word List

Your instructor may give you a test on the meanings of these words. If so, learn the meanings of any of the words that you do not know. The words are followed by the numbers of the exercises in which they are introduced.

1. calamitous, 10.1
2. comatose, 10.1
3. compilation, 10.1
4. differentiate, 10.2
5. disputant, 10.2
6. distinctive, 10.2
7. enviable, 10.2
8. expiration, 10.2
9. familial, 10.2
10. maniacal, 10.2
11. methodical, 10.3
12. perfectionist, 10.3
13. propriety, 10.3
14. remediable, 10.3
15. reparable, 10.4
16. retention, 10.4

17. servile, 10.4
18. sobriety, 10.4
19. victimize, 10.4
20. illegible, 11.1
21. disconsolate, 11.2
22. imprudent, 11.2
23. impropriety, 11.3
24. inimitable, 11.3
25. irreparable, 11.3
26. malodorous, 11.3
27. biennial, 12.2
28. biped, 12.2
29. decimate, 12.2
30. octogenarian, 12.2
31. septuagenarian, 12.2
32. unilateral, 12.2
33. gynecologist, 12.3

34. archaic, 12.4
35. polytheism, 12.4
36. psychic, 12.4
37. seismic, 12.4
38. malevolent, 12.5
39. acrophobia, 12.6
40. claustrophobia, 12.6
41. dipsomania, 12.6
42. egomania, 12.6
43. diffident, 13.4
44. fidelity, 13.4
45. loquacious, 13.5
46. retrospect, 13.6
47. evoke, 13.7
48. omnipotent, 14.1
49. modification, 14.1
50. genocide, 14.2

REVIEW 3.3 Sentence Completion

Complete the following sentences using words that make it clear that you know the meanings of the words that are printed in **boldface**.

1. I made an **expenditure** *of fifty dollars for an unexpected automobile repair.*

2. I mailed my **remittance** _____

3. It is **atypical** _____

4. It is **malicious** to _____

5. **Maniacal** behaviors include _____

6. I was **disconsolate** when _____

7. It is **imprudent** to _____

8. Well-known **octogenarians** include _____

9. **Seismic** activity _____

_____

10. Those who suffer from **claustrophobia** _____

_____

___**REVIEW 3.4** **Writing Applications**

Your instructor may assign one or more of the following writing activities.

1. Write six sentences, each of which includes a word from the Basic Word List on page 127 or the Advanced Word List on pages 127–128. Underline the six words in your sentences.

2. Write six sentences, each of which includes one of the following words specified by your instructor. Underline the six words in your sentences.

   a. _____   d. _____

   b. _____   e. _____

   c. _____   f. _____

3. Write a paragraph on a topic of your choice using six of the words from the Basic Word List on page 127 or the Advanced Word List on pages 127–128. Underline the six words in your paragraph.

4. Write a paragraph on a topic of your choice that includes the following six words specified by your instructor. Underline the six words in your paragraph.

   a. _____   d. _____

   b. _____   e. _____

   c. _____   f. _____

5. Describe a time when you experienced **adversity.**

6. Tell about your favorite television program and explain why you **invariably** enjoy watching it.

7. Describe what you would look for in a **prospective** employer.

8. Recount an instance when you had a **psychic** experience.

9. Describe a **malevolent** person whom you have encountered.

10. What are some characteristics you would expect to find in people who suffer from **egomania?**

REVIEW 3.5   Fill-in Questions

Write on the lines the words that have been deleted from the following definitions of terminology introduced in Chapters 10, 11, and 12.

1. A _____ is a letter or group of letters that is added to the end of a base word.

2. A _____ is a letter or group of letters that is added to the beginning of a base word.

3. A _____ _____ is a Greek or Latin word part that is joined to other word parts or to base words.

REVIEW 3.6   Short-Answer Questions

Refer to Chapters 11 and 12 for the meanings of any of the following prefixes and combining forms that you do not know.

1. Write the meanings of the *prefixes* that are printed in boldface in the following words.

   a. **dis**trust   _____

   b. **a**social   _____

   c. **de**forest   _____

   d. **inter**state   _____

   e. **mis**calculate   _____

   f. **pseudo**science   _____

   g. **semi**public   _____

2. Write the meanings of the combining forms that are printed in boldface in the following words.

   a. **uni**lateral   _____

   b. **anthropo**logy   _____

   c. **patho**gen   _____

   d. **bene**volent   _____

   e. bi**gamy**   _____

   f. **ego**centric   _____

   g. **biblio**phile   _____

Four

Locate Word Meanings

Learning Goals for Unit Four

In studying Chapters 15 and 16 you will learn:

- How dictionaries use definitions, synonyms, and examples to explain the meanings of words (Chapter 15).

- How to select from several definitions for a word the one that pertains to a specific context (Chapter 15).

- How to figure out the meanings of words such as *rotundity* and *semiautonomous* when they are not defined in dictionaries (Chapter 15).

- The importance of learning the terminology of your college courses (Chapter 16).

- How to locate words that are important to learn in the books you study for your college courses (Chapter 16).

Words in Dictionaries

When you cannot determine the meaning of a word by studying context or analyzing word structure, you may need to locate its definition in a dictionary. This chapter contains information that will be helpful to you if you sometimes have difficulty finding or understanding definitions in a dictionary. As you study this chapter, keep in mind the following suggestions that are given in Chapter 4:

■ Purchase a dictionary that states the meanings of words in ways that are easy for you to understand.

■ Determine what method was used to arrange the sequence of definitions in your dictionary.

■ Use subject labels to locate definitions that pertain to college subjects.

These three suggestions and the information in this chapter will help you improve your ability to locate definitions in a dictionary.

Definitions, Synonyms, and Examples

Dictionaries explain the meanings of words using definitions, synonyms, and examples. **Definitions** are statements of the meaning of words; the definition of *happy* is "having a feeling of great pleasure." **Synonyms** are words that have the same or nearly the same meaning; synonyms of *happy* include *glad, pleased, delighted,* and *joyous.* **Examples,** in dictionary entries, are phrases or sentences that illustrate the ways words are used. The following sentence is an example of the way *happy* is used: "We are *happy* that it didn't rain the day of the picnic."

The following entry includes definitions, a synonym, and an example.

> **be·seech** (bĭ-sēch′) *tr.v.* **-sought** (-sôt′) or **-seeched, -seech·ing, -seech·es. 1.** To address an earnest or urgent request to; implore: *beseech them for help.* **2.** To request earnestly; beg for: *beseech help.* See Synonyms at **beg.** [Middle English *bisechen,* from Old English *besēcan : be-,* be- + *sēcan,* to seek; see SEEK.] **—be·seech′er** *n.*

Notice that a semicolon separates the first definition and a synonym and that a colon introduces the example, which is printed in italics.

- The first definition is "To address an earnest or urgent request to."
- The synonym is *implore.*
- The example is "beseech them for help."

Multiple Meanings

Since most words have more than one meaning, it is usually necessary to read two or more definitions of a word to locate the one that pertains to a specific context. The italicized word in the following sentence has several meanings:

Albert Einstein is the *personification* of brains.

Which of the following four definitions of *personification* pertains to the word as it is used in this sentence?

per·son·i·fi·ca·tion (pər-sŏn′ə-fĭ-kā′shən) *n.* **1.** The act of personifying. **2.** A person or thing typifying a certain quality or idea; an embodiment or exemplification: *"He's invisible, a walking personification of the Negative"* (Ralph Ellison). **3.** A figure of speech in which inanimate objects or abstractions are endowed with human qualities or are represented as possessing human form, as in *Hunger sat shivering on the road* or *Flowers danced about the lawn.* Also called *prosopopeia.* **4.** Artistic representation of an abstract quality or idea as a person.

The second definition states the meaning that applies to *personification* as it is used in the sentence about Einstein.

Sequences of Definitions

Another problem in locating the right definition is that entries often have two or more sequences of definitions. The following entry for *hackney* has three numbered sequences of definitions.

hack·ney (hăk′nē) *n., pl.* **-neys. 1.** Often **Hackney.** A horse of a breed developed in England, having a gait characterized by pronounced flexion of the knee. **2.** A trotting horse suited for routine riding or driving; a hack. **3.** A coach or carriage for hire. **—hackney** *tr.v.* **-neyed, -ney·ing, -neys. 1.** To cause to become banal and trite through overuse. **2.** To hire out; let. **—hackney** *adj.* **1.** Banal; trite. **2.** Having been hired. [Middle English *hakenei,* probably after *Hakenei,* Hackney, a borough of London, England, where such horses were raised.]

In this entry, three noun definitions are followed by two verb definitions, and the verb definitions are followed by two adjective definitions.

Unknown Words in Definitions

Sometimes definitions may include words that you do not know. For instance, the first adjective definition for *hackney* is "Banal; trite." If you do not know the meanings of these words, you will need to locate them to completely understand the first adjective definition of *hackney*.

> **ba·nal** (bə-năl′, bā′nəl, bə-näl′) *adj.* Drearily commonplace and often predictable; trite. See Synonyms at **trite.** [French, from Old French, shared by tenants in a feudal jurisdiction, from *ban,* summons to military service, of Germanic origin. See **bhā-²** in Appendix.] —**ba·nal′ize′** *v.* —**ba·nal′ly** *adv.*
>
> **trite** (trīt) *adj.* **trit·er, trit·est. 1.** Lacking power to evoke interest through overuse or repetition; hackneyed. **2.** *Archaic.* Frayed or worn out by use. [Latin *trītus,* from past participle of *terere,* to wear out. See **tere-¹** in Appendix.] —**trite′ly** *adv.* —**trite′ness** *n.*

Notice that the entry for *banal* includes *trite* as a synonym and the entry for *trite* includes *hackneyed* as a synonym.

Undefined Words

Dictionaries provide the spellings, but not the definitions of many words formed by joining suffixes to base words.

> **ro·tund** (rō-tŭnd′) *adj.* **1.** Rounded in figure; plump. See Synonyms at **fat. 2.** Having a full, rich sound; sonorous. [Latin *rotundus.* See **ret-** in Appendix.] —**ro·tun′di·ty** *n.* —**ro·tund′ly** *adv.* —**ro·tund′ness** *n.*

This entry for the adjective *rotund* includes the spellings, but not the meanings, of noun and adverbial forms of the word: *rotundity, rotundly,* and *rotundness.* If you studied Chapter 10, you know that when suffixes are added to a base word, they usually change the base word's part of speech without changing its meaning. As a result, when you know the meaning of a base word, you can usually figure out the meanings of derivatives formed by adding suffixes to it.

In addition, most words that begin with prefixes are not defined in desk dictionaries. For instance, if you want to know the meaning of *semiautonomous* (sĕm′ē-ô-tŏn′ə-məs), you will not find it in a desk dictionary. However, if you studied Chapter 11, you should be able to analyze the word as a derivative that contains the prefix *semi-* and the base *autonomous.*

> **au·ton·o·mous** (ô-tŏn′ə-məs) *adj.* **1.** Not controlled by others or by outside forces; independent: *an autonomous judiciary; an autonomous division of a corporate conglomerate.* **2.** Independent in mind or judgment; self-directed. **3. a.** Independent of the laws of another state or government; self-governing. **b.** Of or relating to a self-governing entity: *an autonomous legislature.* **c.** Self-governing with respect to local or internal affairs: *an autonomous region of a country.* **4.** Autonomic. [From Greek *autonomos : auto-,* auto- + *nomos,* law; see **nem-** in Appendix.] —**au·ton′o·mous·ly** *adv.*

By studying the definitions of *autonomous* and recalling the meaning of *semi-,* you should conclude correctly that *semiautonomous* means "partially or somewhat independent, self-directed, or self-governing."

EXERCISE 15.1   Multiple Meanings

Referring to the entries at the bottom of this page, write the number of the definition that pertain to the words printed in **boldface**.

_____ 1. The 2,000-page manuscript of a novel was **abridged** to a reasonable length before publication.

_____ 2. *Indian* is an **ambiguous** word, because it can refer to natives of India or to natives of North and South America.

_____ 3. I don't mind little white lies, but I am offended by **blatant** lies.

_____ 4. His wife suggested that he **compose** himself before responding to an insulting letter.

_____ 5. It used to be a **convention** for men to remove their hats in the presence of women.

_____ 6. The painting **depicts** Abraham Lincoln addressing a crowd at Gettysburg, Pennsylvania.

_____ 7. They hired a **dynamic**, young lawyer to represent them in court.

_____ 8. Missionaries persuaded many natives of Hawaii to **embrace** Christianity.

_____ 9. A bottle of **generic** aspirin costs $1.99, compared to a brand name aspirin that costs $4.49.

---

a·bridge (ə-brĭj′) *tr.v.* **a·bridged, a·bridg·ing, a·bridg·es. 1.** To reduce the length of (a written text); condense. **2.** To cut short; curtail. See Synonyms at **shorten.**

am·big·u·ous (ăm-bĭg′yōō-əs) *adj.* **1.** Open to more than one interpretation: *an ambiguous reply.* **2.** Doubtful or uncertain: *"The theatrical status of her frequently derided but constantly revived plays remained ambiguous"* (Frank Rich). See Synonyms at **vocifer·ous.**

bla·tant (blāt′nt) *adj.* **1.** Unpleasantly loud and noisy: *"There are those who find the trombones blatant and the triangle silly, but both add effective color"* (Musical Heritage Review). See Synonyms at **vociferous. 2.** *Usage Problem.* Totally or offensively conspicuous or obtrusive: *a blatant lie.*

com·pose (kəm-pōz′) *v.* **-posed, -pos·ing, -pos·es.** *Abbr.* **comp.** —*tr.* **1.** To make up the constituent parts of; constitute or form: *an exhibit composed of French paintings; the many ethnic groups that compose our nation.* See Usage Note at **comprise. 2.** To make or create by putting together parts or elements. **3.** To create or produce (a literary or musical piece). **4.** To make (oneself) calm or tranquil: *Compose yourself and deal with the problems logically.* **5.** To settle or adjust; reconcile: *They managed to compose their differences.* **6.** To arrange aesthetically or artistically.

con·ven·tion (kən-věn′shən) *n.* *Abbr.* **conv. 1.a.** A formal meeting of members, representatives, or delegates, as of a political party, fraternal society, profession, or industry. **b.** The body of persons attending such an assembly: *called the convention to order.* **2.** An agreement between states, sides, or military forces, especially an international agreement dealing with a specific subject, such as the treatment of prisoners of war. **3.** General agreement on or acceptance of certain practices or attitudes: *By convention, north is at the top of most maps.* **4.** A practice or procedure widely observed in a group, especially to facilitate social interaction; a custom: *the convention of shaking hands.* **5.** A widely used and accepted device or technique, as in drama, literature, or painting: *the theatrical convention of the aside.*

de·pict (dĭ-pĭkt′) *tr.v.* **-pict·ed, -pict·ing, -picts. 1.** To represent in a picture or sculpture. **2.** To represent in words; describe. See Synonyms at **represent.**

dy·nam·ic (dī-năm′ĭk) also **dy·nam·i·cal** (-ĭ-kəl) *adj.* **1.a.** Of or relating to energy or to objects in motion. **b.** Of or relating to the study of dynamics. **2.** Characterized by continuous change, activity, or progress: *a dynamic market.* **3.** Marked by intensity and vigor; forceful. See Synonyms at **active. 4.** Of or relating to variation of intensity, as in musical sound.

em·brace (ĕm-brās′) *v.* **-braced, -brac·ing, -brac·es.** —*tr.* **1.** To clasp or hold close with the arms, usually as an expression of affection. **2.a.** To surround; enclose: *We allowed the warm water to embrace us.* **b.** To twine around: *a trellis that was embraced by vines.* **3.** To include as part of something broader. See Synonyms at **include. 4.** To take up willingly or eagerly: *embrace a social cause.* **5.** To avail oneself of: *"I only regret, in my chilled age, certain occasions and possibilities I didn't embrace"* (Henry James).

ge·ner·ic (jə-něr′ĭk) *adj.* *Abbr.* **gen. 1.** Relating to or descriptive of an entire group or class; general. See Synonyms at **general. 2.** *Biology.* Of or relating to a genus. **3.** Not having a trademark or brand name.

EXERCISE 15.2   Multiple Meanings

Referring to the entries at the bottom of this page, write the numbers of the definitions that pertain to the words printed in **boldface.**

_____ 1. In biology, animal life is arranged in a **hierarchy,** with one-celled protozoa at the bottom and apes very near the top.

_____ 2. Disappointed in love, he **immersed** himself in work.

_____ 3. Those who are very rich have the **latitude** to work or not to work.

_____ 4. Our professor told a joke as he was passing out a test, but we didn't laugh, because we didn't appreciate the **levity.**

_____ 5. The entire student body was attracted by the **magnetism** of the speaker's personality.

_____ 6. She doesn't own a car because she knows she can **manipulate** others into driving her where she wants to go.

_____ 7. The wealthy parents worried that the poor young man wanted to marry their daughter for **mercenary** reasons.

_____ 8. The enjoyment she derives from her work makes it clear that she has found her **niche.**

_____ 9. Audiophiles have **omnivorous** appetites for listening to high-fidelity sound reproduction.

hi·er·ar·chy (hī′ə-rär′kē, hī′rär′-) *n., pl.* **-chies. 1.** A body of persons having authority. **2.a.** Categorization of a group of people according to ability or status. **b.** The group so categorized. **3.** A series in which each element is graded or ranked: *put honesty first in her hierarchy of values.* **4.a.** A body of clergy organized into successive ranks or grades with each level subordinate to the one above. **b.** Religious rule by a group of ranked clergy. **5.** One of the divisions of angels.
im·merse (ĭ-mûrs′) *tr.v.* **-mersed, -mers·ing, -mers·es. 1.** To cover completely in a liquid; submerge. See Synonyms at **dip. 2.** To baptize by submerging in water. **3.** To engage wholly or deeply; absorb: *scholars who immerse themselves in their subjects.*
lat·i·tude (lăt′ĭ-tood′, -tyood′) *n. Abbr.* **lat. 1.a.** The angular distance north or south of the earth's equator, measured in degrees along a meridian, as on a map or globe. **b.** A region of the earth considered in relation to its distance from the equator: *temperate latitudes.* **2.** *Astronomy.* The angular distance of a celestial body north or south of the ecliptic. **3.** Freedom from normal restraints, limitations, or regulations. See Synonyms at **room.**
lev·i·ty (lĕv′ĭ-tē) *n., pl.* **-ties. 1.** Lightness of manner or speech, especially when inappropriate; frivolity. **2.** Inconstancy; changeableness. **3.** The state or quality of being light; buoyancy.
mag·net·ism (măg′nĭ-tĭz′əm) *n. Abbr.* **mag. 1.** The class of phenomena exhibited by a magnetic field. **2.** The study of magnets and their effects. **3.** The force exerted by a magnetic field.

4. Unusual power to attract, fascinate, or influence: *the magnetism of money.* **5.** Animal magnetism.
ma·nip·u·late (mə-nĭp′yə-lāt′) *tr.v.* **-lat·ed, -lat·ing, -lates. 1.** To operate or control by skilled use of the hands; handle: *She manipulated the lights to get just the effect she wanted.* **2.** To influence or manage shrewdly or deviously: *He manipulated public opinion in his favor.* **3.** To tamper with or falsify for personal gain: *tried to manipulate stock prices.* **4.** *Medicine.* To handle and move in an examination or for therapeutic purposes: *manipulate a joint; manipulate the position of a fetus during delivery.*
mer·ce·nar·y (mûr′sə-nĕr′ē) *adj.* **1.** Motivated solely by a desire for monetary or material gain. **2.** Hired for service in a foreign army.
niche (nĭch, nēsh) *n.* **1.** A recess in a wall, as for holding a statue or an urn. **2.** A cranny, hollow, or crevice, as in rock. **3.a.** A situation or an activity specially suited to a person's interests, abilities, or nature: *found her niche in life.* **b.** A special area of demand for a product or service: *"One niche that is approaching mass-market proportions is held by regional magazines"* (Brad Edmondson). **4.** *Ecology.* **a.** The function or position of an organism or a population within an ecological community. **b.** The particular area within a habitat occupied by an organism.
om·niv·o·rous (ŏm-nĭv′ər-əs) *adj.* **1.** Eating both animal and vegetable foods. **2.** Taking in everything available: *an inquiring, omnivorous mind.*

EXERCISE 15.3 Multiple Meanings

Referring to the entries at the bottom of this page, write the numbers of the definitions that pertain to the words printed in **boldface**.

_____ 1. Most employers provide **orientation** for new employees.

_____ 2. "Give and you will receive" is a well-known **paradox**.

_____ 3. The mayor's campaign promise to favor the death penalty was nothing but a **placebo**—the mayor cannot inflict the death penalty.

_____ 4. I try not to disturb my friends when they are **preoccupied** with study for their college courses.

_____ 5. The party was a **qualified** success—the band was good, but there wasn't enough food and drinks.

_____ 6. The museum wants to acquire a painting that is **representative** of the artist's work when she was an art student.

_____ 7. She says whatever comes into her mind, but her husband is **reserved**.

_____ 8. They purchased fifteen acres of lakefront property, **speculating** that many people would soon consider it to be a desirable place to build vacation homes.

_____ 9. He was fired when his employer discovered that his excuse for constant lateness was **spurious**.

o·ri·en·ta·tion (ôr′ē-ĕn-tā′shən, -ən-, ōr′-) *n.* **1.** The act of orienting or the state of being oriented. **2.** Location or position relative to the points of the compass. **3.** The construction of a church so that its longitudinal axis is from west to east and its main altar is at the eastern end. **4.** The direction followed in the course of a trend, movement, or development. **5.a.** A tendency of thought; a general inclination: *a Marxist orientation.* **b.** Sexual orientation. **6.a.** An adjustment or adaptation to a new environment, situation, custom, or set of ideas. **b.** Introductory instruction concerning a new situation: *orientation for incoming students.* **7.** *Psychology.* Awareness of the objective world in relation to one's self.

par·a·dox (păr′ə-dŏks′) *n.* **1.** A seemingly contradictory statement that may nonetheless be true: *the paradox that standing is more tiring than walking.* **2.** One exhibiting inexplicable or contradictory aspects: *"You have the paradox of a Celt being the smooth Oxonian"* (Anthony Burgess). **3.** An assertion that is essentially self-contradictory, though based on a valid deduction from acceptable premises. **4.** A statement contrary to received opinion.

pla·ce·bo (plə-sē′bō) *n.,* *pl.* **-bos** or **-boes. 1.a.** *Medicine.* A substance containing no medication and prescribed or given to reinforce a patient's expectation to get well. **b.** An inactive substance or preparation used as a control in an experiment or test to determine the effectiveness of a medicinal drug. **2.** Something of no intrinsic remedial value that is used to appease or reassure another. **3.** (plä-chā′bō). *Roman Catholic Church.* The service or office of vespers for the dead.

pre·oc·cu·pied (prē-ŏk′yə-pīd′) *adj.* **1.a.** Absorbed in thought; engrossed. **b.** Excessively concerned with something; distracted. **2.** Formerly or already occupied. **3.** Already used and therefore unavailable for further use. Used of taxonomic names.

qual·i·fied (kwŏl′ə-fīd′) *adj.* **1.** Having the appropriate qualifications for an office, a position, or a task. **2.** Limited, restricted, or modified: *a qualified plan for expansion.* **—qual′i·fied′ly** (-fīd′lē, -fī′ĭd-lē) *adv.*

rep·re·sen·ta·tive (rĕp′rĭ-zĕn′tə-tĭv) *n.* *Abbr.* **rep., Rep. 1.** One that serves as an example or a type for others of the same classification. **2.** One that serves as a delegate or an agent for another. **3.a.** A member of a governmental body, usually legislative, chosen by popular vote. **b.** A member of the U.S. House of Representatives or of the lower house of a state legislature.

re·served (rĭ-zûrvd′) *adj.* **1.** Held in reserve; kept back or set aside. **2.** Marked by self-restraint and reticence. See Synonyms at **silent. —re·serv′ed·ly** (-zûr′vĭd-lē) *adv.* **—re·serv′ed·ness** *n.*

spec·u·late (spĕk′yə-lāt′) *v.* **-lat·ed, -lat·ing, -lates. —intr. 1.** To meditate on a subject; reflect. **2.** To engage in a course of reasoning often based on inconclusive evidence. See Synonyms at **conjecture, think. 3.** To engage in the buying or selling of a commodity with an element of risk on the chance of profit. — *tr.* To assume to be true without conclusive evidence: *speculated that high cholesterol was a contributing factor to the patient's health problems.*

spu·ri·ous (spyŏŏr′ē-əs) *adj.* **1.** Lacking authenticity or validity in essence or origin; not genuine; false. **2.** Of illegitimate birth. **3.** *Botany.* Similar in appearance but unlike in structure or function. Used of plant parts.

EXERCISE 15.4 **Undefined Words**

Following are definitions for some of the undefined words that are listed at the end of dictionary entries at the bottom of this page. Write the words that pertain to the definitions on the lines, and write the abbreviations of the words' parts of speech within the parentheses.

1. _amicability_ (**n.**) Friendliness or agreeableness.

2. _____ ( ) Done in an extremely evil or cruel manner.

3. _____ ( ) An instance of emotionally hardened or unfeeling behavior.

4. _____ ( ) Pertaining to the art of creating and arranging ballets or dances.

5. _____ ( ) Done in a roundabout, lengthy manner.

6. _____ ( ) An instance of working together in a joint intellectual effort.

7. _____ ( ) Done in a quick and skillful manner.

8. _____ ( ) Possessing a feeling of great happiness or well-being.

9. _____ ( ) The quality of being extremely bad or offensive.

am·i·ca·ble (ăm′ĭ-kə-bəl) *adj.* Characterized by or exhibiting friendliness or good will; friendly. [Middle English, from Late Latin *amīcābilis,* from Latin *amīcus,* friend.] —**am′i·ca·bil′i·ty, am′i·ca·ble·ness** *n.* —**am′i·ca·bly** *adv.*

a·tro·cious (ə-trō′shəs) *adj.* **1.** Extremely evil or cruel; monstrous: *an atrocious crime.* See Synonyms at **outrageous. 2.** Exceptionally bad; abominable: *atrocious decor; atrocious behavior.* [From Latin *atrōx, atrōc-,* frightful, cruel. See **āter-** in Appendix.] —**a·tro′cious·ly** *adv.* —**a·tro′cious·ness** *n.*

cal·lous (kăl′əs) *adj.* **1.** Having calluses; toughened: *callous skin on the elbow.* **2.** Emotionally hardened; unfeeling: *a callous indifference to the suffering of others.* —**callous** *tr. & intr.v.* **-loused, -lous·ing, -lous·es.** To make or become callous. [Middle English, from Old French *cailleux,* from Latin *callōsus,* from *callum,* hard skin.] —**cal′lous·ly** *adv.* —**cal′lous·ness** *n.*

cho·re·og·ra·phy (kôr′ē-ŏg′rə-fē, kōr′-) *n.,* *pl.* **-phies. 1.a.** The art of creating and arranging dances or ballets. **b.** A work created by this art. **2.** Something, such as a situation or series of situations or a plan or series of plans, likened to dance arrangements: *"There are times when the choreography of frustration and violence seems rather too rich"* (John Simon). [French *chorégraphie* : Greek *khoreia,* choral dance; see CHOREA + *-graphia,* writing (from Latin *-graphia, -graphy*).] —**cho′re·o·graph′ic** (-ə-grăf′ĭk) *adj.* —**cho′re·o·graph′i·cal·ly** *adv.*

cir·cu·i·tous (sər-kyōō′ĭ-təs) *adj.* Being or taking a roundabout, lengthy course. See Synonyms at **indirect.** [From Medieval Latin *circuitōsus,* from Latin *circuitus,* a going around. See CIRCUIT.] —**cir·cu′i·tous·ly** *adv.* —**cir·cu′i·ty, cir·cu′i·tous·ness** *n.*

col·lab·o·rate (kə-lăb′ə-rāt′) *intr.v.* **-rat·ed, -rat·ing, -rates. 1.** To work together, especially in a joint intellectual effort. **2.** To cooperate treasonably, as with an enemy occupation force. [Late Latin *collabōrāre, collabōrāt-* : Latin *com-,* com- + Latin *labōrāre,* to work (from *labor,* toil).] —**col·lab′o·ra′tion** *n.* —**col·lab′o·ra′tive** *adj.* —**col·lab′o·ra′tor** *n.*

deft (dĕft) *adj.* **deft·er, deft·est.** Quick and skillful; adroit. See Synonyms at **dexterous.** [Middle English, gentle, humble, variant of *dafte,* foolish. See DAFT.] —**deft′ly** *adv.* —**deft′ness** *n.*

eu·pho·ri·a (yōō-fôr′ē-ə, -fōr′-) *n.* A feeling of great happiness or well-being. [New Latin, from Greek, from *euphoros,* healthy : *eu-,* eu- + *pherein,* to bear; see **bher-**[1] in Appendix.] —**eu·phor′ic** (-fôr′ĭk, -fōr′-) *adj.* —**eu·phor′i·cal·ly** *adv.*

fla·grant (flā′grənt) *adj.* **1.** Conspicuously bad, offensive, or reprehensible: *a flagrant miscarriage of justice; flagrant cases of wrongdoing at the highest levels of government.* See Usage Note at **blatant. 2.** *Obsolete.* Flaming; blazing. [Latin *flagrāns, flagrant-,* present participle of *flagrāre,* to burn. See **bhel-**[1] in Appendix.] —**fla′gran·cy, fla′grance** *n.* —**fla′grant·ly** *adv.*

EXERCISE 15.5 Undefined Words

Following are definitions for some of the undefined words that are listed at the end of dictionary entries at the bottom of this page. Write the words that pertain to the definitions on the lines, and write the abbreviations of the words' parts of speech within the parentheses.

1. _gregariousness_ (*n.*) The act of seeking and enjoying the company of others.

2. _____ ( ) Possessing a physiological or temperamental peculiarity.

3. _____ ( ) The capacity to be unshakably calm and collected.

4. _____ ( ) The inability to make an error or mistake.

5. _____ ( ) Done in a way that does not offend or provoke strong emotion.

6. _____ ( ) Longing for things, persons, or situations of the past.

7. _____ ( ) Being an original instance that serves as a model on which later stages are based.

8. _____ ( ) Restoration to an earlier condition by repairing or remodeling.

9. _____ ( ) Done in a stealthy or secret manner.

---

gre·gar·i·ous (grĭ-gâr′ē-əs) *adj.* **1.** Seeking and enjoying the company of others; sociable. See Synonyms at **social. 2.** Tending to move in or form a group with others of the same kind: *gregarious bird species.* **3.** *Botany.* Growing in groups that are close together but not densely clustered or matted. [Latin *gregārius,* belonging to a flock, from *grex, greg-,* flock. See **ger-** in Appendix.] —**gre·gar′i·ous·ly** *adv.* —**gre·gar′i·ous·ness** *n.*

id·i·o·syn·cra·sy (ĭd′ē-ō-sĭng′krə-sē) *n., pl.* **-sies. 1.** A structural or behavioral characteristic peculiar to an individual or a group. See Synonyms at **eccentricity. 2.** A physiological or temperamental peculiarity. **3.** An unusual individual reaction to food or a drug. [Greek *idiosunkrasia : idio-,* idio- + *sunkrasis,* mixture, temperament (*sun-,* syn- + *krasis,* a mixing; see *kere-* in Appendix).] —**id′i·o·syn·crat′ic** (-sĭn-krăt′ĭk) *adj.* —**id′i·o·syn·crat′i·cal·ly** *adv.*

im·per·turb·a·ble (ĭm′pər-tûr′bə-bəl) *adj.* Unshakably calm and collected. See Synonyms at **cool.** —**im′per·turb′a·bil′i·ty, im′per·turb′a·ble·ness** *n.* —**im′per·turb′a·bly** *adv.*

in·fal·li·ble (ĭn-făl′ə-bəl) *adj.* **1.** Incapable of erring: *an infallible guide; an infallible source of information.* **2.** Incapable of failing; certain: *an infallible antidote; an infallible rule.* **3.** *Roman Catholic Church.* Incapable of error in expounding doctrine on faith or morals. [Middle English, from Medieval Latin *īnfallibilis* : Latin *in-,* not; see **IN**—¹ + Medieval Latin *fallibilis,* fallible; see FALLIBLE.] —**in·fal′li·bil′i·ty, in·fal′li·ble·ness** *n.* —**in·fal′li·bly** *adv.*

in·noc·u·ous (ĭ-nŏk′yōō-əs) *adj.* **1.** Having no adverse effect; harmless. **2.** Not likely to offend or provoke to strong emotion; insipid. [From Latin *innocuus : in-,* not; see **IN**—¹ + *nocuus,* harmful (from *nocēre,* to harm; see **nek-**¹ in Appendix).] —**in·noc′u·ous·ly** *adv.* —**in·noc′u·ous·ness** *n.*

nos·tal·gi·a (nŏ-stăl′jə, nə-) *n.* **1.** A bittersweet longing for things, persons, or situations of the past. **2.** The condition of being homesick; homesickness. [Greek *nostos,* a return home; see **nes-**¹ in Appendix + —ALGIA.] —**nos·tal′gic** (-jĭk) *adj.* —**nos·tal′gi·cal·ly** *adv.*

pro·to·type (prō′tə-tīp′) *n.* **1.** An original type, form, or instance that serves as a model on which later stages are based or judged. **2.** An early, typical example. **3.** *Biology.* A primitive or ancestral form or species. [French, from Greek *prōtotupon,* from neuter of *prōtotupos,* original : *prōto-,* proto- + *tupos,* model.] —**pro′to·typ′al** (-tī′pəl), **pro·to·typ′ic** (-tĭp′ĭk), **pro·to·typ′·i·cal** (-ĭ-kəl) *adj.*

ren·o·vate (rĕn′ə-vāt′) *tr.v.* **-vat·ed, -vat·ing, -vates. 1.** To restore to an earlier condition, as by repairing or remodeling. **2.** To impart new vigor to; revive. [Latin *renovāre, renovāt- : re-,* re- + *novāre,* to make new (from *novus,* new; see **newo-** in Appendix).] —**ren′o·va′tion** *n.* —**ren′o·va′tor** *n.*

sur·rep·ti·tious (sûr′əp-tĭsh′əs) *adj.* **1.** Obtained, done, or made by clandestine or stealthy means. **2.** Acting with or marked by stealth. See Synonyms at **secret.** [Middle English, from Latin *surreptīcius,* from *surreptus,* past participle of *surripere,* to take away secretly : *sub-,* secretly; see SUB– + *rapere,* to seize; see **rep-** in Appendix.] —**sur·rep·ti′tious·ly** *adv.* —**sur·rep·ti′tious·ness** *n.*

Words Across the Curriculum

Each college subject has its own **terminology**—words or phrases that have specific meanings within that subject. For example, *depression* is a term used with different meanings in the study of business, psychology, and meteorology. In business it means "a period of low employment, wages, and prices." In psychology, *depression* refers to feelings of hopelessness and inadequacy, and in meteorology it specifies a condition that is associated with low barometric pressure. Sometimes terms are phrases of two or more words. For instance, the phrase *fruits of a crime* is a term used in law and criminology to refer to anything that comes into a criminal's possession as the result of a crime.

Many of the words in the exercises in Chapers 1–15 of *College Vocabulary Skills* are words college students know because they learn them as terminology of college subjects. Some of these terms are listed on page 142.

Since over half of test questions in some college courses directly or indirectly test students' knowledge of terminology, it is extremely important that you identify and learn the terminology in your courses. This chapter explains three methods textbook authors and publishers use to emphasize terminology: printing them in boldface, listing them at the beginning or end of chapters, and defining them in glossaries.

Terms in Boldface

Important terminology in textbooks may be printed in **boldface** or a special color, such as blue. The terms *phoneme* (fō′nēm′) and *morpheme* (môr′fēm′) are printed in boldface in the following excerpt from a psychology textbook.

Phonemes and Morphemes

A **phoneme** is the smallest unit of sound that affects the meaning of speech. Changing a phoneme changes the meaning of a word, much as changing a letter in a printed word changes its meaning. *Tea* has a meaning different from *sea*, and *sight* is different from *sit*. English had twenty-six letters, but it has forty phonemes. The *a* in *cat* and the *a* in *cake*, for example, are different English phonemes.

Although changing a phoneme affects meaning, phonemes themselves are not meaningful. They are combined to form a second level of organiza-

141

Terminology in *College Vocabulary Skills Exercises*

Many of the words introduced in Chapters 1–15 of *College Vocabulary Skills* are terminology of college subjects. Some of these words are listed below.

Natural Sciences	Business and Government	Social Sciences
abiotic	acquit	acrophobia
benign	act of God	adultery
biennial	bigamy	anthropology
biochemistry	bilateral	aphrodisiac
biology	boycott	asocial
biosphere	bureaucracy	claustrophobia
biotic	caveat emptor	deviance
biped	CEO	dysfunctional
carcinogen	constituent	egomania
comatose	CPA	ESP
dilate	dictatorial	genocide
exploratory	edict	heterosexual
geology	GNP	introspection
geophysics	interstate	matriarch
gerontology	laissez faire	megalopolis
gynecology	modus operandi	monogamy
hierarchy	Murphy's Law	monotheism
instinct	nepotism	narcissism
linear	non compos mentis	nomadic
malignant	per capita	nouveau riche
niche	per diem	patriarch
omnivorous	personnel	peer
pathogen	quid pro quo	plaintiff
pathology	remittance	polygamy
phenomena	seniority	polytheism
placebo	sovereign	pseudoscience
prognosis	status quo	psychic
quadruped	totalitarianism	sadism
seismology	unilateral	socioeconomic
Typhoid Mary	verdict	taboo

tion: morphemes. A **morpheme** is the smallest unit of language that has meaning. Word stems like *dog* and *run* are morphemes, but so are prefixes like *un-* and suffixes like *-ed,* because they have meaning even though they cannot stand alone.

The meanings of *phoneme* and *morpheme* are stated in this excerpt from a psychology textbook, and they are also defined in a glossary at the back of the book in which this passage appears.

Lists of Terminology

Important terminology is also sometimes listed at the beginning or end of textbook chapters under a heading such as "Important Words," "Key Concepts," or "Terms Used in This Chapter." When a book has lists of this kind, the words in the lists are usually also defined in a glossary.

Glossaries

Most textbooks have a **glossary,** which is a list of specialized words used in the book and their definitions. It is usually located at the back of a book following the last chapter.

Textbooks also sometimes include little glossaries in margins next to the places where terms are introduced. Figure 16.1 below is an excerpt from a business textbook in which the terms *personal income, disposable income,* and *discretionary income* are printed in boldface and also defined in the margin.

The exercises in this chapter feature glossaries of words for five subject areas.

FIGURE 16.1 **A Marginal Glossary**

Consumer Income

personal income
the income an individual receives from all sources *less* the Social Security taxes the individual must pay

disposable income
personal income *less* all additional personal taxes

discretionary income
disposable income *less* savings and expenditures on food, clothing, and housing

Purchasing power is created by income. However, as every taxpayer knows, not all income is available for spending. For this reason, marketers consider income in three different ways: **Personal income** is the income an individual receives from all sources *less* the Social Security taxes the individual must pay. **Disposable income** is personal income *less* all additional personal taxes. These taxes include income, estate, gift, and property taxes levied by local, state, and federal governments. About 5 percent of all disposable income is saved. **Discretionary income** is disposable income *less* savings and expenditures on food, clothing, and housing. Discretionary income is of particular interest to marketers because consumers have the most choice in spending it. Consumers use their discretionary income to purchase items ranging from automobiles and vacations to movies and pet food.

Psychology and Sociology

Exercise 16.1 on page 145 is about the terminology in this glossary.

alienation (āl'yən-ā'shən) *n.* A feeling of separation or isolation from society brought about by rapid social change, industrialization, and automation.

anxiety (ăng-zī'ə-tē) *n.* Uneasiness or worry about what may happen in the future, accompanied by the feeling of being unable to cope with the future event.

delusion (dĭ-lōo'zhən) *n.* A belief in something that is contrary to reality, such as the belief that one's thoughts are controlled by God or the devil. (Compare with *hallucination.*)

deviance (dē'vē-əns) *n.* Behavior that differs from important social standards and that is, as a result, disapproved by large numbers of people. These behaviors include drug abuse, some sexual behaviors, and serious crimes such as homicide, robbery, rape, aggravated assault, burglary, larceny, auto theft, and arson.

empathy (ĕm'pə-thē) *n.* The ability to share the emotions, thoughts, or feelings of others and to understand their problems from their own points of view.

extrovert (ĕk'strə-vûrt') *n.* A person whose attention is directed outward toward others and the environment rather than inward toward his or her own thoughts and feelings. (Compare with *introvert.*)

hallucination (hə-lōo'sə-nā'shən) *n.* The perception (hearing or seeing) of sights or sounds that are not actually present, such as hearing a voice when no source of a voice is present.

hypochondria (hī'pə-kŏn'drē-ə) *n.* Abnormal anxiety over one's health that sometimes includes experiencing imaginary illnesses.

introvert (ĭn'trə-vûrt') *n.* A person whose thought and interest is turned inward and who is preoccupied with his or her own ideas and feelings. (Compare with *extrovert.*)

masochism (măs'ə-kĭz'əm) *n.* The abnormal behavior of deriving pleasure from experiencing physical or psychological pain.

mores (môr'āz) *pl. n.* Norms that are essential for the survival and welfare of a society, such as the norms that prohibit stealing and murdering. (See *norm.*)

neurosis (nōo-rō'sĭs) *n.* A mental disorder characterized by anxiety, obsessions, phobias, or other abnormal behavior patterns. (See *anxiety* and *obsession.*)

norm (nôrm) *n.* A standard or guideline for behavior that is appropriate in a certain situation, such as the generally accepted standards for behavior in college classrooms. (See *mores.*)

obsession (əb-sĕsh'ən) *n.* Preoccupation with an idea or with an unwanted feeling or desire.

paranoia (păr'ə-noi'ə) *n.* A psychosis characterized by delusions of persecution or grandeur and accompanied by anxiety or anger that sometimes leads to violence. (See *anxiety, delusions,* and *psychosis.*)

psychosis (sī'kō'sĭs) *n.* A major mental disorder characterized by partial or complete withdrawal from reality.

psychosomatic (sī'kō-sō-măt'ĭk) *adj.* Pertaining to physical disorders that originate in or are aggravated by an individual's mental processes.

sanction (săngk'shən) *n.* A reward for conforming to social expectations or a punishment for nonconformity.

sexism (sĕks'ĭz'əm) *n.* The belief that men are superior to women and that, therefore, unequal treatment of women is justified; discrimination against women.

stereotype (stĕr'ē-ə-tīp') *n.* A fixed notion or idea about the characteristics of a person or group, such as the preconceived ideas some people have about the characteristics of football players or mathematicians.

EXERCISE 16.1   Psychology and Sociology

The following questions are about the words in the glossary on page 144.

Matching   Match the words on the left with their meanings by writing the letters *a* through *e* on the lines.

_____   1. anxiety   a. feeling of isolation

_____   2. mores   b. worry about one's health

_____   3. norm   c. worry and uneasiness

_____   4. alienation   d. essential guidelines

_____   5. hypochondria   e. standards for behavior

True-False   Write **T** for true statements and **F** for false statements.

_____   6. Auto theft is not an example of **deviance.**

_____   7. If somebody told you that she had seen Elvis Presley, you might infer that she had experienced a **hallucination.**

_____   8. A **sanction** is always a punishment.

_____   9. People suffering from a **neurosis** are likely to experience a **delusion** or **hallucination.**

_____   10. A **psychosomatic** illness exists in the mind and is not a true physical disorder.

Fill-in   Write the words that are missing from the following statements.

11. _____ includes the belief that unequal treatment of women is justified.

12. A _____ is a preconceived notion about a person or group, such as the idea that all football players are stupid.

13. _____ is the ability to understand the problems of others from their own points of view.

14. _____ is the deriving of pleasure from experiencing pain.

15. An _____ is a preoccupation with an unwanted idea, feeling, or desire.

Business and Economics

Exercise 16.2 on page 147 is about the terminology is this glossary.

actuary (ăk′chōō-ĕr′ē) *n.* A mathematician who calculates insurance premiums.

arbitration (är′bə-trā′shən) *n.* The settlement of a dispute by a neutral third party who hears both sides and comes to a decision.

barter (bärt′ər) *v.* To trade goods or services for other goods or services without using money.

cartel (kär-tĕl′) *n.* An association of business-people or firms for the purpose of obtaining a monopoly over the sale of a product. (See *monopoly.*)

collateral (kə-lăt′ər-əl) *n.* Property that is pledged as security for a loan.

commodity (kə-mŏd′ə-tē) *n.* Any product that is bought and sold.

compensation (kŏm′pən-sā′shən) *n.* Payment given to employees for service or labor.

depreciation (dĭ-prē′shē-ā′shən) *n.* A decline in the value of property (such as machinery) due to wear, use, or other cause.

embargo (ĕm-bär′gō) *n.* A governmental restriction on trade with a foreign country.

entrepreneur (än′trə-prə-nûr′) *n.* A person who assumes the risks of starting and operating a business for the possibility of economic gain.

legal tender (lē′gəl tĕn′dər) *n.* Money that a government specifies must be accepted by a creditor in payment for a debt.

liability (lī′ə-bĭl′ə-tē) *n.* Debts or financial obligations.

mediation (mē′dē-ā′shən) *n.* The use of a neutral third party to assist in the settlement of a dispute.

monopoly (mə-nŏp′ə-lē) *n.* The exclusive control of the production or sale of a product or service.

recruitment (rĭ-krōot′mənt) *n.* Pro- cedures used by a firm or organization to attract qualified job applicants.

retailer (rē′-tāl′ər) *n.* A business that sells products directly to consumers.

subsidy (sŭb′sə-dē) *n.* Financial as sistance granted by a government to an individual, business, city, state, or other governmental entity.

syndicate (sĭn′dĭ-kĭt) *n.* An association of people or firms organized to carry out a financial project that requires a great deal of capital.

tycoon (tī-kōon′) *n.* A wealthy and powerful businessperson, industrialist, or financier.

usury (yōo′zhər-ē) *n.* The practice of lending money at an excessively or unlawfully high rate of interest.

EXERCISE 16.2   Business and Economics

The following questions are about the words in the glossary on page 146.

Matching   Match the words on the left with their meanings by writing the letters *a* through *e* on the lines.

_____	1. collateral	a.	dispute settlement
_____	2. compensation	b.	financial assistance
_____	3. mediation	c.	payment for services
_____	4. subsidy	d.	excessively high interest
_____	5. usury	e.	loan security

True-False   Write **T** for true statements and **F** for false statements.

_____   6. It is possible to **barter** milk and butter for the services of a dentist.

_____   7. Stocks and bonds are **legal tender** in the United States of America.

_____   8. Jeans, popcorn, magazines, and automobiles are examples of **commodities.**

_____   9. The placement of advertisements of job openings in newspapers is one method of **recruitment.**

_____   10. An **actuary** is a person who analyzes the actual profit earned by a corporation or firm.

Fill-in   Write the words that are missing from the following statements.

11. A _____ is an association of people or firms that carries out a costly financial project.

12. A _____ is an association organized to secure a monopoly over the sale of a product.

13. A _____ is the exclusive control of the production or sale of a product or service.

14. A _____ is a wealthy and powerful businessperson.

15. A _____ sells products directly to consumers.

Language and Literature

Exercise 16.3 on page 149 is about the terminology is this glossary.

acronym (ăk′rə-nĭm) *n.* A word made from the initial letters of other words. *Scuba* is an acronym made from the first letters of the following words: s(elf)-c(ontained) u(nderwater) b(reathing) a(pparatus).

cliché (klē-shā′) *n.* An overused expression or phrase, such as "blushing bride," "clear as day," and "quick as a flash."

connotation (kŏn′ə-tā′shən) *n.* An idea or notion associated with or suggested by a word. *Mother*, which means "female parent," suggests love, care, and tenderness. (Compare with *denotation*.)

denotation (dē′nō-tā′shən) *n.* The direct meaning or reference of a word. *Mother* means "female parent." (Compare with *connotation*.)

euphemism (yōō′fə-mĭz′əm) *n.* Words or phrases that are substituted for those that are considered to be distasteful or offensive. "Passed away" and "departed this life" are euphemisms for *died*.

exposition (ĕk′spə-zĭsh′ən) *n.* Writing or speech that gives explanations or that states facts or ideas. Dictionaries, cookbooks, and psychology textbooks are examples of exposition. (Compare with *narration*.)

fallacy (făl′ə-sē) *n.* A false or mis taken idea based on inaccurate knowledge or incorrect reasoning.

figure of speech (fĭg′yər əv spēch) *n.* An expression that is meant to be interpreted poetically rather than literally. (See *metaphor*, *personification*, and *simile*.)

genre (zhän′rə) *n.* A kind or type of work of art, such as novel, science fiction, or melodrama.

irony (ī′rə-nē) *n.* A form of humor or sarcasm in which the intended meaning of words is the opposite of their literal meaning, such as calling a stupid action *clever*.

jargon (jär′gən) *n.* Writing or speech that is difficult to understand because it contains many unfamiliar words, or the technical vocabulary of those in the same work or profession.

metaphor (mĕt′ə-fôr′) *n.* A figure of speech that compares two unlike things without using the word *like* or *as*. "All the world's a stage" and "Her mind is a computer" are examples of metaphors. (See *figure of speech*, and compare with *simile*.)

narration (nă-rā′shən) *n.* The telling of an event, a series of events, or a story. (Compare with *exposition*.)

onomatopoeia (ŏn′ə-măt′ə-pē′ə) *n.* The formation of a word by imitating a sound, such as *buzz* and *meow*.

paraphrase (păr′ə-frāz′) *n.* Restatement of writing or speech that keeps the meaning of the original but expresses it in different words.

personification (pər-sŏn′ə-fĭ-kā′shən) *n.* A figure of speech in which things that are not people or animals are described as having characteristics of human or animal life. "The waves licked the shore" and "The wind roared" are examples of personification. (See *figure of speech*.)

plagiarism (plā′jə-rĭz′əm) *n.* The act of taking the words or ideas of another and passing them off as one's own.

redundancy (rĭ-dŭn′dən-sē) *n.* The use of words that are unnecessary to the meaning, such as "same exact," "freedom and liberty," and "afternoon matinee."

simile (sĭm′ə-lē′) *n.* A figure of speech that compares two unlike things using the word *like* or *as*. "The world is *like* a stage" and "Her mind is quick *as* a computer" are similes. (See *figure of speech*, and compare with *metaphor*.)

spoonerism (spōō′nə-rĭz′əm) *n.* The unintentional transposition of sounds in two or more words, such as "Is the bean dizzy?" for "Is the dean busy?"

EXERCISE 16.3 Language and Literature

The following questions are about the words in the glossary on page 148.

Matching Match the words on the left with the correct examples by writing the letters *a* through *e* on the lines.

_____ 1. euphemism   a. moo and cock-a-doodle-do

_____ 2. metaphor   b. Flames ate the house.

_____ 3. onomatopoeia   c. a heart as big as the world

_____ 4. personification d. a sanitation engineer

_____ 5. simile   e. the curtain of night

True-False Write **T** for true statements and **F** for false statements.

_____ 6. "It is kisstomary to cuss the bride" is an example of a **spoonerism.**

_____ 7. Memorandums sent between computer specialists are not likely to contain **jargon.**

_____ 8. The **denotation** of *acronym* is "scuba."

_____ 9. Exposition and narration are **figures of speech.**

_____ 10. "Blind as a bat" and "as poor as church mice" are **clichés.**

Fill-in Write the words that are missing from the following statements.

11. _____ is the offering of the words or ideas of another as one's own.

12. A _____ is a restatement of writing or speech.

13. A _____ is a story.

14. A _____ is an idea or notion associated with a word.

15. _____ is the use of more words than are needed.

Law and Government

Exercise 16.4 on page 151 is about the terminology is this glossary.

allege (ə-lĕj′) *v.* To assert, declare, or affirm without providing supporting proof.

capital punishment (kăp′ə-təl pŭn′-ĭsh-mənt) *n.* The penalty of death for committing a crime.

conservative (kən-sûr′və-tĭv) *adj.* Tends to oppose change in society. (Compare with *liberal.*)

demagogue (dĕm′ə-gŏg′) *n.* A political leader who wins and holds power by appealing to the emotions and prejudices of the common people.

extradition (ĕk′strə-dĭsh′ən) *n.* The legal procedure by which a government surrenders a person accused of a crime to another state, country, or government so the person can stand trial.

felony (fĕl′ə-nē) *n.* A crime such as murder, rape, or arson that is punishable by imprisonment of one year or more in a state or federal penitentiary or by death. (Compare with *misdemeanor.*)

ideology (ī′dē-ŏl′ə-jē) *n.* The ideas and beliefs on which a political, economic, or social system is based.

incumbent (ĭn-kŭm′bənt) *n.* A person who holds a political office.

indict (ĭn-dīt′) *v.* Formally to accuse a person of a crime after the charges have been investigated.

larceny (lär′sə-nē) *n.* The act of taking another person's property without permission and with the intention of permanently depriving the owner of it.

left wing (lĕft wĭng) *n.* The more liberal or radical section of a political party. (See *liberal, radical,* and *right wing.*)

liberal (lĭb′rəl) *adj.* Open to ideas that challenge tradition and established institutions.

lobby (lŏb′ē) *n.* A group that tries to influence legislation and governmental decisions on behalf of a special interest group, such as the automobile industry.

misdemeanor (mĭs′dĭ-mē′nər) *n.* A minor crime that is punished by fine or imprisonment for a short time in a local jail or workhouse. (Compare with *felony.*)

patronage (pā′trə-nĭj) *n.* The power of a government official to appoint to office, give employment, and offer other favors.

plaintiff (plān′tĭf) *n.* One who, claiming a wrong has been done, institutes a law suit in a court.

radical (răd′ĭ-kəl) *adj.* Demanding substantial or extreme changes in an existing political system.

reactionary (rē-ăk′shə-nĕr′ē) *adj.* Opposing progress and liberalism, resisting change in the existing political system, and promoting return to an earlier social order.

recidivism (rĕ-sĭd′ə-vĭz′əm) *n.* The tendency for a criminal to return to crime or antisocial behavior.

right wing (rīt wĭng) *n.* The more conservative or reactionary section of a political party. (See *conservative* and *reactionary,* and compare with *left wing.*)

EXERCISE 16.4 **Law and Government**

The following questions are about the words in the glossary on page 150.

Matching Match the words on the left with their meanings by writing the letters *a* through *e* on the lines.

_____ 1. conservative   a. demanding political change

_____ 2. liberal   b. liberal or radical

_____ 3. radical   c. opposing social change

_____ 4. right wing   d. favoring social change

_____ 5. left wing   e. conservative or reactionary

True-False Write **T** for true statements and **F** for false statements.

_____ 6. **Capital punishment** is administered by hanging, electrocution, and lethal injection.

_____ 7. A dictator cannot also be a **demagogue.**

_____ 8. The current governor of the state in which you live is the **incumbent** in that office.

_____ 9. To **allege** that a person committed a crime is to find the person guilty of the crime.

_____ 10. A **felony** may be punished by death.

Fill-in Write the words that are missing from the following statements.

11. To _____ is formally to accuse a person of a crime.

12. _____ is the legal term for stealing and thievery.

13. _____ is the tendency for imprisoned people to return to crime when they are released from prison.

14. A _____ is a crime that is not as serious as a felony.

15. A _____ is a party that institutes a suit in a court.

Natural Sciences

Exercise 16.5 on page 153 is about the terminology is this glossary.

acoustics (ə-kōō′stĭks) *n.* The branch of physics dealing with the transmission of sound.

biosphere (bī′ə-sfîr′) *n.* The soil, air, and water at or near the surface of the planet Earth in which all life naturally occurs.

carcinogen (kär-sĭn′ə-jən) *n.* A substance that causes cancer.

congenital (kən-jĕn′ə-təl) *adj.* Pertaining to a disease or condition that is present at birth but that is not hereditary. (See *heredity.*)

decibel (dĕs′ĭ-bəl) *n.* A unit for measuring the loudness of sound.

ecosystem (ĕk′ō-sĭs′təm) *n.* Animals, plants, and other living organisms and the environment in which they live, such as deserts, plains, lakes, and swamps.

embryo (ĕm′brē-ō) *n.* A developing plant or animal at the earliest stages of development—in humans the stage from conception to about the eighth week of development. (See *fetus.*)

fauna (fô′nə) *n.* Animals, especially the animals of a particular place or time. (Compare with *flora.*)

fetus (fē′təs) *n.* The unborn young of an animal that bears young alive rather than laying eggs. In humans the embryo is called a fetus beginning about eight weeks after conception, when major body parts have formed.

flora (flôr′ə) *n.* Plants, especially the plants of a particular place or time. (Compare with *fauna.*)

habitat (hăb′ə-tăt′) *n.* An area or environment in which a specific plant or animal generally lives.

heredity (hə-rĕd′ə-tē) *n.* The passing of characteristics from parent to offspring and the tendency of offspring to resemble parents.

horticulture (hôr′tə-kŭl′chər) *n.* The science of growing and developing garden plants.

hypothesis (hī-pŏth′ə-sĭs) *n.* A tentative explanation used as a basis for investigation.

mean (mēn) *n.* The average, found by adding numbers together and dividing the sum by the total number of numbers. The mean of 4, 6, and 8 is found by adding the numbers (18) and dividing the sum by the total number of numbers (3); the mean is 6. (Compare with *median* and *mode.*)

median (mē′dē-ən) *n.* The middle number in a series of numbers—it has the same number of numbers above and below it. The median of the following numbers is 12: 3, 3, 4, *12*, 14, 20, 22. (Compare with *mean* and *mode.*)

meteorology (mē′tē-ə-rŏl′ə-jē) *n.* The scientific study of weather and weather conditions.

mode (mōd) *n.* The number that occurs most frequently in a series of numbers. The mode of the following series is 9: 2, 4, 9, 9, 9, 24. (Compare with *mean* and *median.*)

syndrome (sĭn′drōm′) *n.* Several symptoms that occur together and that are characteristic of a specific disease or condition.

theory (thîr′ē) *n.* A more or less verified or established explanation offered to account for known facts or phenomena, such as the theory of evolution, which accounts for the origin of living things.

154

<u>**EXERCISE 16.5**</u>   **Natural Sciences**

The following questions are about the words

Matching   Match the words on the left with their ·
letters *a* through *e* on the lines.

_____   1. fauna   a. science of growing plants

_____   2. acoustics   b. plants in a particular place

_____   3. meteorology   c. science of sound transmission

_____   4. horticulture   d. animals in a particular place

_____   5. flora   e. science of weather conditions

True-False   Write **T** for true statements and **F** for false statements.

_____   6. The **biosphere** is the natural habitat for all living things.

_____   7. A **carcinogen** is a cure for benign forms of cancer.

_____   8. An unborn human is called a **fetus** from conception until about
               the eighth week of development.

_____   9. The **mean** of 8, 4, and 15 is 9.

_____ 10. The **median** of 8, 4, and 15 is 4.

Fill-in   Write the words that are missing from the following statements.

11. A _____ is a unit for measuring the loudness of sound.

12. _____ accounts for the tendency for offspring to resemble
     their parents.

13. A _____ is an explanation to account for known facts for
     which no certain explanation is available.

14. A _____ is a tentative explanation used as the basis for
     investigation.

15. A _____ condition exists at birth but is not hereditary.

Unit Four Review

REVIEW 4.1 **Basic Word List**

Your instructor may give you a test on the meanings of these words. If so, learn the meanings of any of the words that you do not know. The words are followed by the exercise numbers in which they are introduced.

1. abridge, 15.1
2. ambiguous, 15.1
3. blatant, 15.1
4. compose, 15.1
5. convention, 15.1
6. depict, 15.1
7. embrace, 15.1
8. immerse, 15.2
9. mercenary, 15.2
10. orientation, 15.3
11. representative, 15.3
12. reserved, 15.3
13. speculate, 15.3
14. amicable, 15.4
15. callous, 15.4
16. euphoria, 15.4
17. flagrant, 15.4
18. gregarious, 15.5
19. idiosyncrasy, 15.5
20. renovate, 15.5
21. delusion, 16.1
22. extrovert, 16.1
23. hallucination, 16.1
24. introvert, 16.1
25. masochism, 16.1
26. norm, 16.1
27. obsession, 16.1
28. barter, 16.2
29. collateral, 16.2
30. commodity, 16.2
31. compensation, 16.2
32. entrepreneur, 16.2
33. mediation, 16.2
34. retailer, 16.2
35. cliché, 16.3
36. connotation, 16.3
37. denotation, 16.3
38. exposition, 16.3
39. irony, 16.3
40. paraphrase, 16.3
41. plagiarism, 16.3
42. allege, 16.4
43. felony, 16.4
44. ideology, 16.4
45. indict, 16.4
46. left wing, 16.4
47. misdemeanor, 16.4
48. right wing, 16.4
49. biosphere, 16.5
50. ecosystem, 16.5
51. embryo, 16.5
52. heredity, 16.5
53. hypothesis, 16.5
54. meteorology, 16.5
55. theory, 16.5

REVIEW 4.2 **Advanced Word List**

Your instructor may give you a test on the meanings of these words. If so, learn the meanings of any of the words that you do not know. The words are followed by the numbers of the exercises in which they are introduced.

1. dynamic, 15.1
2. generic, 15.1
3. hierarchy, 15.2
4. latitude, 15.2
5. levity, 15.2
6. magnetism, 15.2
7. manipulate, 15.2
8. niche, 15.2
9. omnivorous, 15.2
10. placebo, 15.3

11. preoccupied, 15.3
12. qualified, 15.3
13. spurious, 15.3
14. choreography, 15.4
15. deft, 15.4
16. imperturbable, 15.5
17. infallible, 15.5
18. innocuous, 15.5
19. nostalgia, 15.5
20. prototype, 15.5
21. surreptitious, 15.5
22. alienation, 16.1
23. deviance, 16.1
24. empathy, 16.1
25. mores, 16.1
26. sanction, 16.1
27. sexism, 16.1
28. stereotype, 16.1
29. actuary, 16.2
30. arbitration, 16.2
31. cartel, 16.2
32. recruitment, 16.2
33. subsidy, 16.2
34. tycoon, 16.2
35. usury, 16.2
36. acronym, 16.3
37. euphemism, 16.3
38. metaphor, 16.3
39. onomatopoeia, 16.3
40. redundancy, 16.3
41. simile, 16.3
42. spoonerism, 16.3
43. demagogue, 16.4
44. extradition, 16.4
45. incumbent, 16.4
46. patronage, 16.4
47. radical, 16.4
48. reactionary, 16.4
49. carcinogen, 16.5
50. congenital, 16.5
51. fauna, 16.5
52. fetus, 16.5
53. flora, 16.5
54. horticulture, 16.5
55. syndrome, 16.5

___REVIEW 4.3___ Sentence Completion

Complete the following sentences using words that make it clear that you know the meanings of the words that are printed in **boldface.**

1. I took a photograph that **depicts** _my mother sitting on my father's lap._

2. It was **callous** of him to _____

3. One of her **idiosyncrasies** is _____

4. My favorite **retailer** _____

5. It is my **theory** that _____

6. In a moment of **levity** she _____

7. The most interesting thing about the **choreography** was _____

_____

8. One common **stereotype** is _____

_____

9. Local **fauna** includes _____

_____

10. Those interested in **horticulture** _____

_____

REVIEW 4.4   Writing Applications

Your instructor may assign one or more of the following writing activities.

1. Write six sentences, each of which includes a word from the Basic Word List on page 154 or the Advanced Word List on pages 154–155. Underline the six words in your sentences.

2. Write six sentences, each of which includes one of the following words specified by your instructor. Underline the six words in your sentences.

   a. _____   d. _____

   b. _____   e. _____

   c. _____   f. _____

3. Write a paragraph on a topic of your choice using six of the words from the Basic Word List on page 154 or the Advanced Word List on pages 154–155. Underline the six words in your paragraph.

4. Write a paragraph on a topic of your choice which includes the following six words specified by your instructor. Underline the six words in your paragraph.

   a. _____   d. _____

   b. _____   e. _____

   c. _____   f. _____

5. Tell about a time when you experienced **euphoria** while at an amusement park or playing a game.

6. Describe the most **amicable** person you know.

7. Explain whether you believe you are an **introvert** or an **extrovert.**

8. Relate an instance when you had an accident because you were **preoccupied.**

9. Describe a time that you experienced **nostalgia.**

10. Give two of the **euphemisms** for "May I use your toilet?"

REVIEW 4.5   **Fill-in Questions**

Write on the lines the words that are missing from the following definitions of terminology that are introduced in Chapters 15 and 16.

1. A _____ is a statement of the meaning of a word.

2. _____ are words that have the same or nearly the same meaning, such as *happy* and *glad.*

3. In dictionary entries, _____ are phrases or sentences that illustrate the ways words are used.

4. The _____ of a subject is the words or phrases that are used with specific meanings when the subject is discussed.

5. A _____ is a list at the end of a textbook that states definitions of terminology.

REVIEW 4.6   **Short-Answer Questions**

Refer to Chapters 15 and 16 to write the answers to the following questions.

1. What are three methods dictionaries use to explain the meanings of words?

a. _____

b. _____

c. _____

2. Describe two types of words that are frequently not defined in standard desk dictionaries.

_____

_____

_____

_____

_____

_____

3. Why is it important for students to learn the terminology of their college subjects?

   _____

   _____

   _____

4. What are the three methods textbooks frequently use to emphasize important terminology?

   a. _____

   b. _____

   c. _____

Use Words Precisely

Learning Goals for Unit Five

In studying Chapters 17, 18, and 19 you will learn:

- How to locate the words you need to express your thoughts accurately and precisely (Chapters 17, 18, and 19).

- How to use a thesaurus or a dictionary to locate synonyms (Chapter 17).

- How to avoid confusing words which are pronounced alike, such as *cite* and *site* (Chapter 18).

- How to avoid confusing words which are pronounced similarly, such as *affect* and *effect* (Chapter 18).

- How to use a dictionary to determine appropriate word usages when writing serious papers for college credit (Chapter 19).

Synonyms

Synonyms are words that have the same or nearly the same meaning. For example, synonyms of *big* include *large, huge, enormous, monumental, gigantic, immense,* and *colossal.* You probably know all of these words, but chances are that when you speak and write you use *big, large,* and *huge* rather than other synonyms of *big.*

Most college students use only a small portion of the words they know when they express their thoughts in writing. If you analyze papers you have written for your college courses, you are likely to discover that you often use common words such as *big, happy,* and *poor* when you could have expressed your thoughts better by using synonyms of these words, such as *immense, elated,* and *impoverished.* This chapter explains the characteristics of synonyms and how to locate them in a thesaurus or dictionary.

Characteristics of Synonyms

Synonyms have two characteristics that you must understand in order to use appropriate ones in papers you write for college credit.

First, most synonyms have similar meanings in only one of their senses. For example, *bright* and *smart* are synonyms when they are used to describe intelligent people.

> He is a *bright* person.
> She is a *smart* person.

Bright and *smart* may be used interchangeably to mean "intelligent," but they have other meanings that they do not share. *Bright* may mean "shining with light," but *smart* does not have this meaning.

> He wears sunglasses on *bright* days.

Smart may not be used interchangeably with *bright* in this sentence. On the other hand, *smart* may mean "stylish," but *bright* does not.

> She wore a *smart* outfit to the party.

Bright may not be used interchangeably with *smart* in this sentence.

Second, synonyms often have shades of meaning in addition to the meaning they share that makes them synonyms. For instance, *blame* and *denounce* are synonyms that refer to the act of making an unfavorable judgment. However, to *blame* is to fix the responsibility for an error, while to *denounce* is to state intense disapproval publicly.

If you received an advertisement in your mailbox that should have been delivered to a neighbor, you may blame the mail carrier. You may fix the responsibility for the mistake on this postal employee, but you are not likely to denounce the mail carrier for this trivial error. On the other hand, if elected officials are found guilty of stealing taxpayers' money, they are denounced—severely criticized in public—and probably thrown out of office. *Blame* does not convey the unfavorable judgment that elected officials receive when they betray the trust of those who elected them.

Keeping these characteristics of synonyms in mind will help you avoid problems in selecting and using them.

Synonyms in a Thesaurus

A **thesaurus** (thĭ-sôr′əs) is a book that lists synonyms. I especially recommend *The Random House Thesaurus* (1984), from which the following entry is taken.

> **enormous** *adj. The banquet was held in an enormous room:* huge, vast, immense, tremendous, colossal, gigantic, mammoth, gargantuan, Brobdingnagian, titanic, elephantine; massive, prodigious. **Ant.** small, little, tiny, minute, minuscule, Lilliputian, diminutive, trivial, insignificant, meager, midget, dwarf, peewee, itty-bitty, teeny, *(fem.)* petite.

This entry begins with a sentence that shows how *enormous* is used, and it lists thirteen synonyms for the word. The abbreviation *Ant.* stands for *antonym.* An **antonym** (ăn′tə-nĭm′) is a word that is opposite in meaning to another word—*small, little,* and *tiny* are some antonyms of *enormous.*

A thesaurus does not give definitions. If you want to know the exact meanings of synonyms listed in a thesaurus entry, you must locate them in a dictionary.

Synonyms in a Dictionary

A dictionary entry may use a synonym to explain the meaning of a word or include a cross-reference to a discussion of synonyms, as in the following entry for *huge.*

> **huge** (hyōōj) *adj.* **hug·er, hug·est. 1.** Of exceedingly great size, extent, or quantity; tremendous. See Synonyms at **enormous. 2.** Of exceedingly great scope or nature: *the huge influence of the Hellenic world.* [Middle English, from Old French *ahuge.*] **—huge′ly** *adv.* **—huge′ness** *n.*

This entry gives *tremendous* as a synonym of *huge* and the phrase "See Synonyms at **enormous**" is a cross-reference to a discussion of synonyms.

e·nor·mous (ĭ-nôr′məs) *adj.* **1.** Very great in size, extent, number, or degree. **2.** *Archaic.* Very wicked; heinous. [From Latin *ēnormis,* unusual, huge : *ē-, ex-,* ex- + *norma,* norm; see **gnō-** in Appendix. Sense 2, from Middle English *enormious,* from Latin *ēnormis,* monstrous.] **—e·nor′mous·ly** *adv.* **—e·nor′- mous·ness** *n.*

SYNONYMS: *enormous, immense, huge, gigantic, colossal, mammoth, tremendous, stupendous, gargantuan, vast.* These adjectives describe what is extraordinarily large. *Enormous* suggests a marked excess beyond the norm in size, amount, or degree: *an enormous boulder; enormous expenses. Immense* refers to boundless or immeasurable size or extent: *an immense crowd of people; immense pleasure. Huge* especially implies greatness of size or capacity: *a huge wave; a huge success. Gigantic* refers to size likened to that of a giant: *a gigantic redwood tree; a gigantic disappointment. Colossal* suggests a hugeness that elicits awe or taxes belief: *colossal crumbling ruins of an ancient temple; has a colossal nerve. Mammoth* is applied to something of clumsy or unwieldy hugeness: *a mammoth ship; a mammoth multinational corporation. Tremendous* suggests awe-inspiring or fearsome size: *a tremendous monument 100 feet high; ate a tremendous meal. Stupendous* implies size that astounds or defies description: *an undertaking of stupendous difficulty.* "The whole thing was a stupendous, incomprehensible farce" (W. Somerset Maugham). *Gargantuan* especially stresses greatness of capacity, as for food or pleasure: *a gargantuan appetite. Vast* refers to greatness of extent, size, area, or scope: "All the land was shrouded in one vast forest" (Theodore Roosevelt). "Of creatures, how few vast as the whale" (Herman Melville).

This entry for *enormous* is followed by a discussion of adjectives that "describe what is extraordinarily large." Study the discussion of synonyms to complete the following sentences using *gigantic, mammoth,* and *vast.*

1. The universe is _____.

2. Some dinosaurs were _____.

3. I ate a _____ baked potato.

If you wrote *vast, mammoth,* and *gigantic,* you made good choices.

    The following exercises provide practice locating synonyms in a thesaurus and a dictionary.

EXERCISE 17.1   Synonyms in a Thesaurus

Use the following thesaurus entries to answer the questions in this exercise.

old *adj.* **1.** *She's forty years old:* of age. **2.** *Father's an old man now. What an old car!:* elderly, aged, hoary, grizzled, gray-headed, gray with age, white with age, venerable; antiquated, ancient, vintage, timeworn, age-old, antique, old-fashioned, out-of-date, outdated, archaic, obsolete, obsolescent. **3.** *She and I are old friends. Do you remember the good old days?:* of long standing, long established, time-honored, traditional, age-old, of the past, from the past, of yore, bygone. **4.** *This old coat doesn't fit any more. That's an old joke:* worn-out, outworn, decrepit, dilapidated, used, much-used, timeworn, weathered, *Slang* beat-up; weatherbeaten, deteriorated, battered, ramshackle, crumbling, tumbledown, rundown, broken-down; familiar, hackneyed.

new *adj.* **1.** *Did you see Sam's new car?:* recently acquired, of recent make, brand-new, just out, spanking new, up-to-date, modern, current, up-to-the-minute, newly or lately issued, *Informal* newfangled; novel, original, late, fresh, recent. **2.** *We have several new clerks this week:* untried, unseasoned, unessayed, unaccustomed, unfamiliar; unused, unexercised, unventured; uncharted, unexplored; remote, out-of-the-way; untouched, ungathered, uncollected, *Informal* green, wet behind the ears. **3.** *He says he feels like a new man:* restored, reinvigorated, renewed, renovated, revivified, reborn, re-created, regenerated, refreshed; fixed, repaired; rebuilt, reconstructed, remodeled; resumed, reopened; changed, altered.

1. Select two synonyms for **old** that describe people who are eighty years old.

   _____   _____

2. Select two synonyms for **old** that describe horse-drawn carriages in which tourists ride through city parks.

   _____   _____

3. Select two synonyms for **old** that describe ethical teachings written hundreds of years ago.

   _____   _____

4. Select two synonyms for **old** that describe a house that has not been cared for or lived in for twenty years.

   _____   _____

5. Select two synonyms for **new** that describe clothing styles that were not available until yesterday.

   _____   _____

6. Select two synonyms for **new** that describe police officers on their first day on the job.

   _____   _____

7. Select two synonyms for **new** that describe the way people feel after a refreshing three-week vacation.

   _____   _____

8. Select two synonyms for **new** that describe an old house that has been modernized.

   _____   _____

EXERCISE 17.2   Synonyms in a Thesaurus

Use the following thesaurus entries to answer the questions in this exercise.

like[2] *v.* **1.** *Most children like music:* enjoy, take pleasure in, find agreeable, relish, fancy, be partial to, dote, savor, relish. **2.** *The students like the new dean:* esteem, admire, find agreeable, have a friendly feeling for, be partial to, be fond of, fancy, approve, endorse; favor, support; *Informal* take a shine to, have a crush on. **3.** *Would you like to join us?:* care, think fit, feel inclined, wish, have a mind, choose. —*n.* **4. likes** *Everyone has different likes and dislikes:* partialities, favorites, inclinations, prejudices. preferences.

hate *v.* **1.** *Those girls have hated each other since high school. I hate mice!:* dislike, despise, detest, abhor, loathe, abominate, execrate, hold in contempt, bear malice toward, be hostile to, not be able to bear, have no use for, recoil from, shrink from, be repelled by, be sick of, be tired of, give one a pain, give one a pain in the neck. **2.** *Mother hated to move from such a nice neighborhood:* be sorry, be reluctant, be unwilling, feel disinclined to, be averse to, shrink from, not care to, would rather not, not have the heart to, dread, wish to avoid, feel sick at, have no taste for, have no stomach for, wince at, regard as distasteful. —*n.* **3.** *Never trust a man who is full of hate:* hatred, dislike, distaste, disliking, aversion, loathing, repugnance, abomination, abhorrence; enmity, hostility, detestation, rancor, malice, antipathy, animosity, animus, venom, malevolence, resentment, vindictiveness, revengefulness, acrimony.

1. Select two synonyms for **like** in the sentence "She *likes* peaches, strawberries, and other fresh fruit."

   _____   _____

2. Select two synonyms for **like** in the sentence "He *likes* several well-known athletes."

   _____   _____

3. Select two synonyms for **like** in the sentence "She *likes* the boy who lives next door."

   _____   _____

4. Select two synonyms for **like** in the sentence "I would *like* to go to a movie."

   _____   _____

5. Select two synonyms for **hate** in the sentence "She *hates* parents who abuse their children."

   _____   _____

6. Select two synonyms for **hate** in the sentence "He *hates* to be served bloody meat."

   _____   _____

7. Select two synonyms for **hate** in the sentence "We *hated* to be out of town while Mother was ill."

   _____   _____

8. Select two synonyms for **hate** in the sentence "*Hate* in his heart caused him to go on a killing spree."

   _____   _____

EXERCISE 17.3   Synonyms in a Dictionary

Use the following discussions of synonyms to match sentences *1* through *4* with words *a* through *d*, and sentences *5* through *8* with words *e* through *h*.

fan·tas·tic (făn-tăs′tĭk) also **fan·tas·ti·cal** (-tĭ-kəl) *adj.* **1.** Quaint or strange in form, conception, or appearance. **2.a.** Unrestrainedly fanciful; extravagant: *fantastic hopes.* **b.** Bizarre, as in form or appearance; strange: *fantastic attire; fantastic behavior.* **c.** Based on or existing only in fantasy; unreal. **3.** Wonderful or superb; remarkable: *a fantastic trip to Europe.* [Middle English *fantastik,* imagined, from Old French *fantastique,* from Late Latin *phantasticus,* imaginary, from Greek *phantastikos,* able to create mental images, from *phantazesthai,* to appear. See FANTASY.] **—fan·tas′ti·cal′i·ty** (-tĭ-kăl′ĭ-tē) *n.* **—fan·tas′ti·cal·ly** *adv.* **—fan·tas′ti·cal·ness** *n.*

SYNONYMS: *fantastic, bizarre, grotesque, fanciful, exotic.* These adjectives apply to what is very strange or strikingly unusual. *Fantastic* in this comparison describes what seems to have slight relation to the real world because of its strangeness or extravagance: *fantastic imaginary beasts such as the unicorn. Bizarre* stresses oddness of character or appearance that is heightened by striking contrasts and incongruities and that shocks or fascinates: *a bizarre art nouveau façade. Grotesque* refers principally to appearance or aspect in which deformity and distortion approach the point of caricature or even absurdity: *rainspouts terminating in gargoyles and other grotesque creatures. Fanciful* applies to a character, nature, or design strongly influenced by imagination, caprice, or whimsy: *a fanciful pattern with intertwined vines and flowers.* Something *exotic* is unusual and intriguing in appearance or effect: *exotic birds.*

triv·i·al (trĭv′ē-əl) *adj.* **1.** Of little significance or value. **2.** Ordinary; commonplace. **3.** Concerned with or involving trivia. **4.** *Biology.* Relating to or designating a species; specific. **5.** *Mathematics.* **a.** Of, relating to, or being the solution of an equation in which every variable is equal to zero. **b.** Of, relating to, or being the simplest possible case; self-evident. [Middle English *trivialle,* of the trivium (from Medieval Latin *triviālis,* from *trivium,* trivium; see TRIVIUM) and Latin *triviālis,* ordinary (from *trivium,* crossroads).] **—triv′i·al·ly** *adv.*

SYNONYMS: *trivial, trifling, paltry, petty, picayune.* These adjectives all apply to what is small and unimportant. *Trivial* refers principally to what is so insignificant as to be utterly commonplace or unremarkable: *"I think all Christians . . . agree in the essential articles, and that their differences are trivial, and rather political than religious"* (Samuel Johnson). Something *trifling* is so unimportant or so small as to be scarcely worth notice: *"I regret the trifling narrow contracted education of the females of my own country"* (Abigail Adams). *Paltry* especially describes what falls so far short of what is required or desired that it arouses contempt: *"He . . . considered the prize too paltry for the lives it must cost"* (John Lothrop Motley). *Petty* can refer to what is of minor or secondary significance or size; the term can suggest meanness of spirit: *"Our knights are limited to petty enterprises"* (Sir Walter Scott). *"Always give your best, never get discouraged, never be petty"* (Richard M. Nixon). What is *picayune* is of negligible value or importance: *Giving a police officer a free meal may be against the law, but it seems to be a picayune infraction.*

_____ 1. A black, windowless, fifty-story building would be

_____ 2. A restaurant decorated with a waterfall, a stream, and trees to recreate a forest setting would be

_____ 3. Those who have never traveled down the Amazon River in a banana boat may find the experience to be

_____ 4. Students might view a professor who comes to class wearing a red cape and top hat to be a bit

   a. bizarre.   b. grotesque.   c. fanciful.   d. exotic.

_____ 5. The difference between $4.95 and $5.00 is

_____ 6. Employers who complain bitterly the first time an employee is one minute late to work are

_____ 7. To charge money for one toothpick would be

_____ 8. A weekly salary of $35 for full-time work is

   e. trivial.   f. paltry.   g. petty.   h. picayune.

EXERCISE 17.4 Synonyms in a Dictionary

Use the following discussions of synonyms to match sentences *1* through *4* with words *a* through *d*, and sentencees *5* through *8* with words *e* through *h*.

ha·rass (hăr′əs, hə-răs′) *tr.v.* **-rassed, -rass·ing, -rass·es.**
1. To irritate or torment persistently. **2.** To wear out; exhaust.
3. To impede and exhaust (an enemy) by repeated attacks or raids.
[French *harasser*, possibly from Old French *harer*, to set a dog on,
from *hare*, interjection used to set a dog on, of Germanic origin.]
—**ha·rass′er** *n.* —**ha·rass′ment** *n.*

SYNONYMS: *harass, harry, hound, badger, pester, plague, bait.*
These verbs are compared as they mean to trouble persistently or
incessantly. *Harass* and *harry* imply systematic persecution by be-
sieging with repeated annoyances, threats, demands, or misfor-
tunes: *The landlord harassed tenants who were behind in their
rent.* "*Of all the griefs that harass the distress'd*" (Samuel Johnson). *A gang of delinquents harried the storekeeper.* *Hound* suggests unrelenting pursuit to gain a desired end: *Reporters hounded
the celebrity for an interview.* To *badger* is to nag or tease persistently: *The child badgered his parents to buy him a new bicycle.*
To *pester* is to inflict a succession of petty annoyances: "*How she
would have pursued and pestered me with questions and surmis-
es*" (Charlotte Brontë). *Plague* refers to the infliction of tribula-
tions, such as worry or vexation, likened to an epidemic disease:
"*As I have no estate, I am plagued with no tenants or stewards*"
(Henry Fielding). To *bait* is to torment by or as if by taunting,
insulting, or ridiculing: *Hecklers baited the speaker mercilessly.*

re·veal¹ (rĭ-vēl′) *tr.v.* **-vealed, -veal·ing, -veals. 1. a.** To
make known (something concealed or secret): *revealed a confidence.* **b.** To bring to view; show. **2.** To make known by super-
natural or divine means: "*For the wrath of God is revealed from
heaven*" (Romans 1:18). [Middle English *revelen*, from Old
French *reveler*, from Latin *revēlāre* : *re-*, re- + *vēlāre*, to cover
(from *vēlum*, veil).] —**re·veal′a·ble** *adj.* —**re·veal′er** *n.* —**re·
veal′ment** *n.*

SYNONYMS: *reveal, expose, disclose, divulge, betray.* These verbs
signify to make known what has been or ought to be kept from the
knowledge of others. *Reveal* suggests uncovering what has been
concealed: "*He was glad it was to him she had revealed her secret*" (Edith Wharton). To *expose* is to lay bare to public scrutiny:
In a slip of the tongue the schemer exposed his true motivation.
Disclose means to make known as if by removing a cover: *The
journalist refused to disclose the source of her information.* *Divulge* often implies the improper revelation of something private
or secret: "*And whatsoever I shall see or hear in the course of my
profession . . . if it be what should not be published abroad, I will
never divulge, holding such things to be holy secrets*" (Hippocratic
Oath). To *betray* is to make known in a breach of trust or confidence: "*A servant . . . betrayed their presence . . . to the Germans*"
(William Styron). The term can also mean to reveal against one's
desire or will: *Her comment betrayed annoyance.*

_____ 1. Her children continually interrupted her while she was studying. She was

_____ 2. His parents constantly complained that he must clean his messy bedroom. He was

_____ 3. The authorities pursued the escapee for three years until he was captured. The escapee was

_____ 4. Though she refused every time, her employer wouldn't stop ask-ing her to go with him to dinner. She was

  a. harassed.   b. hounded.   c. badgered.   d. pestered.

_____ 5. He told her that he would not reveal secrets about her childhood, but he did. She was

_____ 6. An automobile dealer was reported to have sold used cars as new. An unfair business practice was

_____ 7. After a long investigation, detectives reported that the death was a suicide. Information was

_____ 8. When he told others the secrets of her childhood, her secrets were

  e. exposed.   f. disclosed.   g. divulged.   h. betrayed.

EXERCISE 17.5   Synonyms in a Dictionary

Use the following discussions of synonyms to match sentences *1* through *4* with words *a* through *d,* and sentences *5* through *8* with words *e* through *h.*

spar·ing (spâr′ĭng) *adj.* **1.** Given to or marked by prudence and restraint in the use of material resources. **2.** Deficient or limited in quantity, fullness, or extent. **3.** Forbearing; lenient. **—spar′ing·ly** *adv.* **—spar′ing·ness** *n.*

SYNONYMS: *sparing, frugal, thrifty, economical.* These adjectives mean exercising or reflecting care in the use of resources, such as money. *Sparing* stresses restraint, as in expenditure: *sparing in bestowing gifts; neither profligate nor sparing of her time. Frugal* implies self-denial and abstention from luxury: *a frugal diet; a frugal farmer. Thrifty* suggests industry, care, and diligence in conserving means: *is excessively thrifty because he remembers the Depression. Economical* emphasizes prudence, skillful management, and the avoidance of waste: *an economical shopper; the most economical use of energy.*

hin·der[1] (hĭn′dər) *v.* **-dered, -der·ing, -ders.** —*tr.* **1.** To be or get in the way of. **2.** To obstruct or delay the progress of. —*intr.* To interfere with action or progress. [Middle English *hindren,* from Old English *hindrian.* See **ko-** in Appendix.] **—hin′der·er** *n.*

SYNONYMS: *hinder, hamper, impede, obstruct, block, dam, bar.* These verbs mean to slow or prevent progress or movement. To *hinder* is to hold back, as by delaying: *The travelers were hindered by storms throughout their journey.* Often the word implies stopping or prevention: *What is to hinder you from trying?* To *hamper* is to hinder by or as if by fastening or entangling: *A suit and an overcoat hampered the efforts of the accident victim to swim to safety. She was hampered by ill health in building up her business.* To *impede* is to slow by making action or movement difficult: *"Sentiment and eloquence serve only to impede the pursuit of truth"* (Macaulay). *Obstruct* implies the presence of obstacles that interfere with progress: *A building under construction obstructs our view of the mountains. One of the mugger's accomplices tried to obstruct the police officer from upholding the law. Block* refers to complete obstruction that prevents progress, passage, or action: *A huge snowdrift is blocking the entrance to the driveway. "Do not block the way of inquiry"* (Charles S. Peirce). *Dam* suggests obstruction of the flow, progress, or release of something, such as water or emotion: *dammed the brook to form a swimming pool; dammed up his emotions.* To *bar* is to prevent entry or exit or prohibit a course of action: *mounted troops barring access to the presidential palace; laws that bar price fixing.*

_____ 1. She serves enough food and no more. She is

_____ 2. He has enough money to go on vacation, but he never goes. He is

_____ 3. She mends holes in socks to extend their wear. She is

_____ 4. They read grocery advertisements each week and purchase items that are on sale. They are

     a. sparing.   b. frugal.   c. thrifty.   d. economical.

_____ 5. They wouldn't let my friend into the party because he isn't a student at my college. He was

_____ 6. She had difficulty making herself understood in Mexico because she doesn't speak Spanish. Communication was

_____ 7. The highway was covered with two feet of flood water. Travel on the highway was

_____ 8. Some streets were covered with an inch of slippery mud. Travel on these streets was

     e. hampered.   f. impeded.   g. obstructed.   h. barred.

Words Frequently Confused

Writers often use *who's* when they should use *whose, personal* when they should use *personnel*, or *imply* when they mean *infer*. This chapter explains how to eliminate confusion between words of these kinds.

Words Pronounced Alike

A word pronounced the same as another word but spelled differently is called a **homophone** (hŏm'ə-fōn'). *Know* and *no, steak* and *stake*, and *die* and *dye* are some common pairs of words that are pronounced identically.

Avoid confusing homophones by associating their spellings with their meanings.

Homophones	Meanings	Examples
cite (sīt)	to refer to	*Cite* the books you used in writing your term paper.
sight (sīt)	vision	A delicate operation restored his lost *sight*.
site (sīt)	a location	They selected a *site* to camp for the night.

Exercise 18.1 on pages 171–172 and Exercise 18.4 on pages 177–178 contain words that are frequently confused because they are pronounced alike.

Words Pronounced Similarly

Words pronounced similarly are also frequently confused. For instance, *advice* (əd-vīs') and *advise* (əd-vīz') are pronounced the same except that *advice* ends with the sound of *s* and *advise* ends with the sound of *z*. Other words of this type include *affect* and *effect, loose* and *lose*, and *moral* and *morale*.

Avoid confusing words pronounced similarly by associating their spellings with their pronunciations *and* meanings.

Words Pronounced Similarly	Meanings	Examples
desert (dĕz′ərt)	a dry, barren region	We picked a cactus in the *desert*.
dessert (dĭ-zûrt′)	sweet food	We ate cake for *dessert*.

Notice that *desert* is accented on the first syllable and that *dessert* is accented on the last syllable.

Exercise 18.2 on pages 173–174 and Exercise 18.4 on pages 177–178 contain words that are often confused because they are pronounced similarly.

Words Pronounced Differently

Some words are frequently used incorrectly even though they are pronounced differently and have different meanings. For instance, many students confuse *flaunt* (flŏnt) and *flout* (flout) even though these words have different pronunciations and meanings. *Flaunt* means "to show off," as in "She *flaunted* her wealth by wearing a mink coat to class." *Flout*, on the other hand, means "to scorn or show contempt for," as in "He *flouted* the law by driving while drunk."

When you transpose words such as *flaunt* and *flout*, you create a malapropism. If you did Exercise 6.3 on page 55, you learned that a malapropism is a ludicrous or laughable misuse of a word. It would be ridiculous to say "She *flouted* her wealth by wearing a mink coat to class." Wearing a mink coat may show scorn or contempt for mink, but not for one's wealth.

Exercise 18.3 on pages 175–176 and Exercise 18.4 on pages 177–178 contain words that are frequently confused even though they have different pronunciations and meanings.

EXERCISE 18.1 **Words Pronounced Alike**

Write the appropriate homophones on the lines in the following sentences.

1. A **capital** is a city that is a seat of government.
   A **capitol** is a building.

   a. Sacramento is the _____ of California.

   b. We drove through Indianapolis, which is the _____ of Indiana.

   c. The _____ in Albany, New York, is an unusual Victorian building.

2. **Cite** means "to quote or refer to" or "to praise for action."
   Sight is vision.
   A **site** is a location.

   a. They paid $22,000 for the _____ on which they built their house.

   b. Glasses have improved his _____.

   c. Our English teacher wants us to _____ poetry to illustrate our themes.

3. **Its** is the possessive form of "it."
   It's is a contraction of "it is" or "it has."

   a. _____ been three years since he graduated from high school.

   b. Our car has a clock on _____ dashboard.

   c. Her spelling was bad, but _____ become better.

4. **Principal** means "first in importance or degree."
   A **principle** is a basic truth, rule, or standard.

   a. Flour is the _____ ingredient in bread.

   b. His _____ aim in life is to be rich.

   c. Abraham Lincoln is remembered as a man of _____.

   d. She lives by the _____ "Be kind."

5. **Their** is the possessive form of "they."
   There means "at or in this place," and it also often comes before linking verbs such as "is" at the beginning of sentences.
   They're is a contraction of "they are."

   a. If _____ late, we'll have to leave without them.

   b. _____ dog is twenty-two years old.

   c. _____ bringing _____ children to our house for the weekend.

   d. Did they leave _____ children _____ for you to babysit them?

6. **To** means "toward or in the direction of," and it is used before a verb to indicate the infinitive.
   Too means "also," "very," or "overly."
   Two is the number that comes between one and three.

   a. They have _____ dogs and a cat _____.

   b. She is _____ inexperienced _____ get a high-paying job.

   c. He takes _____ buses _____ get to school.

   d. The _____ of them are _____ much in love to think about divorce.

7. **Who's** is a contraction of "who is" or "who has."
   Whose is the possessive form of "who."

   a. Seek advice from those _____ opinions you value and trust.

   b. If he's the one _____ driving, I'm going to walk.

   c. _____ the one _____ company you enjoy the most?

8. **Your** is the possessive form of "you."
   You're is a contraction of "you are."

   a. Do you know where _____ going on _____ vacation?

   b. _____ not pleasant to be with when _____ mood is bad.

   c. However, when _____ mood is good, _____ a joy to be with.

EXERCISE 18.2   **Words Pronounced Similarly**

Write the correct words on the lines in the sentences.

1. **Affect** (ə-fĕct′) means "to influence or produce a change."
   An **effect** (ĭ-fĕct′) is a result, outcome, or consequence.

   a. Widespread unemployment was one _____ of the economic depression of the 1930s.

   b. The ability to get along with others can _____ the speed with which one advances in the work world.

   c. Her kisses have the _____ of making his heart beat faster.

   d. How would it _____ your life to win a million dollars?

2. The **conscience** (kŏn′shəns) is inner knowledge of right and wrong.
   Conscious (kŏn′shəs) means "awake or aware."

   a. Psychopaths do not have the kind of _____ that most people have—they are social misfits.

   b. We are not _____ while we are sleeping soundly.

   c. His _____ will not let him lie.

3. **Eminent** (ĕm′ə-nənt) means "prominent or outstanding."
   Imminent (ĭm′ə-nənt) means "about to happen."

   a. Dark clouds suggest that rain is _____.

   b. An _____ scientist spoke at graduation exercises.

   c. Since birth was _____, the doctor instructed the pregnant woman to go to the hospital.

4. **Farther** (fär′thər) means "more distant."
   Further (fûr′thər) means "additional or more."

   a. If you read _____, you will find the answer.

   b. He ran ten miles, but he couldn't run _____.

   c. If you study _____, you may receive an A on the test rather than a B or C.

5. **Loose** (lōōs) means "free, unbound, or not tight."
   Lose (lōōz) means "to become unable to find."

   a. Take care not to _____ your wallet.

   b. Light, _____ clothing is comfortable to wear in hot weather.

   c. However, shoes too _____ on the feet are uncomfortable and a potential source of danger.

   d. Do you ever _____ your concentration while you are studying?

6. **Moral** (môr′əl) means "concerned with the principles of right and wrong."
   Morale (mə-răl′) is the spirits of a group or person shown by such qualities as cheerfulness and willingness to do required tasks.

   a. The students' _____ is low because their instructor has been out ill for two weeks.

   b. Is it _____ to condemn murderers to death?

   c. When workers' _____ is high, production is high.

7. **Personal** (pûr′sən-əl) means "pertaining to a particular person."
   Personnel (pûr-sə-nĕl′) are the persons employed by an organization.

   a. She trains our assembly line _____.

   b. On the job, avoid _____ arguments with your coworkers.

   c. We were warned that any _____ found using drugs would be fired immediately.

   d. Excuse me for being _____, but have you found yourself somebody to love?

8. **Thorough** (thûr′ō) means "complete."
   Through (thrōō) means "in one side and out the other side," and it also means "finished."

   a. We must give the house a _____ cleaning on Saturday.

   b. We drove _____ a tunnel under the Hudson River.

   c. The doctor gave her a _____ physical examination.

EXERCISE 18.3 **Words Pronounced Differently**

Write the correct words on the lines in the sentences.

1. **continual** (kən-tĭn′yoo̅-əl) *adj.* Repeated regularly and frequently.
   continuous (kən-tĭn′yoo̅-əs) *adj.* Goes on without stopping.

   a. He is suffering _____ pain from the third-degree burns that cover his body.

   b. She has _____ arguments with her mother.

   c. My sleep was interrupted by _____ telephone calls.

   d. A drive across the continent includes a _____ expanse of 2,000 miles of desert.

2. **disinterested** (dĭs-ĭn′trĭ-stĭd) *adj.* Not influenced by selfish motives.
   uninterested (ŭn-ĭn′trĭs-tĭd) *adj.* Not concerned or curious.

   a. The judge was a _____ party in the trial.

   b. He is _____ in visiting museums.

   c. The workers want a _____ third party to help them settle their disagreement with management.

   d. When she's _____ in a subject, she doesn't enjoy studying it.

3. **famous** (fā′məs) *adj.* Well-known and talked about.
   notorious (nō-tôr′ē-əs) *adj.* Unfavorably well-known and talked about.

   a. Thomas Edison is _____ for his many inventions.

   b. Adolf Hitler was a _____ dictator of Germany.

   c. A _____ murderer received the death penalty.

4. **fortuitous** (fôr-too̅′ə-təs) *adj.* Happening by chance or accidentally; unplanned.
   fortunate (fôr′chə-nĭt) *adj.* Having good luck.

   a. Our meeting was _____; I hadn't talked with her in months.

   b. John feels that he is _____ to be enjoying all of the courses he is taking this term.

   c. Parents are _____ to have healthy, happy children.

   d. Any _____ event, such as a power failure or sudden rain shower, can create an opportunity for you to meet a new friend.

5. **imply** (ĭm-plī′) *v.* To give a suggestion or hint.
   infer (ĭn-fûr′) *v.* To draw a conclusion or derive by reasoning.

   a. Does the report _____ that they are guilty?

   b. Reading the report, you may _____ that they are guilty.

   c. Yawning, stretching, and closing eyes _____ the desire to sleep.

   d. When people yawn and stretch, we may _____ that they are tired.

6. **luxuriant** (lŭg-zhoor′ē-ənt) *adj.* Abundant.
   luxurious (lŭg-zhoor′ē-əs) *adj.* Characterized by luxury; splendid, expensive, comfortable.

   a. He ran his fingers through her _____ head of hair.

   b. We were amazed by the _____ growth of vegetation in the rain forest.

   c. We took a _____ cruise around the world.

7. **persecute** (pûr′sə-kyoot′) *v.* To be cruel and cause to suffer.
   prosecute (prŏs′ə-kyoot′) *v.* To engage in legal proceedings in a court of law.

   a. The district attorney will _____ the case for the state.

   b. Most criminals are never _____ because they are never found.

   c. Martyrs are people who are _____ or killed because they refuse to give up their beliefs or principles.

8. **respectfully** (rĭ-spĕkt′-fəl-ē) *adv.* With respect.
   respectively (rĭ-spĕk′tĭv-lē) *adv.* In regard to each in the order named.

   a. Joe and Moe won first and second prize, _____.

   b. It is wise to speak _____ to your supervisors at work.

   c. She likes him because he treats her _____.

   d. Liz, Ben, and Pat were graded B+, B, and A, _____.

__EXERCISE 18.4__ **More Words Frequently Confused**

Following are examples of the three kinds of frequently confused words that are explained in this chapter. Study the lists to find pairs of words you confuse and learn the meanings of those words.

Words Pronounced Alike

1. allowed (permitted)
   aloud (with the voice)

2. altar (sacred table)
   alter (change)

3. bare (uncovered)
   bear (carry)

4. board (plank)
   bored (restless)

5. brake (to slow)
   break (to smash)

6. cell (prison room)
   sell (exchange for money)

7. cent (penny)
   scent (smell)
   sent (transmitted)

8. coarse (rough)
   course (instructional unit)

9. council (advisory group)
   counsel (advice)

10. die (stop living)
    dye (to color)

11. hole (opening)
    whole (complete)

12. know (to have knowledge)
    no (not any)

13. lessen (reduce)
    lesson (something taught)

14. meat (animal flesh)
    meet (to come upon)

15. peace (absence of war)
    piece (part of a whole)

16. right (correct)
    rite (religious ceremony)
    write (to inscribe words)

17. role (function)
    roll (to turn over)

18. stair (a step or steps)
    stare (to look intently)

19. stationary (not moving)
    stationery (writing paper)

20. sundae (ice cream dessert)
    Sunday (first day of the week)

21. wait (remain)
    weight (heaviness)

22. weak (not strong)
    week (seven-day period)

Words Pronounced Similarly

1. accept (to receive)
   except (to leave out)

2. access (admittance)
   excess (surplus)

3. adapt (to make suitable)
   adopt (to take as one's own)

4. advice (suggestion)
   advise (to give a suggestion)

5. alley (narrow passage)
   ally (associate)

6. breath (air taken in)
   breathe (to take in air)

7. choose (to select)
   chose (past tense of *choose*)

8. clothes (body coverings)
   cloths (pieces of cloth)

9. device (simple machine)
   devise (to create)

10. formally (in a formal manner)
    formerly (earlier)

11. hoping (wanting)
    hopping (leaping on one foot)

12. later (after some time)
    latter (last mentioned of two)

13. proceed (to go forward)
    precede (to go before)

14. quiet (free of noise)
    quite (very)

Words Pronounced Differently

1. **abbreviate** (ə-brē′vē-āt′) *v.* To shorten by leaving out parts [to abbreviate New York to NY].
   abridge (ə-brĭj′) *v.* To reduce the length; condense [to abridge a dictionary].

2. **anxious** (ăngk′shəs) *adj.* Worried, uneasy, or apprehensive [anxious about a test for which one has not studied].
   eager (ē′gər) *adj.* Impatient or desirous [eager for vacation to start].

3. **audience** (ô′dē-əns) *n.* A group of people gathered to listen and watch [a motion picture audience].
   spectators (spĕk′tā-tərz) *n.* A group of people gathered primarily to watch [spectators at a football game].

4. **comprehensible** (kŏm′prĭ-hĕn′sə-bəl) *adj.* Understandable [a comprehensible explanation].
   comprehensive (kŏm′prĭ-hĕn′sĭv) *adj.* Including much or almost everything [a comprehensive list of one's friends].

5. **credible** (krĕd′ə-bəl) *adj.* Believable; worthy of being believed [a credible excuse for lateness].
   credulous (krĕj′ o͞o-ləs) *adj.* Believing too easily [a credulous three-year-old child].

6. **deprecate** (dĕp′rĭ-kāt′) *v.* To express an unfavorable opinion [to deprecate someone's best efforts].
   depreciate (dĭ-prē′shē-āt′) *v.* To lessen the worth [a car's value depreciates each year].

7. **expect** (ĕk-spĕkt′) *v.* To look forward to an occurrence [to expect a birthday present].
   suspect (sə-spĕkt′) *v.* To suppose; to think that something is probable [to suspect that a person is guilty].

8. **irrelevant** (ĭ-rĕl′ə-vənt) *adj.* Not relating to the subject [an irrelevant question].
   irreverent (ĭ-rĕv′ər-ənt) *adj.* Not showing proper respect [irreverent laughter during a religious service].

9. **judicial** (jo͞o-dĭsh′əl) *adj.* Pertaining to courts of law and the administration of justice [the judicial branch of government].
   judicious (jo͞o-dĭsh′əs) *adj.* Having good judgment [the judicious choice of nutritious foods].

10. **percent** (pər-sĕnt′) *n.* Per hundred, used with a number [75 percent of the students].
    percentage (pər-sĕn′tĭj) *n.* A given part, used when no number is given [a large percentage of the students].

Usages

Usage refers to the customary ways in which words and phrases are used in language. The serious papers students write for college credit are usually judged in part on the extent to which words and phrases are used in the ways customarily employed by those who have a good command of English.

Standard English

Millions of people speak English; they live in different places, they have different social backgrounds, and they use English in different ways. These differences are differences of **dialect**—regional variations of a language which involve pronunciation, grammar, and vocabulary. One difficulty that many students have in English courses is that colleges and universities usually teach **Standard English,** which is a kind of English that is free of the differences in pronunciation, grammar, and vocabulary found in dialect. It is the English used by educated people in conversation, formal speeches, and serious papers.

Instructors at most colleges and universities judge students' writing by the extent to which spelling, grammatical constructions, and vocabulary correspond to Standard English. In addition, most large businesses and organizations seek to hire employees who use Standard English.

If you want to ensure that your writing corresponds to Standard English, the following discussions explain some ways in which you may use a dictionary for this purpose. However, only you can decide if you want to use Standard English. Dictionaries do not dictate how you must use words. Rather, they give information so you can, if you wish, use words as they are used by those who speak and write Standard English.

Colloquialism

In every language there are words that are formal and always appropriate and other words that are informal, often inappropriate, and even vulgar. For instance, it is appropriate to refer to phlegm in the nose as nasal mucus, but it is vulgar to refer to this phlegm as *snot*. The vulgarity of words such as *snot* is obvious, but informal usages of words are often not apparent.

179

As a result, dictionaries label some definitions **Informal,** or **Colloquial,** to indicate that they are senses that are appropriate to use in everyday conversation but that are avoided by careful users of English when they give formal speeches or write formal papers. A definition is labeled *Informal* in the following entry:

> **some·bod·y** (sŭm′bŏd′ē, -bŭd′ē, -bə-dē) *pron.* An unspecified or unknown person; someone. See Usage Note at **he**¹.
> **—somebody** *n.*, pl. **-ies.** *Informal.* A person of importance: *"Obviously she was somebody—a real presence in the room"* (Oleg Cassini).

The absence of a label for the first definition indicates that it is always appropriate to use *somebody* to mean "an unspecified or unknown person," as in "*Somebody* lost these keys." On the other hand, the *Informal* label before the second definition advises against using *somebody* to mean "a person of importance" in formal speech or writing. Careful users of English would not, for instance, write "Shakespeare was a *somebody*" in a serious paper.

Slang

Slang is highly informal language that is usually considered appropriate in everyday conversation, but not in formal speech or formal writing. The third definition is labeled *Slang* in the following entry:

> **croak** (krōk) *n.* A low, hoarse sound, as that characteristic of frogs and crows. **—croak** *v.* **croaked, croak·ing, croaks.** *—tr.* **1.** To utter in a low, hoarse sound. **2.** *Slang.* To kill. *—intr.* **1.a.** To utter a low, hoarse sound. **b.** To speak with a low, hoarse voice. **2.** To mutter discontentedly; grumble. **3.** *Slang.* To die. [From Middle English *croken,* to croak, probably of imitative origin.] **—croak′i·ly** *adv.* **—croak′y** *adj.*

Careful users of English may use *croak* to mean "to die" in everyday conversation: "When we learned that our dinner for two cost eighty dollars, we almost *croaked.*" However, those who have good command of English would not use *croak* in this sense when writing serious papers. They would not, for instance, write "George Washington was born in 1732, and he *croaked* in 1799."

Nonstandard

The term **nonstandard** is sometimes used to refer to usages that are not generally approved by educated native users of English. The following dictionary entry indicates that *nowheres* is a nonstandard usage.

> **no·wheres** (nō′hwârz′, -wârz′) *adv.* *Non-Standard.* Nowhere.

This entry states that it is nonstandard to say or write, "He is *nowheres* to be found."

   Words usually considered to be nonstandard include *alright, everywheres,* and *hisself,* and nonstandard grammatical constructions include "could of" for "could have" and "he don't" for "he doesn't."

Other Usage Information

English handbooks and English composition textbooks are sources of information about usage. For instance, the following usage entry is included in *Writing with a Purpose,* tenth edition, by Joseph F. Trimmer (Houghton Mifflin, 1992):

> **and/or** Many people object to *and/or* in college writing because the expression is associated with legal and commercial writing. Generally avoid it.

The American Heritage Dictionary (third edition) includes the following usage note:

> **and/or** (ăn′dôr′) *conj.* Used to indicate that either or both of the items connected by it are involved.
>
> ***USAGE NOTE:*** *And/or* is widely used in legal and business writing. Its use in general writing to mean "one or the other or both" is acceptable but can appear stilted. See Usage Note at **or**[1].

In stating that the use of *and/or* in general writing is stilted (artificially formal), this dictionary entry suggests that the construction should be avoided.

EXERCISE 19.1   Usage

Referring to the entries at the bottom of this page, decide whether the **boldface** words are used in formal, informal, or slang senses, or whether they are nonstandard. On the lines, write **F** for *formal*, **I** for *informal*, **S** for *slang*, and **N** for *nonstandard*.

_____   1. Is you is or is you **ain't** my baby?

_____   2. I'm not invited to the party, but I don't want to go **anyways.**

_____   3. We saw an **awful** automobile accident.

_____   4. I'm **awful** tired because I slept only four hours last night.

_____   5. He gave her a beautiful **bunch** of flowers.

_____   6. I ate lunch with a **bunch** of my friends.

_____   7. There were a **couple** of candlesticks on the table—one at each end.

_____   8. She said, "I'll be there in a **couple** of minutes."

_____   9. She signed her letter, "**Heaps** of love, Jane."

_____   10. There is a **heap** of dirty clothes on the closet floor.

_____   11. I had a **hunk** of cheese and an apple for lunch.

_____   12. She likes him because he is hardworking and intelligent, and he's a **hunk.**

ain't (ānt). *Non-Standard.* **1.** Am not. **2.** Used also as a contraction for *are not, is not, has not,* and *have not.*

an·y·ways (ĕn′ē-wāz′) *adv. Non-Standard.* In any case.

aw·ful (ô′fəl) *adj.* **1.** Extremely bad or unpleasant; terrible: *had an awful day at the office.* **2.** Commanding awe: *"this sea, whose gently awful stirrings seem to speak of some hidden soul beneath"* (Herman Melville). **3.** Filled with awe, especially: **a.** Filled with or displaying great reverence. **b.** *Obsolete.* Afraid. **4.** Formidable in nature or extent: *an awful burden; an awful risk.* **—awful** *adv. Informal.* Extremely; very: *was awful sick.*

bunch (bŭnch) *n.* **1.a.** A group of things growing close together; a cluster or clump: *a bunch of grapes; grass growing in bunches.* **b.** A group of like items or individuals gathered or placed together: *a bunch of keys on a ring; people standing around in bunches.* **2.** *Informal.* A group of people usually having a common interest or association: *My brother and his bunch are basketball fanatics.* **3.** *Informal.* A considerable number or amount; a lot: *a bunch of*

trouble; *a whole bunch of food.* **4.** A small lump or swelling; a bump.

cou·ple (kŭp′əl) *n.* **1.** Two items of the same kind; a pair. **2.** Something that joins or connects two things together; a link. **3.** *(used with a sing. or pl. verb).* **a.** Two people united, as by betrothal or marriage. **b.** Two people together. **4.** *Informal.* A few; several: *a couple of days.* **5.** *Physics.* A pair of forces of equal magnitude acting in parallel but opposite directions, capable of causing rotation but not translation.

heap (hēp) *n.* **1.** A group of things placed or thrown, one on top of the other: *a heap of dirty rags lying in the corner.* **2.** Often **heaps.** *Informal.* A great deal; a lot: *We have heaps of homework tonight.* **3.** *Slang.* An old or run-down car.

hunk (hŭngk) *n.* **1.** *Informal.* A large piece; a chunk: *a hunk of fresh bread.* **2.** *Slang.* A sexually attractive man with a well-developed physique. [Perhaps from Flemish *hunke,* a piece of food.]

EXERCISE 19.2   Usage

Referring to the entries at the bottom of this page, decide whether the **boldface** words are used in formal, informal, or slang senses, or whether they are nonstandard. On the lines, write **F** for *formal,* **I** for *informal,* **S** for *slang,* and **N** for *nonstandard.*

_____ 1. Some people continue to smoke cigarettes **irregardless** of the dangers to their health.

_____ 2. Nestor may act like a **nerd,** but he is actually an exceptionally fine young man.

_____ 3. If you want to cook dinner, it's **OK** with me.

_____ 4. There is **plenty** of food for all of us.

_____ 5. I was **plenty** tired and ready for a good night's sleep.

_____ 6. He can't stay awake in class because he's a **pothead.**

_____ 7. My English teacher read a **quote** from a play by Tennessee Williams.

_____ 8. "Life is sweet," and you may **quote** me.

_____ 9. Candy may not be good for you, but it **sure** tastes good.

_____ 10. If we avoid foolish errors, we are **sure** to win the game.

_____ 11. The players on our football team are all **tough.**

_____ 12. It is **tough** that you lost your wallet.

---

ir·re·gard·less (ĭr′ĭ-gärd′lĭs) *adv. Non-Standard.* Regardless. [Perhaps from IR(RESPECTIVE) + REGARDLESS.]

nerd *also* **nurd** (nûrd) *n. Slang.* **1.** A person regarded as stupid, inept, or unattractive. **2.** A person who is single-minded or accomplished in scientific pursuits but is felt to be socially inept. [Perhaps after *Nerd,* a character in *If I Ran the Zoo,* by Theodor Seuss Geisel.] —**nerd′y** *adj.*

OK[1] *or* **O.K.** *or* **o·kay** (ō-kā′) *Informal.—n., pl.* **OK's** *or* **O.K.'s** *or* **o·kays.** Approval; agreement: *got her supervisor's OK before taking a day off.* —*tr.v.* **OK'd, OK'ing, OK's** *or* **O.K.'d, O.K.'ing, O.K.'s** *or* **o·kayed, o·kay·ing, o·kays.** To approve of or agree to; authorize. —*interj.* Used to express approval or agreement. [Abbreviation of *oll korrect,* slang respelling of *all correct.*] —**OK** *adv. & adj.*

plen·ty (plĕn′tē) *n.* **1.** A full or completely adequate amount or supply: *plenty of time.* **2.** A large quantity or amount; an abundance: *"Awards and honors came to her in plenty"* (Joyce Carol Oates). **3.** A condition of general abundance or prosperity: *"fruitful regions gladdened by plenty and lulled by peace!"* (Samuel Johnson). —**plenty** *adj.* Plentiful; abundant: *"Ships were then not so plenty in those waters as now"* (Herman Melville). —**plenty** *adv. Informal.* Sufficiently; very: *It's plenty hot.*

pot·head (pŏt′hĕd′) *n. Slang.* One who habitually smokes marijuana.

quote (kwōt) *v.* **quot·ed, quot·ing, quotes.** —*tr.* **1.** To repeat or copy the words of (another), usually with acknowledgment of the source. **2.** To cite or refer to for illustration or proof. **3.** To repeat a brief passage or excerpt from: *The saxophonist quoted a Duke Ellington melody in his solo.* **4.** To state (a price) for securities, goods, or services. —*intr.* To give a quotation, as from a book. —**quote** *n.* **1.** *Informal.* A quotation. **2.** A quotation mark. **3.** Used by a speaker to indicate the beginning of a quotation.

sure (shŏor) *adj.* **sur·er, sur·est.** **1.** Impossible to doubt or dispute; certain. **2.** Not hesitating or wavering; firm: *sure convictions.* **3.** Confident, as of something awaited or expected: *sure of ultimate victory.* **4.a.** Bound to come about or happen; inevitable: *sure defeat.* **b.** Having one's course directed; destined or bound: *sure to succeed.* **5.** Certain not to miss or err; steady: *a sure hand on the throttle.* **6.a.** Worthy of being trusted or depended on; reliable. **b.** Free from or marked by freedom from doubt: *sure of her friends.* **7.** Careful to do something: *asked me to be sure to turn off the stove.* **8.** *Obsolete.* Free from harm or danger; safe. —**sure** *adv. Informal.* Surely; certainly.

tough (tŭf) *adj.* **tough·er, tough·est.** **1.** Able to withstand great strain without tearing or breaking; strong and resilient: *a tough all-weather fabric.* **2.** Hard to cut or chew: *tough meat.* **3.** Physically hardy; rugged: *tough mountaineers; a tough cop.* See Synonyms at **strong.** **4.** Severe; harsh: *a tough winter.* **5.a.** Aggressive; pugnacious. **b.** Inclined to violent or disruptive behavior; rowdy or rough: *a tough street group.* **6.** Demanding or troubling; difficult: *skipping the toughest questions.* **7.** Strong-minded; resolute: *a tough negotiator.* **8.** *Slang.* Unfortunate; too bad: *a tough break.* **9.** *Slang.* Fine; great.

EXERCISE 19.3 Usage Notes

Consult the usage notes at the bottom of this page to cross out the answers in parentheses that are *not* preferred. For instance, in the first sentence cross out *in the affirmative* or *yes*, whichever is *not* preferred.

1. I hoped she would answer (in the affirmative, yes).

2. But she answered (in the negative, no).

3. He compared the human body (to, with) a machine.

4. He compared his receipts (to, with) the statement he received from his credit card company.

5. There are (fewer, less) days in February than in March.

6. It is (fewer, less) than two weeks until my birthday.

7. The actors in *Robin Hood* wore (historic, historical) costumes.

8. The signing of the Declaration of Independence is a (historic, historical) moment in our history.

9. I can't wait to get (off, off of) this airplane.

10. We went to the movies spending money we got (off, from) my father.

---

af·fir·ma·tive (ə-fûr′mə-tĭv) *adj.* **1.** Asserting that something is true or correct, as with the answer "yes": *an affirmative reply.*

USAGE NOTE: The expressions *in the affirmative* and *in the negative*, as in *She answered in the affirmative*, are generally regarded as pompous. *She answered yes* would be more acceptable even at the most formal levels of style.

com·pare (kəm-pâr′) *v.* **-pared, -par·ing, -pares.** —*tr.* **1.** To consider or describe as similar, equal, or analogous; liken.

USAGE NOTE: *Compare* usually takes the preposition *to* when it refers to the activity of describing the resemblances between unlike things: *He compared her to a summer day. Scientists sometimes compare the human brain to a computer.* It takes *with* when it refers to the act of examining two like things in order to discern their similarities or differences: *The police compared the forged signature with the original. The committee will have to compare the Senate's version of the bill with the version that was passed by the House.* When *compare* is used to mean "to liken (one) with another," *with* is traditionally held to be the correct form: *That little bauble is not to be compared with (not to) this enormous jewel.* But *to* is frequently used in this context and is not incorrect.

few (fyōō) *adj.* **few·er, few·est. 1.** Amounting to or consisting of a small number: *one of my few bad habits.*

USAGE NOTE: The traditional rule holds that *fewer* is used with expressions denoting things that can be counted (*fewer than four players*), while *less* is used with mass terms denoting things of measurable extent (*less paper; less than a gallon of paint*). How-

ever, *less* is idiomatic in certain constructions where *fewer* would occur according to the traditional rule. *Less than* is used before a plural noun that denotes a measure of time, amount, or distance: *less than three weeks; less than $400; less than 50 miles. Less* is sometimes used with plural nouns in the expressions *no less than* (as in *No less than 30 of his colleagues signed the letter*) and *or less* (as in *Give your reasons in 25 words or less*).

his·tor·ic (hĭ-stôr′ĭk, -stŏr′-) *adj.* **1.** Having importance in or influence on history. **2.** Historical.

USAGE NOTE: *Historic* and *historical* are differentiated in usage, though their senses overlap. *Historic* refers to what is important in history: *the historic first voyage to outer space.* It is also used of what is famous or interesting because of its association with persons or events in history: *a historic house. Historical* refers to whatever existed in the past, whether regarded as important or not: *a historical character. Historical* refers also to anything concerned with history or the study of the past: *a historical novel; historical discoveries.* The differentiation between the words is not complete. They are often used interchangeably: *historic times* or *historical times.*

off (ôf, ŏf) *adv.* **1.** From a place or position: *drove off.*

USAGE NOTE: In Modern English the compound preposition *off of* is generally regarded as informal and is best avoided in formal speech and writing: *He stepped off (not off of) the platform. Off* is informal as well in its use to indicate a source: formal style requires *I borrowed it from (not off) my brother.*

Unit Five Review

REVIEW 5.1 Basic Word List

Your instructor may give you a test on the meanings of these words. If so, learn the meanings of any of the words that you do not know. The words are followed by the exercise numbers in which they are introduced.

1. exotic, 17.3
2. grotesque, 17.3
3. trivial, 17.3
4. betray, 17.4
5. disclose, 17.4
6. divulge, 17.4
7. expose, 17.4
8. hound, 17.4
9. obstruct, 17.5
10. frugal, 17.5
11. capital, 18.1
12. capitol, 18.1
13. cite, 18.1

14. site, 18.1
15. principal, 18.1
16. principle, 18.1
17. affect, 18.2
18. effect, 18.2
19. conscience, 18.2
20. conscious, 18.2
21. farther, 18.2
22. further, 18.2
23. imply, 18.3
24. infer, 18.3
25. notorious, 18.3

REVIEW 5.2 Advanced Word List

Your instructor may give you a test on the meanings of these words. If so, learn the meanings of any of the words that you do not know. The words are followed by the numbers of the exercises in which they are introduced.

1. bizarre, 17.3
2. fanciful, 17.3
3. paltry, 17.3
4. petty, 17.3
5. badger, 17.4
6. harass, 17.4
7. bar, 17.5
8. hamper, 17.5
9. impede, 17.5
10. sparing, 17.5
11. eminent, 18.2
12. imminent, 18.2
13. moral, 18.2

14. morale, 18.2
15. personal, 18.2
16. personnel, 18.2
17. disinterested, 18.3
18. fortuitous, 18.3
19. fortunate, 18.3
20. persecute, 18.3
21. prosecute, 18.3
22. luxuriant, 18.3
23. luxurious, 18.3
24. respectively, 18.3
25. uninterested, 18.3

___**REVIEW 5.3**   **Sentence Completion**

Complete the following sentences using words that make it clear that you know the meanings of the words that are printed in **boldface.**

1. The most **exotic** *place I've ever visited is the*
   ancient city of Fez, Morroco.

2. I saw a **grotesque** _____
   _____

3. Please don't **divulge** _____
   _____

4. I was **harassed** by _____
   _____

5. One **principle** _____
   _____

6. I would never **betray** _____
   _____

7. Our progress was **impeded** _____
   _____

8. The most **trivial** _____
   _____

9. Our **morale** _____
   _____

10. The most **luxuriant** _____
    _____

___**REVIEW 5.4**   **Writing Applications**

Your instructor may assign one or more of the following writing activities.

1. Write six sentences, each of which includes a word from the Basic Word List or the Advanced Word List on page 185. Underline the six words in your sentences.

2. Write six sentences, each of which includes one of the following words specified by your instructor. Underline the six words in your sentences.

   a. _____   d. _____

   b. _____   e. _____

   c. _____   f. _____

3. Write a paragraph on a topic of your choice using six of the words from the Basic Word List or the Advanced Word List on page 185. Underline the six words in your paragraph.

4. Write a paragraph on a topic of your choice which includes the following six words specified by your instructor. Underline the six words in your paragraph.

   a. _____   d. _____

   b. _____   e. _____

   c. _____   f. _____

5. Describe the **capitol** of your state or a capitol you have visited.

6. Explain how you **infer** your mother's or father's mood or the mood of some other relative or friend.

7. **Cite** some of the lyrics of your favorite song.

8. Recount ways you have seen students **persecuted** by their classmates.

9. Describe a **luxurious** bedroom.

10. Explain the difference between the words **disinterested** and **uninterested.**

REVIEW 5.5   **Fill-in Questions**

Write on the lines the words that are missing from the following definitions of terminology that are introduced in Chapters 17, 18, and 19.

1. _____ are words that have opposite meanings, such as *big* and *little*.

2. A _____ is a book that lists synonyms.

3. _____ are words that are pronounced the same but are spelled differently, such as *know* and *no*.

4. A _____ is a regional variation of a language which involves pronunciation, grammar, and vocabulary.

5. American colleges usually teach _____ English, which is a kind of English that is free of the differences in pronunciation, grammar, and vocabulary found in dialects.

6. Dictionaries label some definitions _____ to indicate that they are senses that are avoided by careful users of English when they give formal speeches or write formal papers.

7. _____ is highly informal language that is usually considered inappropriate in formal speech or formal writing.

8. The term _____ is sometimes used to refer to usages that are not generally approved by educated native users of English.

REVIEW 5.6 Short-Answer Questions

Refer to Chapters 17, 18, and 19 to answer the following questions.

1. What two characteristics of synonyms must you consider to select appropriate ones?

   a. _____

   _____

   b. _____

   _____

2. Why is it important for college students to know the difference between Standard English and nonstandard English?

   _____

   _____

   _____

3. When is it usually considered appropriate to use colloquialisms and slang?

   _____

   _____

   _____

Six

Improve Your Spelling

Learning Goals for Unit Six

In studying Chapters 20, 21, and 22 you will learn:

- How to make fewer spelling errors (Chapter 20).
- How to locate words in a dictionary even when their spellings are very different from their pronunciations (Chapter 21).
- How to spell words such as *mischievous* and *receipt,* which contain *ie* and *ei* (Chapter 22).
- How to spell words such as *earring,* which contains two words; *misspell,* which contains a prefix and a word; and *usually,* which contains a word and a suffix (Chapter 22).
- How to spell words such as *achieving,* which has a base that ends in *e; emptiness,* which has a base that ends in *y;* and *referring,* which has a base that ends in one consonant preceded by one vowel (Chapter 22).

How to Improve Spelling

This chapter explains several methods you can use to improve your spelling. Other chapters in this unit of *College Vocabulary Skills* explain how to use a dictionary to locate spellings (Chapter 21) and how to use rules to spell hundreds of words correctly (Chapter 22).

Keep a List of Words You Misspell

Keep a list of the words you misspell in papers you write for college credit and the words whose spellings you look up frequently. When a teacher marks a misspelled word on a paper you wrote, add the word to your list of misspelled words. In addition, each time you look up a spelling in your dictionary, place a pencil check next to the spelling. When there are three checks next to a word, you use that word often enough to learn its spelling instead of consulting a dictionary each time you want to use it.

You may find it helpful to keep your list in the following format.

Correct Spelling	My Misspelling	Note
dining	dinning	dine + -ing (drop *e*)
all right	alright	two words, not one
vacuum	vacume	uu
really	realy	real + -ly

By keeping records of this type, you may identify patterns in your errors.

Use the Six-Step Study Method

Use the following procedure to learn the correct spellings of words.

1. Study the word to learn how its consonant and vowel sounds are spelled and possibly to locate a familiar prefix, suffix, or base word.

2. Read the word aloud.

3. Spell the word letter by letter.

4. Write the word without looking at it.

5. Check to see whether you spelled the word correctly.

6. Repeat steps 1 through 5 until you are able to spell the word correctly from memory.

The purpose of the first step is to locate possible sources of difficulty in spelling a word correctly. For instance, the difficulty in spelling *concern* correctly may be that the sound of *s* is spelled by the letter *c* (concern).

Use Mnemonic Devices

A **mnemonic** (nĭ-mŏn'ĭk) **device** is any device used to aid memory. You can use three basic types of mnemonic devices to remember spellings.

1. Use a statement of fact about the spelling of a word, such as "There are three *e*'s in *therefore*."

2. Use an observation about the sequence of letters in a word, such as "*Together* spells the phrase *to get her*."

3. Use one of the spelling rules that are explained in Chapter 22. For example, use the jingle "*i* before *e* except after *c*" to remember to spell *achieve* rather than *acheive*.

The most useful mnemonic devices are the spelling rules explained in Chapter 22 and the mnemonic devices that you make up for yourself.

Pronounce Words Correctly

Incorrect pronunciation is a frequent cause of spelling errors. The most common pronunciation error is to leave out a sound that belongs in a word.

Correct	Incorrect
candidate (kăn'də-dāt')	canidate (kăn'ə-dāt')
government (gŭv'ərn-mənt)	goverment (gŭv'ər-mĕnt)
literature (lĭt'ər-ə-chŏor')	literture (lĭt'ər-chŏor')

Some words are misspelled because they may be correctly pronounced by omitting a sound in them. For instance, *chocolate* may be pronounced (chŏ'kə-lĭt) or (chŏk'lĭt); those who use the second pronunciation may spell the word incorrectly.

Use a Dictionary

Dictionaries are the most authoritative sources of information about the correct spellings of words, and dictionaries probably contain more information than you are aware of about the correct spellings of words. Chapter 21 explains the various types of information about spelling you can find in a dictionary and how to locate the correct spellings of words with pronunciations that are very different from their spellings.

Master Spelling Rules

One of the most efficient ways to improve spelling is to master the spelling rules that are explained in Chapter 22. When you learn those rules, you will be certain of the answers to questions such as the following.

1. Why is there an *ie* in *brief* but an *ei* in *ceiling?*

2. Why are there two *t*'s in *nighttime?*

3. Why are there two *s*'s in *dissimilar?*

4. Why are there two *l*'s in *really?*

5. Why is there no *e* in *lovable?*

6. Why is there an *i* in *penniless?*

7. Why are there two *r*'s in *referred* and one *r* in *reference?*

If there is any question in this list that you cannot answer, you will benefit by studying Chapter 22 with care.

Proofread Your Writing Carefully

If your written work often contains misspellings of words that you know how to spell correctly, you have not developed sufficient skill in proofreading for spelling errors. If you want to produce written material that is free of misspellings, you must carefully read what you have written to make absolutely certain that no word is misspelled. Use Exercise 20.3 on page 196 to assess your ability to proofread written material.

EXERCISE 20.1   Mnemonic Devices

This exercise provides practice in making mnemonic devices for remembering the correct spellings of words.

1. The spelling of some words can be remembered by finding and remembering the spelling of words embedded within them. For instance, some people remember to spell *resistance* (rather than *resistence*) by remembering that the spelling of *tan* is embedded in *resistance*. Locate the words that are embedded in the following words. The numbers in parentheses indicate the number of letters in the words you are to locate. For example, find a four-letter word in *balloon*.

   a. balloon (4)   _____   g. juice (3)   _____

   b. outrageous (4)   _____   h. sincerely (4)   _____

   c. incentive (4)   _____   i. laboratory (5)   _____

   d. attendance (5)   _____   j. hear (3)   _____

   e. conscience (7)   _____   k. tragedy (3)   _____

   f. believe (3)   _____   l. amateur (3)   _____

2. The spellings of some words can be remembered by the number of vowels of a specific kind there are in them. For instance, some people spell *therefore* correctly by remembering that it contains three *e*'s. Make mnemonic devices for remembering the spellings of the following words.

   a. sophomore   _____   b. cemetery   _____

3. Make a mnemonic device for remembering that *stationery*, referring to writing material, is spelled with an *e* rather than an *a*.

   _____

   _____

4. Make a mnemonic device for remembering that *compliment*, meaning "praise," is spelled with an *i* rather than an *e*.

   _____

   _____

5. Make a mnemonic device for remembering the correct spellings of *dessert* (sweet food) and *desert* (dry land).

   _____

   _____

EXERCISE 20.2 Mispronunciation

Spell correctly the words that are partially spelled and italicized in the following sentences. They are words that are frequently misspelled because they are mispronounced.

_____	1. She is a *can*date* for mayor.
_____	2. I like *choc** ice cream.
_____	3. Pollution harms the *envi*ment.*
_____	4. It is often cold in *Feb*ry.*
_____	5. Our *gov*ment* taxes us.
_____	6. He's *int*ested* in getting married.
_____	7. There was an explosion in the chemistry *lab*ory.*
_____	8. If you laugh, I'm *l*ble* to laugh.
_____	9. I must return books to the *lib*.*
_____	10. She is studying English *lit*ture.*
_____	11. Algebra is one branch of *math*ics.*
_____	12. She collects *min*ture* penguins.
_____	13. You'll *prob*ly* get married.
_____	14. He drank a great *quant*ty* of beer.
_____	15. She doesn't *rec*nize* when she's wrong.
_____	16. I had a tuna *san*ich* for lunch.
_____	17. He is muscular, but he has little *str*th.*
_____	18. A *su*ise* is something that is unexpected.
_____	19. The *temp*ure* dropped, and it snowed.
_____	20. Corn is his favorite *veg*ble.*

EXERCISE 20.3   Proofreading

Cross out the misspelled words and write the correct spellings above them.
There are seventeen errors.

Here is one of the best pieces of advice that any college student can   *1*

be given: Attend classes faithfully and take good class notes. In case your   *2*

not use to taking lecture notes, some of the following suggestions may   *3*

be helpful to you.   *4*

When you study dificult subjects, read assigned material before class.   *5*

In the classroom, eliminate any sources of distraction that may effect   *6*

your ability to consentrate. For instance, eat so you won't be hungry and   *7*

avoid sitting next to annoying classmates.   *8*

Chose notebook paper that measures 8½ by 11 inches—the size   *9*

preferred by experienced note takers. Begin each days notes with a   *10*

heading that includes the date and name or number of the course. Than   *11*

listen carefully with the goal in mine of organizing your notes so that   *12*

major details stand out clearly and minor details are listed under major   *13*

details in an orderly fashion. Make notes that summarize what teacher's   *14*

say; the trick is to write enough but not to much.   *15*

Anything written on the board may be used as the basis for a test   *16*

question. Therefor, include in your notes everything that is written on   *17*

the board and devise a method for marking the material for special   *18*

attention when you study. You might draw a star in the margin next to   *19*

the information, or you might underline it.   *20*

Copy classmates notes if you are absent from classes or if you loose   *21*

notes. Unfortunately, you are likely to fine that other students' notes are   *22*

not very helpful to you. Except that you must attend classes so that you   *23*

will have your personnel notes to study for tests.   *24*

The Dictionary and Spelling

If you own a good desk dictionary, you own an excellent spelling textbook. Modern desk dictionaries give the answers to virtually all your questions about correct spellings.

Variant Spellings

Many words have two correct spellings—a preferred spelling and a variant spelling. The entry below shows that *judgment* is a preferred spelling and that *judgement* is a variant spelling.

> **judg·ment** also **judge·ment** (jŭj′mənt) *n.* **1.** The act or process of judging; the formation of an opinion after consideration or deliberation. **2. a.** The mental ability to perceive and distinguish relationships; discernment: *Fatigue may affect a pilot's judgment of distances.* **b.** The capacity to form an opinion by distinguishing and evaluating: *His judgment of fine music is impeccable.*

When a word has two spellings, the spelling that is listed first is the preferred spelling. If you use preferred spellings, you will spell words as they are usually spelled in carefully edited writing.

Plurals

If there is anything unusual about the spelling of a plural noun, that spelling is shown in desk dictionaries. The entry below shows that there are two ways to spell the plural of *thesaurus.*

> **the·sau·rus** (thĭ-sôr′əs) *n., pl.* **-sau·ri** (-sôr′ī′) or **-sau·rus·es. 1.** A book of synonyms, often including related and contrasting words and antonyms. **2.** A book of selected words or concepts, such as a specialized vocabulary of a particular field, as of medicine or music.

This entry states that the plural of *thesaurus* may be spelled *thesauri* or *thesauruses.*

Principal Parts of Verbs

If there is anything unusual about the spellings of verbs ending with *-ed, -ing,* or *-s,* those spellings are shown at the beginnings of verb definitions.

The entry below shows that when *-ed* and *-ing* are added to *confer,* the final *r* is doubled: *conferred* and *conferring.*

> **con·fer** (kən-fûr′) *v.* **-ferred, -fer·ring, -fers.** —*tr.* **1.** To be-stow (an honor, for example): *conferred a medal on the hero; con-ferred an honorary degree on her.* **2.** To invest with (a charac-teristic, for example): *a carefully worded statement that conferred an aura of credibility onto the administration's actions.* —*intr.* To meet in order to deliberate together or compare views.

When a dictionary gives no information about the spellings of the principal parts of verbs, there is nothing unusual about the way they are spelled. For example, most dictionaries do not provide the spellings of *walked, walking,* and *walks* because there is nothing unusual about them.

Comparatives and Superlatives

When adjectives have comparative and superlative forms, these forms are shown at the beginning of adjective definitions. The entry below shows that the comparative of *tiny* is spelled *tinier* and that the superlative is spelled *tiniest.*

> **ti·ny** (tī′nē) *adj.* **-ni·er, -ni·est.** Extremely small; minute. See Synonyms at **small.** [Alteration of Middle English *tine.*] —**ti′-ni·ness** *n.*

If no comparative or superlative form is given for an adjective, it has none. For instance, an entry for *beautiful* does not show *beautifuler* or *beautifulest* because these words do not exist.

Derivatives

Derivatives are words formed by joining prefixes or suffixes to bases. For example, *resell* and *seller* are derivatives formed by joining the prefix *re-* and the suffix *-er* to the base *sell.* When a derivative is not listed as an entry word, it may be listed at the end of the entry for its base word.

> **in·sep·a·ra·ble** (ĭn-sĕp′ər-ə-bəl, -sĕp′rə-) *adj.* **1.** Impossi-ble to separate or part: *inseparable pieces of rock.* **2.** Very closely associated; constant: *inseparable companions.* —**in·sep′a·ra·bil′i·ty, in·sep′a·ra·ble·ness** *n.* —**in·sep′a·ra·ble** *n.* —**in·sep′a·ra·bly** *adv.*

This entry for *inseparable* includes the spellings *inseparability, inseparable-ness,* and *inseparably.*

Compounds

Compounds are words such as *fireworks* and *roommate* that are formed by joining two words. Compounds are usually written without spaces between the joined words, but they may be written with spaces *(wedding ring)* or with hyphens between the words *(sister-in-law)*. Since there are no rules that explain when to leave spaces or use hyphens in compounds, consult a dictionary when you are uncertain of the correct form to use.

> **part-time** (pärt′tīm′) *adj.* For or during less than the customary or standard time: *a part-time job.* —**part′-time′** *adv.* —**part′-tim′er** *n.*

This entry shows that *part-time* is written with a hyphen.

Contractions

A **contraction** is a word that contains an apostrophe to indicate the omission of a letter or letters. For instance, *it's* is a contraction of *it is* (*it* + *is* = *it's*). Most contractions include the word *are* (you're), *is* (it's), *has* (who's), *would* (they'd), *had* (she'd), *have* (they've), *not* (don't), or *will* (he'll).

> **I'd** (īd). **1.** I had. **2.** I would. **3.** I should.

This entry for *I'd* states that it is a contraction of *I had*, *I would*, and *I should*.

Abbreviations

Desk dictionaries give the correct spellings of **abbreviations,** which are shortened forms of words, such as *lb.* for *pound*.

> **psy·chol·o·gy** (sī-kŏl′ə-jē) *n., pl.* **-gies.** *Abbr.* **psych., psychol. 1.** The science that deals with mental processes and behavior. **2.** The emotional and behavioral characteristics of an individual, a group, or an activity: *the psychology of war.*

This entry shows that *psychology* may be abbreviated *psych.* or *psychol.*

Capitalization

Entry words are capitalized to indicate that they are capitalized in writing.

> **al·a·mo** (ăl′ə-mō′) *n., pl.* **-mos.** *Southwestern U.S.* A poplar tree, especially a cottonwood. [Spanish *álamo.*]
> **Al·a·mo** (ăl′ə-mō′). A chapel built after 1744 as part of a mission in San Antonio, Texas. During the Texas Revolution against Mexican rule some 182 people were besieged here from February 24 to March 6, 1836. All the insurgents, including Davy Crockett and Jim Bowie, were killed.

These entries show that *alamo* is not capitalized when it refers to a tree, but it is capitalized when it refers to a place in San Antonio, Texas.

In the following entry, a label in the second definition states that *president* is usually capitalized when it is used to designate the chief executive of the United States.

> **pres·i·dent** (prĕz′ĭ-dənt, -dĕnt′) *n.* *Abbr.* **pres., Pres., p., P.**
> **1.** One appointed or elected to preside over an organized body of people, such as an assembly or a meeting. **2. a.** Often **President.** The chief executive of a republic. **b. President.** The chief executive of the United States, serving as both chief of state and chief political executive.

It is correct to write, "We elected a new student council *president*," but "The *President's* aircraft is called Air Force One."

Syllabication

When you write papers for college credit, you may sometimes need to divide a word at the end of a line. Entry words are printed in syllables to indicate how they may be divided.

> **Cal·i·for·nia** (kăl′ĭ-fôr′nyə, -fôr′nē-ə). *Abbr.* **CA, Cal., Calif.**
> A state of the western United States on the Pacific Ocean. It was admitted as the 31st state in 1850. The area was colonized by the Spanish and formally ceded to the United States by the Treaty of Guadalupe Hidalgo (1848). Sacramento is the capital and Los Angeles the largest city. Population, 23,667,837. —**Cal′i·for′nian** *adj. & n.*

California is printed in four syllables to indicate that it may be divided at the end of a line in the following ways: *Cal-ifornia, Cali-fornia,* or *Califor-nia.*

Do not divide a word at the end of a line if only one or two letters will appear at the end or the beginning of a line. For example, do not divide *about* (a-bout) because only one letter will be at the end of a line, and do not divide *handed* (hand-ed) because only two letters will be at the beginning of a line.

Key to Common Spellings

It is sometimes difficult to locate the spelling of a word when its spelling is very different from its pronunciation. For instance, you may have difficulty locating the spelling of the word that is pronounced (skēm) and that means "a method for doing something," as in "a (skēm) for making money."

On the inside back cover of this book there is a key to the common spellings of consonant and vowel sounds that may be helpful to you when you have difficulty locating the correct spelling of a word. The key includes information about the common spellings of the sounds of *s* and *k*, as in (skēm). It states that the sound of *s* is sometimes spelled *c* (cent), *sc* (scent), or *ss* (discuss) and that the sound of *k* is sometimes spelled *c* (call), *ch* (chemistry), or *q* (quit). By using this information, you may locate the correct spelling of (skēm), which is *scheme.*

EXERCISE 21.1   The Dictionary and Spelling

Use a desk dictionary to do this exercise.

Plurals   Determine the plural spellings of the following nouns and write them on the lines.

1. crisis   _____   3. hero   _____

2. elf   _____   4. medium   _____

Principal Parts of Verbs   Determine the spellings of the *-ed* and *-ing* forms of the following verbs and write them on the lines.

5. cycle   _____   _____

6. delay   _____   _____

7. ski   _____   _____

8. step   _____   _____

Comparatives and Superlatives   Determine the spellings of the *-er* and *-est* forms of the following adjectives and write them on the lines.

9. big   _____   _____

10. busy   _____   _____

11. fierce   _____   _____

12. happy   _____   _____

Derivatives   Determine the spellings of the following words with *-able* added to them and write them on the lines. The words you are looking for may be listed at the ends of entries rather than as entry words.

13. change _____   15. justify _____

14. regret _____   16. value _____

Compounds   Determine the correct spellings of the following compounds and underline them.

17. nighttime   night-time   night time
18. commonsense   common-sense   common sense
19. fulltime   full-time   full time
20. diningroom   dining-room   dining room

Contractions   Determine the spellings of the contractions of the following words and write them on the lines.

21. they + are   _____   23. I + would   _____

22. he + has   _____   24. will + not   _____

Abbreviations   Determine the abbreviations of the following words and write them on the lines.

25. Arkansas   _____   27. pages   _____

26. colonel   _____   28. quart   _____

Capitalization   Determine which of the italicized words in the following sentences should be capitalized and underline them.

29. He got an A in his *psychology* course.

30. She is studying *spanish* literature.

31. They live in the *west*, near the Pacific Ocean.

32. Our bedroom faces *south*.

33. The planets closest to the *sun* are *mercury*, *venus*, and *earth*.

34. Few men have left the *earth* to walk on the *moon*.

Syllabication   Determine how the following words may be divided into syllables and write their correct syllabications on the lines.

35. importance   _____   37. knowledge   _____

36. information   _____   38. performance   _____

EXERCISE 21.2 Variant Spellings

Consult a dictionary to determine the preferred spellings of the following words, and write these on the lines. If both spellings are listed, the preferred spelling is the one listed first.

1. abridgment, abridgement   _____

2. blond, blonde   _____

3. canceled, cancelled   _____

4. cigarette, cigaret   _____

5. phantasy, fantasy   _____

6. lovable, loveable   _____

7. marihuana, marijuana   _____

8. summersault, somersault   _____

9. yoghurt, yogurt   _____

10. theater, theatre   _____

11. banjos, banjoes   _____

12. bluish, blueish   _____

13. chilli, chili   _____

14. disk, disc   _____

15. exhibitor, exhibiter   _____

16. indorse, endorse   _____

17. nicknack, knickknack   _____

18. pigmy, pygmy   _____

19. Shakespeare, Shakspere   _____

20. T-shirt, tee shirt   _____

EXERCISE 21.3   The Key to Common Spellings

Use the Key to Common Spellings on the inside back cover of this book to locate in a dictionary the correct spellings of the words in this exercise. Write the correct spellings of the words whose pronunciation spellings are given in the following sentences.

1. A (fär′mə-sē) sells drugs. _____

2. Jell-O contains (jĕl′ə-tən). _____

3. Coffee contains (kă-fēn′). _____

4. Old skin (rĭng′kəlz). _____

5. We enjoyed mountain (sē′nə-rē). _____

6. A (sĕl′ə-bĭt) is unmarried. _____

The spelling of the sound of *s* is deleted from the following words. Spell the words correctly by writing, *c, s, sc,* or *ss* on the lines.

7. a ____ end   12. de ____ endant   17. li ____ ense

8. can ____ el   13. di ____ ipline   18. medi ____ ine

9. colo ____ al   14. fa ____ inate   19. nece ____ ary

10. con ____ ensus   15. inno ____ ent   20. resour ____ e

11. con ____ equently   16. insen ____ itive   21. respon ____ e

The spelling of the sound of schwa (ə) is deleted from the following words. Spell the words correctly by writing *a, e, i, o,* or *u* on the lines.

22. comm ____ n   27. lux ____ ry   32. prej ____ dice

23. cust ____ mer   28. maint ____ nance   33. pron ____ nciation

24. d ____ sirable   29. min ____ mum   34. rel ____ vant

25. d ____ vide   30. obst ____ cle   35. sacr ____ fice

26. equiv ____ lent   31. pois ____ n   36. sep ____ rate

Eight Essential Spelling Rules

This chapter explains eight spelling rules that you can use to spell hundreds of words correctly.

The Rule for ie and ei

You can avoid most misspellings of words that contain the *ie* or *ei* vowel combination by learning the rule that is summarized in the following jingle:

> Write *i* before *e*
> Except after *c*
> Or when sounded like *a*
> As in *neighbor* and *weigh*.

The rule for *ie* and *ei* has three parts.

1. Usually spell the combination *ie*, as in *believe*.

2. However, spell *ei* when the combination follows the letter *c*, as in *receive*.

3. Also, spell *ei* when the combination has the sound of *a*, as in *weigh* (wā).

   Exceptions to this rule include words in which the combination should be spelled *ie* but is spelled *ei*: *caffeine, either, foreign, height, leisure, neither, protein, their,* and *weird.* There are also words in which the combination follows *c* and should be spelled *ei* but is spelled *ie*. In all these words, *c* is pronounced *sh: ancient, conscience, deficient, efficient, proficient,* and *sufficient.* Remember to spell *ie* rather than *ei* after *c* when *c* spells the sound *sh.*
   Exercise 22.1 on pages 211–212 provides practice in spelling words with *ie* and *ei.*

The Word + Word Rule

The Word + Word Rule explains how to join words to form compounds such as *fireworks*.

Usually join two words without changing their spellings.

Here are some examples of how to use the Word + Word Rule.

    book + keeper = boo*k*keeper
    room + mate = roo*m*mate
    fire + arms = fir*e*arms

Exceptions to the Word + Word Rule include *almost, already, although, altogether, always, oneself, pastime,* and *wherever.* There is additional information about compounds on page 199.

Exercise 22.2 on page 213 provides practice for the Word + Word Rule.

The Prefix + Word Rule

The Prefix + Word Rule may be used to avoid spelling errors such as *mispell* and *unecessary.*

Join a prefix and a word without changing the spelling of the prefix or the word.

Here are some examples of how to use the Prefix + Word Rule.

    mis- + spell = mis*s*pell
    un- + necessary = u*n*necessary
    dis- + appear = di*s*appear

Exercise 22.3 on page 214 provides practice for the Prefix + Word Rule.

The Word + Suffix Rule

The Word + Suffix Rule states the basic procedure to use when you join words and suffixes.

> Usually join a word and a suffix without changing the spelling of the word or suffix.

Here are some examples of how to use the Word + Suffix Rule.

usual + -ly = usua*ll*y
clean + -ness = clea*nn*ess
poison + -ous = poiso*n*ous

Eighteen is one of the exceptions to this rule; according to the rule, it should be spelled *eightteen*, but it is not. Other exceptions are given in the explanations of the remaining rules in this chapter.

Exercise 22.4 on page 215 provides practice for the Word + Suffix Rule.

The Final e Rule

The Final *e* Rule explains how to join suffixes to words that end in silent *e*.

> When a word ends in silent *e*, usually drop the *e* when you join a suffix that begins with a vowel, but retain the *e* when you join a suffix that begins with a consonant.

Silent *e* is an *e* such as the one in *love*, which you do not hear when *love* is pronounced. Since *love* ends in silent *e* and the suffix *-able* begins with a vowel, drop *e* when you join *love* and *-able*.

love + -able = lovable

However, since the suffix *-less* begins with a consonant, retain the *e* in *love* when you join *love* and *-less*.

love + -less = loveless

Exceptions to this rule include words in which *e* should be retained but is dropped: *acknowledgment, argument, awful, duly, judgment, ninth, truly, wholly,* and *wisdom*. Other exceptions include words ending in *ce* or *ge* when they are joined with *-able* or *-ous*: *advantageous, changeable, courageous, manageable, noticeable, outrageous, peaceable, serviceable,* and *traceable*.

Exercise 22.5 on pages 216–217 provides practice for the Final *e* Rule.

The Final y Rule

The Final *y* Rule explains how to join suffixes to words that end in *y*.

> When a word ends in *y*, usually change the *y* to *i* when you join a suffix
> if the *y* is preceded by a consonant, but do not change it if the *y* is
> preceded by a vowel or if you join the suffix *-ing*.

Notice that the *y* in *study* is preceded by the consonant *d* and that the *y* in
destroy is preceded by the vowel *o*.

stu*d*y   destr*o*y

Since the *y* in *study* is preceded by a consonant, change *y* to *i* when you join
a suffix.

stu*d*y + -ed = stud*i*ed

On the other hand, since the *y* in *destroy* is preceded by a vowel, do not change
y to *i* when you join a suffix.

destroy + -ed = destroyed

In addition, do not change *y* to *i* when you join the suffix *-ing*.

study + -ing = studying

If the *y* were changed to *i* before joining *-ing*, then *studying* would be spelled
studiing, which you should recognize as incorrect because few words contain
the spelling *ii*.

Except for *daily*, the exceptions to the Final *y* Rule are words that you are
not likely to spell often: *dryly, dryness, shyly, shyness, slyly, slyness, gaiety,*
and *gaily*.

Exercise 22.6 on pages 218–219 provides practice for the Final *y* Rule.

Final Consonant Rule 1

Final Consonant Rule 1 pertains to words such as *ship*, which is a one-syllable
word that ends in one consonant preceded by one vowel. Below, the letter *c*
indicates a consonant, and the letter *v* indicates a vowel.

$$s\overset{c}{h}\,\overset{v}{i}\,\overset{c}{p}$$

Final Consonant Rule 1 explains how to join suffixes to one-syllable words
that end in the *cvc* combination.

> When a one-syllable word ends in the *cvc* combination, usually double the final consonant when you join a suffix that begins with a vowel, but do not double it when you join a suffix that begins with a consonant.

Ship is a one-syllable word that ends in the *cvc* combination, so double the final consonant when you join a suffix that begins with a vowel.

ship + -*ing* = shi*pp*ing

However, do not double the final consonant when you join a suffix that begins with a consonant.

ship + -*ment* = shi*p*ment

Final Consonant Rule 1 does not apply to words that end in two consonants preceded by one vowel (*vcc*) or to words that end in one consonant preceded by two vowels (*vvc*).

$$\underset{\text{w a r m}}{\overline{v\ c\ c}} \qquad \underset{\text{n e a t}}{\overline{v\ v\ c}}$$

The rule does not apply to words such as *warm* and *neat* because they do not end in the *cvc* combination.

Do Exercise 22.7 on page 220 before you study Final Consonant Rule 2.

Final Consonant Rule 2

Final Consonant Rule 2 explains how to join suffixes to words of more than one syllable that end in the *cvc* combination.

> When a word of more than one syllable ends in the *cvc* combination and it is accented on the last syllable, usually double the final consonant when you join a suffix that begins with a vowel, but do not double it when you join a suffix that begins with a consonant.

Commit is accented on the last syllable and ends in the *cvc* combination.

(kə-mĭt′)   c o m m i t

Therefore, double the final consonant when you join a suffix that begins with a vowel.

commit + -*ing* = commi*tt*ing

However, do not double the final consonant when you join a suffix that begins with a consonant.

commit + -*ment* = commi*t*ment

Final Consonant Rule 2 does not apply to words that end in two consonants preceded by one vowel *(vcc)* or to words that end in one consonant preceded by two vowels *(vvc)*.

$$\underline{v}\ \underline{c}\ \underline{c}$$
i n t e n d   c o n t a i n
$$\underline{v}\ \underline{v}\ \underline{c}$$

The rule does not apply to words such as *intend* and *contain* because they do not end in the *cvc* combination.

Also notice that Final Consonant Rule 2 does not apply unless words are accented on the last syllable of the base word after a suffix is joined to them. *Confer* and *refer* end in the *cvc* combination.

$$\underline{c}\ \underline{v}\ \underline{c}$$
c o n f e r   r e f e r
$$\underline{c}\ \underline{v}\ \underline{c}$$

However, *confer* and *refer* are not accented on the last syllable after the suffix -*ence* is joined to them.

confer + -ence = conference (kŏn'fə-rəns)
refer + -ence = reference (rĕf'ər-əns)

Since *confer* and *refer* are not accented on the last syllable, their final consonants are not doubled in *conference* and *reference*.

Exceptions to this rule include words in which a consonant should not be doubled but is: *cancellation, crystallize, equipped, excellence, excellent,* and *questionnaire.* There are also two words in which a consonant should be doubled but is not: *transferable* and *transference.*

Exercise 22.8 on pages 221–222 provides practice for Final Consonant Rule 2.

EXERCISE 22.1   The Rule for *ie* and *ei*

Use the Rule for *ie* and *ei*, stated on page 205, to spell the following words correctly by writing the *ie* or *ei* that is deleted from them.

1. aud*nce   _____

2. dec*tful   _____

3. fr*ght   _____

4. gr*f   _____

5. hyg*ne   _____

6. misch*vous   _____

7. v*n   _____

8. p*rce   _____

9. rec*pt   _____

10. qu*t   _____

11. r*gn   _____

12. rev*w   _____

13. sl*gh   _____

14. y*ld   _____

Use the Rule for *ie* and *ei* to spell correctly the words represented by the pronunciation spellings in the following sentences.

_____   15. She works to (ə-chēv') her goals.

_____   16. Her husband's sudden illness caused her great (ăng-zī'ə-tē).

_____   17. He has great (bĭ-lēf') in his ability.

_____   18. Do you (bĭ-lēv') in Santa Claus?

_____   19. There is no (sē'lĭng) to her aspirations.

_____   20. His (chēf) problem is to get a job.

_____   21. Can you (kən-sēv') how we might have peace in our time?

_____   22. Lies are statements that are intended to (dĭ-sēv') others.

_____   23. She tells her best (frĕnd) all of her secrets.

_____   24. My (nā'bər) has twelve cats.

_____   25. He has two nephews and one (nēs).

_____   26. To (pər-sēv') is to become aware through the sense of sight, hearing, touch, taste, or smell.

_____   27. I had a (pēs) of pizza for lunch.

_____ 28. She hopes to (rĭ-sēv′) an A in psychology.

_____ 29. Aspirin gives (rĭ-lēf′) from headaches.

_____ 30. Games can (rĭ-lēv′) boredom on a quiet rainy day.

_____ 31. Always (rĭ-vyōō′) class notes before you take a test.

_____ 32. Biology is the (sī′əns) of living things.

_____ 33. A (thēf) broke into their home while they were away on vacation.

_____ 34. She is dieting because she wants to (wā) less.

Spell correctly the words represented by the pronunciation spellings in the following sentences; they are all exceptions to the Rule for *ie* and *ei*.

_____ 35. He was fired from his job because his work was (dĭ-fĭsh′ənt).

_____ 36. His boss hired a more (ĭ-fĭsh′ənt) worker to replace him.

_____ 37. She can write with (ē′thər) her left or right hand.

_____ 38. He can speak three (fôr′ĭn) languages.

_____ 39. He starred in four movies a year at the (hīt) of his career.

_____ 40. She works so much that she has little (lē′zhər) time.

_____ 41. Only one of them cooks, and (nē′thər) of them washes dishes.

_____ 42. There is always a dictator waiting to (sēz) power.

_____ 43. A word to the wise is (sə-fĭsh′ənt).

_____ 44. My English teacher wears a green cape and red shoes, which give him a (wîrd) appearance.

EXERCISE 22.2 **The Word + Word Rule**

Use the Word + Word Rule, stated on page 206, to join the words enclosed in parentheses in the following sentences.

_____ 1. She was promoted from (book + keeper) to accountant.

_____ 2. It is (extra + ordinary) for a person to be seven feet tall.

_____ 3. The cat is warming (it + self) by the fire.

_____ 4. She wanted to sleep; (never + the + less) she had to awaken to nurse her baby.

_____ 5. He bought a lottery ticket at a (news + stand) in New York City.

_____ 6. There are more women in college (now + a + days) than at any time in the past.

_____ 7. When she cooks, her (room + mate) washes the dishes.

_____ 8. He wears a tattoo on his arm and an (ear + ring) in his left ear.

_____ 9. At the seashore we change clothes at the (bath + house).

_____ 10. Employers must (with + hold) taxes from employees' paychecks.

_____ 11. They are trying to find their son, but they don't know his (where + abouts).

_____ 12. Pat can (out + talk) Chris.

_____ 13. My grandmother used to collect figurines and other (knick + knacks).

_____ 14. She's very smart, but she pretends to be a (dumb + bell).

_____ 15. Mark Twain is the (pen + name) of Samuel Langhorne Clemens.

_____ 16. The chief wore a beautiful (head + dress) of feathers and beads.

_____ 17. On New Year's Eve, the streets are filled with (merry + makers).

214 NAME ____ DATE ____

EXERCISE 22.3 The Prefix + Word Rule

Use the Prefix + Word Rule, stated on page 206, to join the prefixes and words enclosed in parentheses in the following sentences.

_____ 1. They are identical twins, but their facial features are (dis- + similar) in some respects.

_____ 2. It is (ir- + rational) to suppose that we will live forever.

_____ 3. Take care not to (mis- + spell) words.

_____ 4. She dyed her hair an (un- + natural) greenish-blue color.

_____ 5. I shop at a store that refunds my money when I return a product with which I am (dis- + satisfied).

_____ 6. The mayor is hoping to be (re- + elected) for a third term.

_____ 7. He annoyed his teacher by asking (ir- + relevant) questions.

_____ 8. He was so frightened that he was speechless and (im- + mobile).

_____ 9. Many teachers give low grades to written work that is (il- + legible).

_____ 10. The plastic handles of saucepans become (mis- + shapen) when they are exposed to excessive heat.

_____ 11. We like your work, and we would be pleased to (re- + employ) you next summer.

_____ 12. It is (un- + neighborly) of them to let their dogs run wild on our property.

_____ 13. He is (re- + evaluating) his decision to drop out of college.

_____ 14. (Inter- + racial) marriages are still not very common in the United States of America.

_____ 15. The (ir- + resistible) aroma of baking cookies filled the air.

© 1995 by Houghton Mifflin Company. All rights reserved.

EXERCISE 22.4   **The Word + Suffix Rule**

Use the Word + Suffix Rule, stated on page 207, to join the words and suffixes enclosed in parentheses in the following sentences.

_____   1. He lives in a dream world rather than in (real + -ity).

_____   2. Santa Claus does not (real + -ly) exist.

_____   3. My third-grade teacher was one of the (mean + -est) people I ever met.

_____   4. (Mean + -ness) is not a desirable quality for a teacher to possess.

_____   5. Everybody likes her because she has a great (personal + -ity).

_____   6. He claims to be (personal + -ly) acquainted with several movie stars.

_____   7. Since we knew the contents of the will, the lawyer's reading of it was nothing more than a (formal + -ity).

_____   8. We dressed (formal + -ly) for the wedding.

_____   9. She (accidental + -ly) broke her leg.

_____   10. He was often absent from work because of (drunken + -ness).

_____   11. Thanksgiving is celebrated (annual + -ly).

_____   12. Because of his (stubborn + -ness) he would not give in.

_____   13. We thought he would never stop talking, but he did (eventual + -ly).

_____   14. The (sudden + -ness) with which she swerved the car prevented a serious accident.

_____   15. After five years of college, he (final + -ly) graduated.

_____   16. Abbreviations (general + -ly) end with a period.

_____   17. We (occasional + -ly) have Chinese food on Sunday evening.

EXERCISE 22.5   **The Final *e* Rule**

Use the Final *e* Rule, stated on page 207, to join the following words and suffixes correctly.

1. achieve + -ing   _____

2. achieve + -ment   _____

3. sincere + -ity   _____

4. sincere + -ly   _____

5. like + -able   _____

6. like + -ness   _____

7. taste + -y   _____

8. taste + -less   _____

9. pave + -ing   _____

10. pave + -ment   _____

Check your answers for items 1 through 10 before you do problems 11 through 40.

11. measure + -able   _____

12. measure + -ment   _____

13. hate + -ing   _____

14. hate + -ful   _____

15. encourage + -ing   _____

16. encourage + -ment _____

17. false + -ify   _____

18. false + -hood   _____

19. accumulate + -ion _____

20. advise + -able   _____

21. argue + -ing   _____

22. care + -ful   _____

23. aggravate + -ion _____

24. complete + -ing _____

25. continue + -ous _____

26. extreme + -ly _____

27. nine + -ty _____

28. value + -able _____

29. excite + -ation _____

30. ice + -y _____

Some of the following words are exceptions to the Final *e* Rule.

31. change + -less _____

32. change + -able _____

33. change + -ing _____

34. enforce + -able _____

35. enforce + -ment _____

36. manage + -able _____

37. manage + -ment _____

38. courage + -ous _____

39. service + -able _____

40. service + -ing _____

EXERCISE 22.6   The Final *y* Rule

Use the Final *y* Rule, stated on page 208, to join the following words and suffixes correctly.

1. angry + -ly   _____

2. attorney + -s   _____

3. glory + -ous   _____

4. destroy + -ed   _____

5. easy + -ly   _____

Check your answers to items 1 through 5 before you do items 6 through 40.

6. mystery + -ous   _____

7. industry + -al   _____

8. empty + -ness   _____

9. happy + -ness   _____

10. justify + -ed   _____

11. lively + -hood   _____

12. lovely + -ness   _____

13. money + -less   _____

14. employ + -ment   _____

15. ninety + -eth   _____

16. play + -ful   _____

17. remedy + -able   _____

18. survey + -or   _____

19. study + -ous   _____

20. valley + -s   _____

21. hurry + -es   _____

22. marry + -age   _____

23. worry + -ed   _____

24. enjoy + -ment   _____

25. study + -ing   _____

26. lucky + -er   _____

27. monkey + -s   _____

28. lady + -es   _____

29. donkey + -s   _____

30. comply + -ing   _____

31. convey + -ance   _____

32. vary + -ance   _____

33. annoy + -ance   _____

34. unemploy + -able   _____

35. relay + -ed   _____

36. accompany + -ment   _____

37. lobby + -ing   _____

38. pity + -ing   _____

39. comply + -ance   _____

40. misally + -ance   _____

EXERCISE 22.7 Final Consonant Rule 1

Use Final Consonant Rule 1, stated on page 209, to join the following words and suffixes. Answer the two questions before you attempt to spell a word.

	Word ends in *cvc*?	Suffix begins with a vowel?	Word + suffix
1. ship + -ing	_____	_____	_____
2. ship + -ment	_____	_____	_____
3. clear + -ance	_____	_____	_____
4. fit + -ing	_____	_____	_____
5. fit + -ness	_____	_____	_____
6. hand + -ing	_____	_____	_____

Check your answers for items 1 through 6 before you do items 7 through 18.

7. drop + -ed	_____	_____	_____
8. hit + -ing	_____	_____	_____
9. clear + -ly	_____	_____	_____
10. wed + -ing	_____	_____	_____
11. mad + -er	_____	_____	_____
12. mad + -ness	_____	_____	_____
13. think + -er	_____	_____	_____
14. flat + -en	_____	_____	_____
15. flat + -ness	_____	_____	_____
16. bang + -ed	_____	_____	_____
17. plan + -ed	_____	_____	_____
18. step + -ing	_____	_____	_____

EXERCISE 22.8   **Final Consonant Rule 2**

Use Final Consonant Rule 2, stated on page 209, to join the following words and suffixes. Answer the three questions before you attempt to spell a word.

	Word ends in *cvc*?	Word accented on last syllable?	Suffix begins with a vowel?
1. occur + -ed			
_____	_____	_____	_____
2. submit + -ed			
_____	_____	_____	_____
3. commit + -ment			
_____	_____	_____	_____
4. commit + -ing			
_____	_____	_____	_____
5. accept + -able			
_____	_____	_____	_____
6. reveal + -ed			
_____	_____	_____	_____

Check your answers for items 1 through 6 before you do items 7 through 23.

7. admit + -ed			
_____	_____	_____	_____
8. begin + -ing			
_____	_____	_____	_____
9. benefit + -ed			
_____	_____	_____	_____
10. avoid + -ance			
_____	_____	_____	_____

11. cancel + -ed

_____   _____   _____   _____

12. confer + -ence

_____   _____   _____   _____

13. control + -ed

_____   _____   _____   _____

14. intend + -ing

_____   _____   _____   _____

15. forget + -ing

_____   _____   _____   _____

16. label + -ed

_____   _____   _____   _____

17. occur + -ence

_____   _____   _____   _____

18. complain + -ing

_____   _____   _____   _____

19. permit + -ed

_____   _____   _____   _____

20. prefer + -ed

_____   _____   _____   _____

21. prefer + -ence

_____   _____   _____   _____

22. refer + -ence

_____   _____   _____   _____

23. refer + -ed

_____   _____   _____   _____

Unit Six Review

REVIEW 6.1 **The Rule for *ie* and *ei***

Learn the spellings of any of the following words that you sometimes spell incorrectly. The words printed in italics are exceptions to the Rule for *ie* and *ei*.

1. achieve	11. *either*	21. receive
2. anxiety	12. *foreign*	22. relief
3. belief	13. friend	23. relieve
4. believe	14. *height*	24. review
5. ceiling	15. *leisure*	25. *science*
6. chief	16. neighbor	26. *seize*
7. conceive	17. *neither*	27. *sufficient*
8. deceive	18. niece	28. thief
9. *deficient*	19. perceive	29. weigh
10. *efficient*	20. piece	30. *weird*

REVIEW 6.2 **The Word + Word Rule**

Learn the spellings of any of the following words that you sometimes spell incorrectly. Words 2, 4, and 17 are exceptions to the Word + Word Rule, and words 1 and 3 are often written incorrectly as *alright* and *alot*. Notice that words 9 and 10 are written with a space between words, and that words 15, 16, and 20 are written with a hyphen between words.

1. all right	8. gentlemen	15. old-fashioned
2. almost	9. high school	16. part-time
3. a lot	10. ice cream	17. pastime
4. although	11. itself	18. roommate
5. bookkeeper	12. nevertheless	19. therefore
6. earring	13. newsstand	20. white-collar
7. extraordinary	14. nowadays	

REVIEW 6.3 **The Prefix + Word Rule**

Learn the spellings of any of the following words that you sometimes spell incorrectly.

1. disagree	6. impatient	11. inappropriate
2. disappear	7. impersonal	12. inconvenient
3. disappoint	8. impossible	13. indefinite
4. disapprove	9. inaccurate	14. independent
5. immoral	10. inadequate	15. infrequent

16. irrational
17. irrelevant
18. misinterpret
19. misspell
20. misuse

21. rearrange
22. reevaluate
23. reexamine
24. uncommon
25. unconscious

26. unlikely
27. unnecessary
28. unpleasant
29. unsuccessful
30. unusual

REVIEW 6.4   The Word + Suffix Rule

Learn the spellings of any of the following words that you sometimes spell incorrectly.

1. accidentally
2. accomplishment
3. according
4. addressed
5. annually
6. appearance
7. assistance
8. attendance
9. available
10. conception

11. consideration
12. difference
13. discussion
14. drunkenness
15. embarrassed
16. eventually
17. exceedingly
18. finally
19. fourth
20. generally

21. immediately
22. interrupted
23. occasionally
24. original
25. profession
26. really
27. recommendation
28. resistance
29. succeeded
30. suggestion

REVIEW 6.5   The Final *e* Rule

Learn the spellings of any of the following words that you sometimes spell incorrectly. The words printed in italics are exceptions to the Final *e* Rule.

1. achievement
2. aggravation
3. arguing
4. *argument*
5. athletic
6. competition
7. completing
8. confusion
9. continuous
10. dining

11. divided
12. extremely
13. famous
14. hoping
15. invitation
16. *judgment*
17. losing
18. *manageable*
19. nineteen
20. ninety

21. *ninth*
22. *noticeable*
23. *outrageous*
24. safety
25. surprising
26. *truly*
27. using
28. valuable
29. writing
30. *written*

REVIEW 6.6   The Final *y* Rule

Learn the spellings of any of the following words that you sometimes spell incorrectly.

1. accompanied
2. angrily
3. applying
4. buried
5. business
6. destroyed

7. easily
8. employee
9. emptiness
10. funniest
11. happiness
12. hurried

13. hurrying
14. industrial
15. justified
16. livelihood
17. loneliness
18. loveliness

19. luxurious	23. necessarily	27. temporarily
20. marriage	24. ninetieth	28. tried
21. merciful	25. stayed	29. worried
22. mysterious	26. studying	30. worrying

REVIEW 6.7 Final Consonant Rules 1 and 2

Learn the spellings of any of the following words that you sometimes spell incorrectly. The words printed in italics are exceptions to Final Consonant Rule 2.

1. admitted	11. *excellent*	21. *questionnaire*
2. beginning	12. forgetting	22. reference
3. benefited	13. labeled	23. referred
4. canceled	14. occurred	24. shipped
5. commitment	15. occurrence	25. shopping
6. committed	16. omitted	26. stopped
7. committee	17. permitted	27. submitted
8. conference	18. planned	28. swimming
9. controlled	19. preference	29. transferred
10. dropped	20. preferred	30. traveled

REVIEW 6.8 Fill-in Questions

Write on the lines the words that are missing from the following definitions of terminology that are introduced in Chapters 20, 21, and 22.

1. A _____ device is any device used to aid memory.

2. Words such as *resell* and *seller* are _____: words that are formed by joining prefixes or suffixes to base words.

3. Words such as *lipstick* and *flashlight* are _____: words that are formed by joining two words.

4. *Don't* and *they're* are _____: words that contain an apostrophe to indicate the omission of a letter or letters.

REVIEW 6.9 Short-Answer Questions

Refer to Chapters 20, 21, and 22 to write the answers to the following questions.

1. What are the seven basic methods for improving spelling that are explained in Chapter 20?

   a. _____

   b. _____

c. _____

d. _____

e. _____

f. _____

g. _____

2. Write the information that is missing from the Rule for *ie* and *ei*.

Write _____ before _____

Except after _____

Or when sounded like _____

As in _____ and _____.

3. Write the information that is missing from the Final *e* Rule.

When a word ends in silent *e*, usually _____ the *e*

when you join a suffix that begins with a _____, but

_____ the *e* when you join a suffix that begins with

a _____.

4. Write the information that is missing from the Final *y* Rule.

When a word ends in *y*, usually change the *y* to *i* when you join a suffix

if the *y* is preceded by a _____, but do not change it if

the *y* is preceded by a _____ or if you join the suffix

_____.

5. Write the information that is missing from Final Consonant Rule 2.

When a word of more than one syllable ends in the *cvc* combination

and it is accented on the _____ syllable, usually double

the final consonant when you join a suffix that begins with a

_____, but do not double it when you join a suffix that

begins with a _____.

CREDITS (Continued from Copyright Page.)

All other dictionary entries are adapted and reprinted by permission from the standard edition of THE AMERICAN HERITAGE DICTIONARY OF THE ENGLISH LANGUAGE, third edition, copyright © 1992 by Houghton Mifflin Company and paperback edition of THE AMERICAN HERITAGE DICTIONARY, second edition, copyright © 1983 by Houghton Mifflin Company. Reproduced by permission from THE AMERICAN HERITAGE DICTIONARY OF ENGLISH LANGUAGE, third edition and THE AMERICAN HERITAGE DICTIONARY, second college paperback edition.

Extracts featuring the words *dysfunctional, paragon, instinct, taboo, loathsome, rudimentary, virtually, predominantly, infirmity, nonexistent, linear, diagrammatically, coercive, proliferation, recidivism, pseudoscience, obesity, adultery, inconclusive, impoverished, affluent, plight, deprivation, genocide, submissive, disproportionate, gerontology, illegitimate, patrilocal, matrilocal, patriarchy, matriarchy, irreverently, pharmaceutical,* and *megalopolis* in Chapters 9 and 14 are from Ian Robertson, SOCIOLOGY, third edition, 1987, Worth Publishers, New York. Used by permission.

Extracts featuring the words *phoneme* and *morpheme* in Chapter 16 are from Douglas A. Bernstein and others, PSYCHOLOGY, second edition, © 1991 by Houghton Mifflin Company.

Extract featuring the words *and/or* in Chapter 19 is from Joseph F. Trimmer, WRITING WITH A PURPOSE, tenth edition, © 1992 by Houghton Mifflin Company.

Extract entitled "Consumer Income" in Chapter 16 is from William M. Pride and others, BUSINESS, fourth edition, © 1993 by Houghton Mifflin Company.

Extracts featuring the words *reverential, vociferously, defrays, decentralized, reformulated, hyperresponsiveness, counterinfluences, determinant, pronuclear, antinuclear, socioeconomic, undifferentiated, objective, extolling, incentive, seniority, quest, tenure,* and *ensuing* in Chapters 9 and 14 are from Janda, Kenneth, Jeffrey M. Berry, and Jerry Goldman, THE CHALLENGE OF DEMOCRACY: GOVERNMENT IN AMERICA, third edition. Copyright © 1992 by Houghton Mifflin Company. Used with permission.

Subject Index

A page number printed in **boldface** indicates the location of the definition of a term.

Abbreviations, **28**
Accent, 37
Acronyms, **51**
Adjectives, 198
Affixes, **29**
Antonyms, **162**
Assimilation, **100**

Base words, 88
Blends, **51**
Borrowing, **47**–48
Breve, **35**

Capitalization, 199–200
Circumflex, **36**
Clipping, *see* Shortening
Coinage, **50**
Colloquial usages, 180
Combining forms, **101**–102, 118
Compounds, **53**
Consonants, **34**–35
Context
  definition of, **63**
  limitations of, 64, 70
  word meanings implied by, 69–70
  word meanings stated in, 63–64
Contractions, **199**

Definitions
  definition of, **64, 133**
  in dictionaries, 133–135
  examples to illustrate, 133
  implied by context, 69–70
  multiple, in dictionaries, 134
  sequences of, in dictionaries, 134
  stated in contexts, 63–64
  synonyms as, 133
  in textbooks, 141–143
  undefined words in, 135
Derivatives
  definition of, **52**
  in dictionaries, 198
Diacritical marks, 33–36

Dialect, **179**
Dictionaries
  abbreviations in, **28**, 199
  affixes in, **29**
  checklist for evaluating, 30
  combining forms in, 102
  definition sequences in, 23–24
  desk, 21–22
  entry words in, **21**
  etymologies in, **24**, 47–52
  homographs in, **26**
  idioms in, **25**–27
  illustrations in, 29
  paperback, 21–22
  parts of speech in, 23
  pronunciation spellings in, 22–23, 33–37
  recommended, 22
  subject labels in, **25**
  syllabication in, 200
  synonyms in, **25**
  usages in, 29
  variant spellings in, 197
Dieresis, **36**
Digraphs, **34**–35
Diphthongs, **36**

Echoic, *see* Imitation
Entry words, in dictionaries, **21**
Etymology
  acronyms, **51**
  blends, **51**
  borrowing, **47**–48
  coinage, **50**
  compounding, **53**, 199
  contractions, **199**
  definition of, **47**
  derivatives, **53**
  fictitious people and places, 50
  imitation, **51**
  people and places, 48–50
  reduplication, **52**
  shortenings, **50**–51
Examples, **64, 133**
Expressive vocabulary, **3**

Formal usage, *see* Standard English
French phrases, 49

Homographs, **26**
Homophones, **169**

Idioms, **25**–27
Imitation, **51**
Imply, **69**
Infer, **69**
Informal usage, **180**

Key to common spellings, 200

Latin phrases, 48
Latin roots
  characteristics of, 109–110
  examples of, 110
  importance of, 110
Learning words, 9–12
Long vowels, 35

Macron, **35**
Mnemonic devices, **192**

Notes, for learning words, 10–11
Nouns, 197

Parts of Speech
  abbreviations for, 23
  adjectives, 198
  nouns, 197
  verbs, 198
Plural nouns, 197
Prefixes
  and assimilation, 100
  common, 96
  definition of, **95**
  in dictionaries, 29
  and word meanings, 95–96, 117–118
Primary accent marks, **37**
Primary stress, **37**
Pronunciation,
  breve, **35**

circumflex, **36**
consonants, **34**–35
dieresis, **36**
digraphs, **34**–35
diphthongs, **36**
key to, in dictionaries, 33
long vowels, **35**
macron, **35**
primary accent mark, **37**
primary stress, **37**
schwa, **37**
secondary accent mark, **37**
secondary stress, **38**
short vowels, **35**
stress, **37**
syllables, **36**–37
words pronounced alike, 169
words pronounced similarly,
  169–170
vowels, **34**–36
Proofreading, 193

Receptive vocabulary, **3**
Reciting to learn words, 12
Reduplication, **52**
Reviewing to learn words, 12
Roots, **109**

Schwa, **37**
Secondary accent mark, **37**
Secondary stress, **37**
Shortening, **50**–51
Short vowels, **35**
Slang, **180**
Spelling,
  abbreviations, **199**
  capitalization, 199–200
  comparative adjectives, 198
  compounds, **199**

contractions, **199**
derivatives, 198
in dictionaries, 22, 197–200
Final consonant rules,
  208–210
Final *e* Rule, 207
Final *y* Rule, 208
homophones, **169**
Key to common spellings, 200
and mnemonic devices, **192**
noun plurals, 197
Prefix + word Rule, 206
principal parts of verbs, 198
and pronunciations, 192
and proofreading, 193
Rule for *ie* and *ei*, 205
Six-step study method,
  191–192
superlative adjectives, 198
syllabication, 200
variants, 197
Word + suffix rule, 206–207
Word + word rule, 206
Standard English, **179**
Stress, **37**
Subject labels, **25**
Suffixes
  common, 88
  definition of, **87**
  in dictionaries, 29
  and parts of speech, 87–88
  and word meanings, 88, 117
Superscripts, 26
Syllables, **36**–37
Syllabication, 200
Synonyms,
  characteristics of, 161–162
  definition of, **133, 161**
  as definitions, 133

in dictionaries, 162–163
in thesauruses, 162

Terminology
  in business and economics,
    146
  definition of, **141**
  in glossaries, 143
  in language and literature, 148
  in law and government, 150
  listed in textbooks, 143
  in natural sciences, 152
  printed in boldface, 141
  in psychology and sociology,
    144
Tests
  of vocabulary in context, 5–8
  of vocabulary in isolation, 4
Thesauruses, **162**

Usage
  colloquial, 180
  definition of, **179**
  dialect, **179**
  informal, **180**
  nonstandard, **180**
  slang, **180**
  Standard English, **179**

Variant spellings, 197
Verbs, 198
Vowels, **34**–36

Word structure, *see* Base words;
  Combining forms;
  Derivatives; Latin Roots;
  Prefixes; Suffixes

Word Index

This is an index to the words, prefixes, and combining forms that are introduced in *College Vocabulary Skills*.